Dear Yeats, Dear Pound, Dear Ford

*Writing American Women*
Carol A. Kolmerten, *Series Editor*

JRF, 1916. Foster Collection, Chestertown Historical Society, Chestertown, New York.

# Dear Yeats, Dear Pound, Dear Ford

## Jeanne Robert Foster and Her Circle of Friends

Richard Londraville
and Janis Londraville

*With a Foreword by* William M. Murphy

Syracuse University Press

Copyright 2001 by Syracuse University Press

Syracuse, New York 13244-5160

All Rights Reserved

First Edition 2001

01  02  03  04  05  06      6  5  4  3  2  1

The paper used in this publication meets the minimum requirements of American National Standard for Information Sciences—Permanence of paper for Printed Library Materials, ANSI Z39.48–1984.∞™

**Library of Congress Cataloging-in-Publication Data**

Londraville, Richard, 1933–

     Dear Yeats, dear Pound, dear Ford : Jeanne Robert Foster and her circle of friends / Richard Londraville and Janis Londraville ; with a foreword by William M. Murphy. — 1st ed.

        p. cm. — (Writing American women)

     Includes bibliographical references and index.

     ISBN 0-8156-0730-X (alk. Paper)

        1. Foster, Jeanne Robert, 1879–1970. 2. Women and literature—United States—History—20th century. 3. Yeats, W. B. (William Butler), 1865–1939—Friends and associates. 4. Foster, Jeanne Robert, 1879–1970—Friends and associates. 5. Yeats, John Butler, 1839–1922—Friends and associates. 6. Ford, Ford Madox, 1873–1939—Friends and associates. 7. Pound, Ezra, 1885–1972—Friends and associates. 8. Authors, American—20th century—Biography. 9. New York (State) —Biography. I. Londraville, Janis, 1949– II. Title. III. Series.

PS3511.O689 Z7 2001

811'.52—dc21

[B]                                          2001042053

*Manufactured in the United States of America*

For William M. Murphy,
*il miglior fabbro*

RICHARD LONDRAVILLE and JANIS LONDRAVILLE are noted for their publications about Jeanne Foster, John Quinn, W. B. Yeats, and their circle. The Londravilles' work has appeared in many scholarly journals, including *Yeats Annual*, *Yeats: An Annual of Critical and Textual Studies*, *Journal of Modern Literature*, *Paideuma*, *The Independent Shavian*, *English Literature in Transition*, *English*, and *Eire Ireland*. Their book publications include *On Poetry, Painting, and Politics: The Letters of May Morris and John Quinn* (1997) and *Too Long a Sacrifice* (1999), a collection of the letters between Maud Gonne and John Quinn.

Richard Londraville is a professor emeritus of literature at the State University of New York at Potsdam, and Janis Londraville is a fellow at the Center for Independent Scholars of the Associated Colleges of the Saint Lawrence Valley, New York.

# Contents

# Illustrations

# An Accidental Meeting?

WHEN I MET JEANNE ROBERT FOSTER almost a half century ago, I had no idea how important she had been in the lives of others and no suspicion how important she would be in mine.

Shortly after World War II ended, I took my Ph.D. in English literature from Harvard, where I had spent my undergraduate years and taught my first classes. At Union College in Schenectady, I taught Chaucer and Shakespeare and regarded these subjects as my specialties. Although a generalist in nineteenth-century literature, I was certainly not regarded as an authority on the subject of William Butler Yeats and his family. Meeting Jeannie Foster was to change that.

In 1948, as a two-year resident of my congressional district, I was asked to run for the House of Representatives as a sacrificial lamb. The district was so overwhelmingly Republican that no seasoned Democrat wanted the job. Young and innocent and feeling there was nothing to lose, I accepted and was duly defeated. In the following year, the Democrats took temporary control of the Schenectady City Council and, as a reward for my sacrifice, appointed me to a nonpaying job as a member of the Schenectady Municipal Housing Authority (MHA), the public institution that provided inexpensive housing for people with low incomes.

At the office one day, an elderly woman named Jeanne Foster approached me. She was in charge of the Tenant Selection Bureau, the office with the responsibility for choosing the most-deserving applicants for housing. She told me of her admiration for Harvard (having learned somehow of my Harvard connection) and of her having studied there in the early part of the twentieth century. In the course of our conversations, she mentioned familiar names—Charles Townsend Copeland, the celebrated

Harvard teacher whom I had known in his declining years, and Frank Hersey, under whom, as it happened, I had taken a course in composition as an undergraduate, a fact that delighted her. She also mumbled something about "John Butler Yeats," or at least that's what I thought she said, for her speech was somewhat slurred, and I had difficulty understanding her. I was sure she had meant to say "William Butler Yeats" and wondered whether she was aware of the slip.

It wasn't a slip. As she talked, I learned that she had known the father of the poet, John Butler Yeats, during his last years in New York and had indeed been the last friend to see him the night before he died. When his family could not arrange to have his body shipped to Ireland for burial, she donated a plot of her own in the Rural Cemetery in Chestertown, New York, and had been present at his burial there.

From those early talks in the MHA developed a friendship that lasted till her death almost twenty years later. When the Republicans returned to power, I was dumped from the authority, and thereafter my meetings with Jeannie took place mostly at her home or, on a few occasions, at mine. I became embarrassed at visiting her, for she insisted on presenting me with a "small gift" each time I came, the "small gift" being a letter from William Butler Yeats to his father or from Lady Gregory to John Quinn. She was proud to show me her collection of books, many published by the Dun Emer and Cuala Presses of Dublin, run by William Butler Yeats's sister Lollie. On the top of her piano was a pencil portrait of William Butler Yeats by his father, behind it on the wall an oil portrait of her by André Derain; on another wall hung a portrait of her by the Rumanian painter Costin Petrescu. Her living room resembled a Victorian parlor of a hundred years ago.

As some compensation for her generosity, I gave her a copy of a monograph, privately printed, that I had written as a memorial essay on the life and career of David Worcester, who had been my Freshman English teacher at Harvard and had died at the age of thirty-nine while president of Hamilton College. Because much of the book was about Harvard, it only excited her more, and our tie grew stronger.

Some time during the early years of our association, she was approached by a young man who asked if he could catalog her collection, and she sought my advice on the matter. I agreed enthusiastically. The cataloger was Richard Londraville, and it is he and his wife Janis who, with their vast knowledge of every aspect of Jeannie's life, have now fashioned this impressive work.

The subject Jeannie spoke most of to me was John Butler Yeats. She told me how she had been evaluating her materials on him over the years and hoped some day to write his biography. But gradually and imperceptibly she decided I should write it instead, and the flow of "little gifts" became a river of documents, chiefly the letters that the elder Yeats had written to John Quinn and to Jeannie herself. At her death, she bequeathed to me the remainder of her vast collection, which has been of inestimable help to me and others.

Supported by her early gift of documents, I applied for and received grants from the American Philosophical Society and the American Council of Learned Societies to travel to Europe in 1966. In Dublin, my wife and I met the descendants of William Butler Yeats—his daughter Anne, his son Michael, Michael's wife Gráinne, and their children—who still remain among our closest friends. Their generosity provided me with thousands of letters and other documents without which no reliable biography of John Butler Yeats would have been possible.

In Italy, we met her friend Ezra Pound, to whom she had written asking if he would be kind enough to see us. During those years, Pound was not eager to see anybody, having been discharged from a mental hospital in Washington after spending years there because of his support of Mussolini during World War II, and having suffered a mild stroke. But when he received Jeannie's letter, he accepted us at once, and we had a good chat in his house in Venice about his relationship with John Butler Yeats. Through Jeannie's influence also, direct or indirect, I came to meet others who had known the old man: the Irish writer Padraic Colum, the American literary historian Van Wyck Brooks, and the writer Conrad Aiken.

When a few years later I published a monograph, *The Yeats Family and the Pollexfens of Sligo*, which I dedicated to Jeannie, I found myself, quite involuntarily, a member of the universal society of Yeats scholars, an association I had never dreamed of. Without Jeannie Foster, my life would have been quite different.

The most pleasant times with Jeannie, I think, were our periodic visits to John Butler Yeats's grave in Chestertown, where we would take a sip of red wine, as she and JBY had done at dinners in the Petitpas boarding house on West Twenty-ninth Street in New York City, then sprinkle the remainder over his grave. I was sorry that the work required for writing John Butler Yeats's biography was so extensive that the book for which she was in such large measure responsible (*Prodigal Father: The Life of John Butler Yeats, 1839–1922*) didn't appear until eight years after her death.

Jeannie Foster believed in the existence of a metaphysical world, in the influence of the stars and of fate, and she was convinced that our own meeting was somehow predetermined. I had to confess to her, when she put the question to me directly, that I held no such belief and was sure that everything came about by pure chance. Despite my admission, she continued to have faith and confidence in me. I believe one reason may be that she discovered that one of my children had been born on William Butler Yeats's birthday, another on the anniversary of his death. She saw connections not visible to me. But the impact that the great and near great had on her life was as nothing compared to the impact she had on mine, so I often wonder whether she might not have been right.

William M. Murphy

# Acknowledgments

THE WEB that is Jeanne Robert Foster's life could not have been untangled without the aid of many who knew her or who have been students of her work. To them and to all who made this book possible, we give our thanks, but we must acknowledge the guidance of William M. Murphy above all others. When we were in most need of direction, Dr. Murphy was ready to assist. As Jeanne Foster's literary executor, he gave us access to his private collection of Foster papers, as well as permission to publish photographs and letters.

Charles Alexander of Paul Smith's College shared the research he and Joanne Taylor had done for the WCFE (PBS, Plattsburgh) television program *Seasons of a Poet: The Jeanne Foster Story*. The New York Public Library Rare Books and Manuscripts Division—Astor, Lenox, and Tilden Foundations—provided documents from its Foster-Murphy and John Quinn Collections—letters, photographs, articles, and diaries—and granted us permission to publish them. We particularly thank Mimi Bowling at the New York Public Library for her support.

The Chestertown Historical Society, the Crandall Library in Glens Falls, the Adirondack Museum, and the Schenectady Historical Society granted us permission to publish portions of their collections. The Center for Independent Scholars, Associated Colleges of the St. Lawrence Valley, has supported this project and others over the years. Anneke Larrance, director of the Associated Colleges; John A. Fallon III, president of the State University of New York at Potsdam; and Anthony Tyler, chair of the English department at SUNY–Potsdam have been expeditious in recognizing our work.

Other institutions that gave support or provided research facilities were the State University of New York at Potsdam, the John and Mable Ringling Museum of Art, Harvard University, the University at Albany, the University of South Florida–New College, the College of Saint Rose, and Keuka College.

We are grateful to Michael Yeats and his sister Anne Yeats for permission to publish excerpts from John Butler Yeats's and Lily Yeats's letters to Jeanne Foster, and to Michael Yeats and William M. Murphy for permission to publish the photograph of the Murphys and the Yeatses with Jeanne Foster at her home in Schenectady. We thank the Ezra Pound Trust, New Directions Publishing Corporation, for permission to publish excerpts of letters from Ezra Pound to Mrs. Foster; and Houghton Library, Harvard University, for permission to publish excerpts from its collection of Ezra Pound letters. We also thank Omar Pound for his consent to publish excerpts of Dorothy Pound's letters to Mrs. Foster; and Omar Pound and Mary de Rachewiltz for their consent to publish excerpts from Homer Pound's letters. Patrick Gregory, son of Marya Zaturenska and Horace Gregory, allowed us to publish his mother's letters to Jeanne Foster; and Dallas Swan Jr. did likewise for the letters of his uncle, Paul Spencer Swan.

The journal *English Literature in Transition: 1880–1920* (University of North Carolina at Greensboro) granted permission to publish sections of our 1990 article on Ford Madox Ford, "A Portrait of Ford Madox Ford," and the Balliol Corporation allowed us to reproduce Harrison Fisher's sketches of Mrs. Foster.

On several occasions, we consulted Richard Finneran, Warwick Gould, A. Norman Jeffares, Ann Saddlemyer, and Deirdre Toomey, and we appreciate their guidance. Amy Farranto, the acquisitions editor with whom we worked at Syracuse University Press, also supported our project from the beginning and helped guide us through the inevitable changes one must make before publication.

The staff of the Crumb Library at SUNY–Potsdam deserves special mention. We would still be searching for information if not for the patient help of Nancy Alzo, David Trithart, Rebecca Thompson, Marion Blauvelt, Keith Compeau, Jane Subramanian, Holly Chambers, Amy Witzel, Carol Franck, Kathy LaClair, Pat Niles, David Ossenkop, and Germaine Linkins.

Douglas Brown, David Brower, Robert Jewett, Cynthia Lucia, Romeyn

Prescott, and Paula Willard at the Center for Distributed Computing at SUNY–Potsdam provided technical support in New York.

In Venice, Florida, where we did much of our work, Ann M. Herre provided computer support. Lynn Thierry, Mary Waddell, Melanie Odom, Muriel McMasters, Louise Bacacio, Susan Cortright, and Janice Zinn of the Venice Public Library answered all questions and provided ideal facilities in which to work.

John Cross, SUNY–Potsdam Department of Modern Languages; Françoise Hack, the Ringling Museum of Art, Sarasota, Florida; and Paul B. Franklin, now at *Nest* magazine, helped translate text and letters written in French. Dr. Franklin also edited parts of the biography.

Linda R. McKee, director of the John and Mable Ringling Museum of Art Library, helped us in particular with the chapters about John Quinn and the artists Jeanne Foster knew (chapters 9 and 10). She also edited the entire biography and translated text and letters written in German.

Others who have contributed to this book, either directly or indirectly, and for whose help we are grateful are Betty Allen, Bridget Ball, Daniel Berggren, Phyllis Bogle, Warder Cadbury, Bruce Cole, Arthur Collins, Frank Enzien, Rosemarie Enzien, Cathy E. Fagan, Joanne Familio, George Gabor, Julie Gabor, Marilyn Gardner, Delbert Gardner, Alice Gilborn, Larry Hart, Michael Holroyd, David Garrett Izzo, Arthur L. Johnson, Sharon Jordan, Len Kilian, Mary Kilian, Marijke Lee, Paul R. Londraville, Eileen Egan Mack, Lisa McDonough, Ann McGarrell, Richard McKee, Pat McKeown, Berenice Ormsbee, James F. Peck, Gerald Pepper, Elizabeth Sarnowski, Robert Shepherd, James Stamper, Alan Steinberg, Josephine Vrooman, Alex Wachsler, Alice Wheeler, Kate Kealani H. Winter, and Judith Zilczer.

# Abbreviations

THE FOLLOWING ABBREVIATIONS are used throughout the book for economy and clarity.

| | |
|---|---|
| AP | *Adirondack Portraits,* by Jeanne Robert Foster |
| ARR | *American Review of Reviews* |
| CL | Jeanne Foster Papers, Crandall Library, Glens Falls, N.Y. |
| CP | Jeanne Foster Papers, Chestertown Historical Society, Chestertown, N.Y. |
| JL | Janis Londraville |
| JBY | John Butler Yeats |
| JQ | John Quinn |
| JRF | Jeanne Robert Foster |
| LC | Richard Londraville private collection |
| MC | William M. Murphy private collection |
| MFNY | *The Man from New York: John Quinn and His Friends,* by Benjamin L. Reid |
| NOY | *Neighbors of Yesterday,* by Jeanne Robert Foster |
| NYPL | Foster-Murphy Collection, New York Public Library |
| PF | *Prodigal Father: The Life of John Butler Yeats, 1839–1922,* by William M. Murphy |
| RF | *Rock Flower,* by Jeanne Robert Foster |
| RL | Richard Londraville |
| WA | *Wild Apples,* by Jeanne Robert Foster |
| WBY | William Butler Yeats |

# Introduction

THIS BOOK HAS BEEN TOO LONG in the making, although its start was auspicious. With the aid of a faculty research grant from the State University of New York, and with Jeanne Robert Foster's approval and help, I began my research into her life and career in the late 1960s. I had finished part of the biography when William M. Murphy telephoned me in September 1970 with the news that Jeanne Foster had died. She had been in poor health and had been bedridden since her acceptance of an honorary degree from Union College the previous June, but somehow I expected that she would live forever. Without Mrs. Foster as audience, I shifted my attention to other projects, many of which dealt with making items in her collection more accessible.

More than a decade after Mrs. Foster's death, I was pleased with the resurgence of interest in her life and her writing. When Noel Riedinger-Johnson asked to use my collection of Foster material and my biographical notes to aid her editorial work on *Adirondack Portraits* (Foster 1986), I was happy to oblige. Later, I worked with the 1994 WCFE Plattsburgh production team (led by Charles Alexander of Paul Smith's College) on *Seasons of a Poet: The Jeanne Robert Foster Story.* It is the example of such dedicated people that has prompted me to complete this extraordinary woman's story.

I first came across the name Jeanne Robert Foster in 1965, when I was researching the plays of W. B. Yeats. In *J. B. Yeats, Letters to His Son W. B. Yeats and Others, 1869–1922,* edited by Joseph Hone (J. B. Yeats 1946), I read a few tantalizing references to the friendship between Mrs. Foster and the elder Yeats.[1] What was most intriguing to me was that he was buried in Mrs.

1. John Butler Yeats (1839–1922), Irish portrait artist.

Foster's family plot in Chestertown, New York. There were also hints in the book that Mrs. Foster was acquainted with John Quinn (1870–1924), the famous New York lawyer and patron of the arts.

If this mysterious woman was a friend to people such as Yeats and Quinn, why had I read nothing of her before? I recalled that a friend of mine, John Ormsbee, had several times suggested that I contact a woman in Schenectady who "had known Yeats." He had heard about her from his wife, Berenice, whose mother (Ann Healey O'Connor) knew Mrs. Foster as a fellow employee in the Schenectady Municipal Housing Authority. I immediately checked with Berenice to see if this woman was the same Mrs. Foster in Hone's book and found out that she was, indeed, that Mrs. Foster.

I called and asked if I might see her. She consented, after first asking me the purpose of my visit. I told her that I was interested in Yeats, especially his plays. She said that she would be glad to talk to me on that subject. I was more intrigued than ever; I knew that Yeats's plays did not attract the audience that his poetry did. Regardless of Mrs. Foster's expertise on his work, I hoped that I might get some insights about the family from someone who had known them, in whatever capacity. I thought that with her interests in politics and social reform she may have been connected with W. B. Yeats when he was a senator in the Irish Free State.

I parked my car at the curb of 1762 Albany Street, in front of a wine-colored house that, I later discovered, had once been part of a five-acre parcel Mrs. Foster helped her parents purchase in 1901.[2] Because of financial needs, pieces had been sold off over the years. In 1965, it was still a lovely home with a large yard.

I was admitted by a petite elderly woman. My first impression was positive; she was gracious and receptive, dispersing my nervousness with a gentle smile. She ushered me through her foyer and into her living room and asked me if I would have a seat. The room was furnished in a mixture of periods and ringed by paintings that, I later learned, were by André Derain,

2. JRF claimed that she purchased the house, but her cousin, Adorna Wright, said that she understood Frank Oliver (JRF's father) bought the home. It is possible that JRF made a sizeable contribution. (Wright interviewed by RL and JL, 9 September 1998, Warrensburgh, N.Y.)

Costin Petrescu, Gwen John, and J. B. Yeats.[3] I must admit that I did not recognize most of what I hurriedly glanced at, but several portraits caught my
eye. One was an oil of W. B. Yeats done when he was about twenty, painted
by his father.[4]

Mrs. Foster was extremely helpful concerning my specific Yeats interest.
She not only knew a great deal about the plays, but was also interested in
what she called the "Michael Robartes" phase of Yeats's career, and she
thought that the later plays were an important part of that phase.[5] She
talked knowledgeably about material that only scholars knew well and
showed a general appreciation and comprehension of my research.

She then asked me to accompany her from the living room to her dining
room, where the table was neatly spread with several envelopes. A cursory
examination revealed the familiar handwriting of W. B. Yeats, and in addition to his letters to Mrs. Foster there were many more to her from his father, along with autographed proof sheets from the Cuala Press with notes
from Yeats and his sisters. What was most striking, however, was an envelope containing what I later learned were Yeats's unpublished typescripts
of theater speeches that he used during his 1903–4 North American tour.
At the time, I recognized only that these speeches were definitely Yeats's
work; I assumed that texts so central to his drama must have been already
published.[6]

I was dazzled, of course, but had I known more about Yeats I would have
been even more impressed. I didn't know enough to ask the right questions;
Mrs. Foster gently repaired my ignorance and suggested how these treasures might be useful to someone working on Yeats's theater. At the time, I
was much more interested in critical evaluation than in primary materials,
but even I recognized the value of what she had.

---

3. A noted Rumanian portrait painter, Costin Petrescu was born in Pitesti, Romania, in
1873, studied in Vienna, and taught in Bucharest. André Derain (1880–1954), French artist,
most noted for his Fauve period. Gwen John (1876–1939), Welsh painter.

4. The painting is now in MC.

5. JRF's interest in WBY's use of different personalities as a mask is reflected in her occult
studies and in her own poetry. See "The Masker" in RF, 101.

6. See W. B. Yeats 1990.

"Where did you get these things?" I asked bluntly, too excited to be polite.

"Over the years, my friends gave them to me," she said. "At the time, they didn't seem so important—just mementos of good days, but I kept them all. I guess it's a good thing I'm such a squirrel."

We talked for a long time that first day, and when I finally looked at my watch, I had to apologize for taking so much of her time. As I got up to leave, she touched my arm and said, "It was good talking about literature and old friends. Not too many people are interested in such things. Let me know if I can be of further help."

As I drove home, my head was in a whirl. I could not thoroughly examine the papers at that first meeting, so I made another appointment. I still did not know how Mrs. Foster had come to know the Yeatses so well or what her profession had been when she knew them. Surely she had not been working on Schenectady housing all her life.

Before one of our early visits, I called to ask her if I might bring a tape recorder. She so overwhelmed me with her stories that I felt I had to have a record more accurate than my notes. She told me earlier of her regret that little of the conversation of J. B. Yeats and his group at the Petitpas restaurant had been preserved, so I used the opportunity to remind her of the parallel with our conversations. She demurred, saying that there was hardly a comparison; I insisted that there was and finally obtained her permission to bring my recorder on my next visit.

When I arrived with my equipment, she suggested that we have some tea and personal talk before I turned on "the machine." Before I realized it, we had talked an hour and a half, and it was time for me to go. After one more unsuccessful attempt to get some of her reminiscences on tape, I abandoned the project. It was clear that she would discuss nothing of importance with a machine present. I made a last abortive try a couple of years later, when I thought that she might reconsider. We had become close friends during the interim, and I had moved some distance away. I used the excuse of Christmas to send her a recorder and suggested that we use it to exchange letters. My motives were purer this time, for I did miss hearing her voice, but the result was the same. She wrote on 19 December 1968 that she had wept over the present, but that she could not accept it. Instead, to ease my disappointment, she sent me a gift: "Usually I do not shed tears at Christmas but I poured them on your Christmas package when I opened it. (I only opened the end and I did not disturb the contents.) How I would like to express my memories and thoughts over the little dictation camera, but I am a cripple about oral work. I am sending a registered package to you today with a few little things—another item for your present and future."

Enclosed with the tape recorder were proof sheets of an original chapbook of Lionel Johnson's poetry, by Cuala Press, with handwritten emendations by W. B. Yeats and his sisters, Lily and Lollie Yeats. Needless to say, I was thrilled. It was Jeanne Foster's way—tucking gifts in the letters or in the hands of her friends.[7]

I resigned myself to the fact that Mrs. Foster wanted no taped record of what she had to say. Whether her motive was vanity (she thought that a false plate altered her speech) or simply a dislike of the machine itself, I had learned enough not to pursue the matter further.

As I continued with my research—without a tape recorder—I found that her connection with the Yeats family represented only a minuscule part of her collection, for she had known many major American and British writers of the early twentieth century. I found this out gradually and only as it pertained to my research. She rarely volunteered information about her past, not because she was especially reticent, but because she was always more interested in the present and in the project before her. As I would mention Ezra Pound or James Joyce or Lady Gregory in connection with my work, she would have stories to tell about that person and documents relating to him or her.[8] She also had dozens of photographs, most of them taken with her box camera, of literary, artistic, and political figures. She appeared in many of them, like Zelig in Woody Allen's film, a mysterious figure smil-

7. Lionel Pigot Johnson (1867–1902), English poet and critic. Lily (Susan Mary Yeats (1866–1949) and her sister Lollie (Elizabeth Corbet, 1868–1940) helped run the Cuala Press, with Lily organizing the embroidery workshop and Lollie supervising the press. When RL cataloged the Foster collection in 1968, there were more than one thousand items, but it is clear that over the years JRF had given away at least an equal number to her friends and had sold several paintings.

8. Lady Isabella Augusta Gregory, née Persse (1852–1932), Irish playwright; with W. B. Yeats and others, she aided in founding (1899) the Irish Literary Theatre and in 1904 became the director of the Abbey Theatre in Dublin.

ing and at ease with the great men and women of the early twentieth century.

My head was full of questions that would take months to be answered, not that Jeanne Foster was in any way uncommunicative. The problem was instead that the other scholars who visited her from time to time were as focused as I about their topics, and like the blind men with the elephant, few of us were able to see beyond our own interest. In addition to the help she gave William M. Murphy with *Prodigal Father* (1978), which he describes in the preface to this book, she also assisted Aline Saarinen with her chapter on John Quinn in *The Proud Possessors* (1958). Bernard Poli consulted her about his book *Ford Madox Ford and the* Transatlantic Review (1967), and Benjamin Reid was able to use her stories of her years with John Quinn to write his Pulitzer Prize-winning *The Man from New York* (1968). Michael Holroyd sought her assistance while he was collecting research for his biography of Augustus John (1974).[9]

When she agreed to this biography, one of her requests was that she not be spoken of as "a disembodied third person," and I have tried to follow her wishes while maintaining the distance necessary for an unbiased account. I have voluminous notes from my conversations with her over the years, and we exchanged many letters. Much of the information in this volume derives from these conversations and letters.

The organization of this book presented some difficulties, for Mrs. Foster's life through her twenties was crammed with experiences that often overlapped. She was a wife, a model, a student, and a journalist, and she divided her time between Boston and New York during the first decade of the twentieth century. She also knew many writers, artists, and politicians during the next twenty years, so the book begins with a straightforward chronology of her early life, which develops into accounts of her interaction with her famous friends. The final chapter is concerned with Mrs. Foster's later life in Schenectady, and the appendix is a critical evaluation of her poetry, an aspect of her life that reveals a great deal that she did not divulge to her many correspondents.

9. See also Holroyd 1996, the revised edition of this biography. Augustus John (1878–1961), British artist.

Mrs. Foster wished that the biography not be published in her lifetime, for she deemed some of her experiences "too personal." Conversely, she recognized that her story needed to be told without reservation if it was to be a truthful and useful history. She therefore gave to me certain of her papers that recounted hitherto secret aspects of her life. Jeanne Foster was a talented woman, successful in each of her many careers, but she had some frailties common to us all, and these frailties demonstrate the depth of her humanity. Therefore, this book will not be a hagiography, but the chronicle of a woman whose vitality and ability could not be confined by the age in which she lived.

Her dealings with the men in her life were definitional. She was a woman emerging from the nineteenth to the twentieth century, and at that time qualities such as bravery, openness, and assertiveness were often socially stigmatized, especially when exhibited by a female. Behavior that today would be judged as merely independent and autonomous was then deemed scandalous. What was unfortunate for the quality of her life was that Jeanne Foster agreed with that conclusion. She suffered chronically from the need to be "good" and to please others, but there is evidence of a rebellious spirit in her poetry ("The Deacon's Wife" and "Marriage" in NOY) and in her conduct. When she was in Paris in 1913, for example, an ocean away from the restrictions and morality of America, she posed nude for photographer J. J. Henner. Most of the time, however, she assumed the role of a decorous young wife. When her own conduct did not conform to this model, she altered reality to suit.

At the same time that she was married to an older man, she had liaisons with others she met through her work and social contacts. She was adamant that she was unfaithful with none of these men, although her diaries suggest otherwise. Her relationship with John Quinn is the best example of this denial, for although she professed her love for him, she was indignant that others called her his mistress. It may be true, as she insisted, that by the time she met Quinn, he was no longer able to function sexually, but in every important way she gave herself to him while she left her husband to languish in Schenectady. She wrote in her dairy that in order to reach her potential she needed to be attached to a superior man, and Matlack Foster was not, in her judgment, such a man.

JRF "Nude on Couch," photograph by J. J. Henner, 1913. Foster-Murphy Collection, New York Public Library.

In spite of her own considerable talent, Mrs. Foster claimed that genius was a male principle.[10] She had been hailed as an important voice in American poetry as early as 1916, when her first books of poetry, *Neighbors of Yesterday* and *Wild Apples*, were published, but most of her life she had worked, albeit willingly, in the shadow of men whom she considered superior artists. She thus endorsed the fiction of male genius, which assigned to the female a secondary role, a kind of Milton's daughter sitting by the great man, acting as devoted amanuensis.

Decades later, when I met her, she had established herself as a force in Schenectady society. She did not think of herself as the free spirit she had been earlier. Those days were indeed another life, one that did not dovetail with the honored and cherished public figure she had become. In spite of these shortcomings, and sometimes because of them, she was a person almost everyone, women as well as men, admired. Her beauty has been mentioned often, but unlike some beautiful people who do not feel the need to consider others, Jeanne Foster was singularly kind and, most important, at-

10. JRF to RL, 28 December 1968: "I have told you that, to me, all genius is male. I do not live in a state of egotism" (LC).

tentive to everyone she met. This attentiveness, more than any other quality, is what endeared her to friends, whether they were heads of state or
baggage porters. She made each person feel that the world needed his or
her project and that she would not rest until it was completed, attendant
with requisite honors and accolades. Michael Holroyd encapsulates this
feeling we all experienced when he says that the time he spent with Jeanne
Foster was "one of the most romantic episodes of [his] life" (see chapter 14).
She was then in her late eighties.

Characteristically, Mrs. Foster thought that there were many other projects that might better occupy one's time than writing her biography. But
this is one time I have disregarded her advice. In addition to the intrinsic
appeal of her remarkable life, hers is also an important chronicle in the history of women and their place in this nation. At a time when the so-called
weaker sex was considered too emotionally unstable to be allowed the vote,
Jeanne Foster took on a man's world and its restrictions. She not only prevailed against such limitations but flourished against immense odds, creating a life out of her beauty, talent, and uncanny proclivity to make the best
of what fortune granted to her.

Richard Londraville

Dear Yeats, Dear Pound, Dear Ford

# 1

## The Adirondack Years

### 1879—1897

A YOUNG LUMBERMAN is clinging to a rock in a raging river. On the shore, his wife and daughters watch in horror as the icy water tears his numb fingers from their hold. With his last strength, he waves to his family as the torrent carries him to his death.

This was the most powerful memory of one of the lumberman's daughters, Lucia Oliver, Jeanne Robert Foster's mother, but it passed almost intact to her daughter. It speaks of the might, beauty, and terror of the wilderness, an impression that burned itself into the consciousness of the young Lucia and, in the next generation, into that of her daughter Julia. That daughter, who later adopted the name Jeanne in honor of an ancestor, told the story in her own words years later: "Lucia Newell, my mother, was adopted . . . by the Putnams. My grandfather, William Newell, a lumberman and raftsman, was drowned in the Hudson at North River when he was twenty-four, about 1860. His only marker is a white birch tree almost across from the old North River Hotel. Lucinda Weller Newell, his wife, stood on the bank with her four little girls and saw him lose his hold on a rock and wave good-bye. The girls were Hattie, Elizabeth, Lucia (my mother), and Nancy."[1]

All information not identified specifically by source throughout the volume is from notes RL took in conversations with JRF (LC).

1. Enos Putnam (son of Enos Sr. and Sybil Putnam) married Margaret Little and took over the family farm where Jeanne Foster was born. Francis Putnam (Enos's brother) and his wife gave Lucia a home not long after her father drowned. Her biological mother simply could not care for all the children by herself (JRF to Caroline Fish [Chestertown historian], not

Her Grandfather Newell was Irish, and Jeanne said that all that she ever did she owed to his Celtic blood, for with it came the heritage of Deirdre, the Irish Helen.[2]

Jeanne Robert Foster was born Julia Elizabeth Oliver in Johnsburg, New York, on 10 March 1879, one of four children. Frank and Lucia Oliver chose to name their daughter after Julia Oliver (Jeanne's grandmother) and after Lucia's own sister, Elizabeth. Jeanne and her siblings, Cara (1882–1947), Frances (1886–1959), and Elwyn (1893–1932), learned early that children in the Adirondacks had little time for the games and pastimes of city boys and girls.[3] They knew that survival required every member of the family to pitch in, for a few more vegetables put up in the root cellar might well make the difference for the family over a hard winter.

Jeanne's father was a lumberjack, and her mother was a schoolteacher, with a degree from Albany Normal School. One can only speculate why this woman left a promising career as a teacher (she taught previously at Peekskill and Elmira) to cast her lot with the relatively uneducated and underemployed Frank Oliver. The reason may have been as simple as love, or it may have been a desire to return to the Adirondacks. Whatever the cause, Lucia Oliver had a stronger sense of what the world had to offer than did some of her neighbors, and she was largely responsible for encouraging the young Jeanne to set her sights beyond the nearest hills.

It is difficult to imagine a less-auspicious beginning for a life that spanned more than ninety years and several careers. Jeanne's place of birth was the modest York-brown farmhouse of Enos Putnam Jr. (1835–1912) and Margaret Little Putnam (1834–86), off Mill Creek Road, near Johnsburg in Warren County.[4] Enos Sr. and his wife, Sybil, had been the original

---

dated, CP). The 1855 Census lists William Newell (born in Massachusetts) as being thirty-six years old, and his wife, Lucinda, as twenty-six. William Newell is not listed in the 1860 Census, perhaps because he had died by then, at the age of forty-one, not twenty-four as JRF thought (CL).

2. JRF to Helen Shevlin, dated 11 December 1967 (CP).

3. Cara was originally "Clara," named after an aunt. Like their mother, the Oliver girls occasionally changed their names. Frances, often called "Fan," became Francesca and, later, Fanette.

4. York brown is the pigment found in the streambed soil between Whortleberry and Crane Mountains (AP, 73). There are many stories, some having been told by JRF herself,

tenants. The elder Enos, a Wesleyan Methodist preacher, had seceded from the Methodist Episcopal Church in 1848 because the organization would not formally condemn slavery (*AP,* 73, 76, 80). Enos Jr.'s brother, Francis Putnam (1836–97), had taken in Jeanne's mother (renamed Eliza or "Lizzy" Putnam) when she was a child.

There had once been a log cabin on the Putnam property for hiding runaway slaves on their way to Canada and freedom (Enos Putnam finally tore it down after the liberation). The runaways also occasionally hid in the cellar of the main house. Lucia Oliver told an interesting tale once about a time when she and her adoptive family were staying at the Putnams' farm:

> I came down the stairs in my nightgown. Father was just opening the cellar door. He had a lighted candle in one hand and a plate of food in the other. He did not see me and I followed him part way down the cellar stairs. He set the plate of food on a box and took a key from his pocket and unlocked the door of a room in the cellar where mother kept her preserves. I could see from my perch, two or three steps down, that there was a kind of bed in the room and a young man, very black, sat on it. I was frightened for I had never seen a black man before and I hurried to go back to bed.[5]

"Lizzy" was at the farm when she gave birth to her first child. The delivery was especially difficult on that cold March day in 1879, and the baby showed no signs of life. Dr. Wallace Aldrich, the attending physician from North Creek, wrapped the child in a blanket and turned his efforts to Mrs. Oliver.[6] When he later checked the baby, which he had placed on the windowsill, he was surprised to find that she was alive. Infant mortality at that time was all too common, but even at birth Jeanne was quietly determined. Later, when Dr. Aldrich would meet young Jeanne on the streets of Chestertown, he never failed to tell her that her survival was still a mystery to him.

---

that she was born in a log cabin. The Putnams had three children, George (1861–1931), Martha (1867–1971), and Kate (dates of birth and death unknown) (*AP,* 80).

5. Lucia Oliver quoted in "Reverend" 1962, 3.

6. JRF, interviewed by RL, 14 July 1968. Unless otherwise noted, all JRF interviews by RL took place in Schenectady, N.Y. The story about JRF's birth is partially repeated in "Author of Book" 1964.

Thus begins the story of a woman who was to become a nationally noted model (once called "homely" by a neighbor and later an "international play-girl" by a journalist [Frank 1984, H-1]), a commentator on art and litera-ture, a fine poet in her own right, and an editor of two prestigious early-twentieth-century periodicals.

Jeanne Robert Foster's genealogy perhaps gives some clues to her re-markable life force. She thought her family originated in France's olive country, Provence, but could more directly trace the Oliver family from Samuel Ollivier, who sailed over from England in 1658 to join the Massa-chusetts Bay Colony. The "Robert" part is more vague, but Jeanne thought they too originated in France. Samuel Ollivier's eldest son, Jean, was killed at twenty-five while defending the colony against an attack by a native tribe, and his death was recorded as the first written obituary in the records of the Bay State Colony. It was this Jean Ollivier whose name Jeanne Foster adopted.[7]

The family later moved to Bennington, Vermont, and another ancestor, John T. Ollivier, served as an officer in the Revolutionary War. From Ben-nington, some members of the family moved to Hoffman, Essex County, New York. There, Jeanne's great-grandfather, Aaron Ollivier, purchased one thousand acres of Adirondack land. Aaron chose to call all of his chil-dren by names starting with the letter A. After Aaron Jr., came Alva and then Almeron, Jeanne's grandfather. Almeron married Julia Whitman of Poughkeepsie, a cousin of New York governor Charles Whitman.[8] Jeanne's first memory was of her grandfather Almeron's funeral. She was about three years old at the time, and her father lifted her in his arms so that she might see her grandfather for the last time.

The Olivers (who by this time had simplified the spelling of their name) had not fared as well in the Adirondacks as they had in Massachusetts and Vermont, and when Jeanne was a child there was nothing left of the origi-nal family holdings. She explained by saying that the men of the family had no "financial sense." In 1881, when she was two years old, her family moved to Leonardsville, near Olmstedville, in the township of Minerva. There

7. After the family moved to Schenectady in the early 1900s, Lucia changed the *Oliver* spelling to *Oliviere*.

8. Charles Seymour Whitman, governor of New York State (1915–1919).

they lived for six years in a log cabin on the property of her mother's aunt, Joanna Lavery.[9]

Her father struggled to become a farmer, but did not prosper. Farming was not an easy task in Adirondack soil—what there was of it. After a few inches of sandy soil, there was only Adirondack bedrock, usually granite. When farms were cleared, the arable land was planted again and again because there were not enough fields to let some lie fallow. The result was a weak soil where only pines and hemlocks seemed to thrive. But little Jeanne was not fully aware of the family's hardships. She enjoyed learning about her neighbors—the Supernants, the Wamsleys, and the Wilsons—and she liked exploring the hillsides around her new home.

One particularly poignant story Jeanne told of her years in Leonardsville was about her Christmases. They never had a Christmas tree in their log cabin, and all she remembered having as a gift was a rag doll named Peggy. Often the snows made travel impossible, and when drifts blocked the roads, her father had to snowshoe into Olmstedville for supplies. One year, the Olivers did not see another female for three months. Christmas in such a land was often only another day in a long winter: "I never saw [a Christmas tree] until I was five years old when, the weather being moderate, father drove me in the cutter out to the Methodist Church in Olmstedville. . . . I was overcome by the tree blazing with snowy candles; toys I had never seen; candy canes and little net bags of candy and nuts. The doll-angel at the top of the tree held my eyes. To me she was *real*, and I gazed at her with awe and delight" (*AP*, 21).

Lucia Oliver, reasonably enough, had a great deal to do with the formation of Jeanne's character. A schoolteacher in her youth and later in Chestertown, Mrs. Oliver was responsible for her daughter's early love of learning. A native of the Adirondacks herself, she was determined to overcome the rigors of the life and instill her children with the hope of better

9. The house was locally known as the Burteau or Burto home because Benjamin Burteau was the previous tenant. In *AP*, JRF says that Joanna Lavery was her father's aunt, but Joanna was the sister of JRF's maternal grandmother (16). Although JRF sometimes wrote that she moved to Chestertown when she was seven (*AP*, 42), at other times she wrote that she was eight. She insisted to RL that she was eight and that 1887 was the date of the family's move to Chestertown.

days. She had an acute concern for social inequities and, during later years when the family moved to Schenectady, was active in the Socialist Party, serving as a delegate to her party's convention, running twice for state senator, and campaigning for women's rights (Winter 1989, 42).

Lucia could accommodate herself to almost any condition, but was satisfied with nothing less than perfection from herself or her children, so her eldest daughter presented a dilemma. By the time Jeanne was six, her mother had almost given up hope that the child would ever talk coherently. It took a visit from one of Mrs. Oliver's friends, a schoolteacher with whom she had boarded in Peekskill, to convince her that her child was normal:

> Here is the cause, probably, of my being unable to think—speaking or composing—or record correctly:
>
> Up to the log house from Peekskill came an angel. This angel was old Mrs. Stuart with whom my mother had boarded at Peekskill. She must have been a speech teacher. She asked my mother why I kept away from her and all others. My mother told her I had some defect that prevented my enunciating words, that the family could understand me but no one else could and that I was solitary and shy on that account.
>
> Mrs. Stuart asked my mother to bring me to her. She took me out in the yard. I remember the scent of the petunias in the bed so poignantly. She encouraged me to talk to her.
>
> Then she called my mother and said: "Luci"—my mother's name was Lucia—"I am ashamed of you. This child simply needs instruction. She cannot give the 'th' sound; she has no gutturals," etc. etc. "I shall be here less than two weeks but I will teach her to speak." Mrs. Stuart taught me how to breathe, the position of my tongue to create certain sounds, used in speech therapy. Before she left for her home in Peekskill, I was speaking correctly, slowly, for I had to use the mechanics of speech. I have loved her memory.
>
> At this time, I was six; I could write the old Spencerian. I had read "The Lady of the Lake," anything I could find. (JRF to RL, 19 December 1968, LC)

Once it became apparent that Jeanne was not only normal but bright, her mother spent more time on her education. Mrs. Oliver always wanted her children to excel, and her firstborn became the child destined to carry her mother's hopes. The two became closer, and the mother instilled in the daughter some of the dreams and love of literature later realized in Jeanne

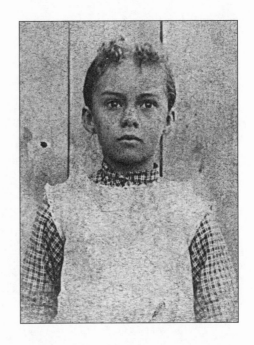

Jeanne Robert Foster at eight years,
1887. Foster-Murphy Collection,
New York Public Library.

Foster's career. But in the early
years, finances were of more
immediate concern to the
Oliver family than any literary
ambitions.

The Olivers finally had to
move again because Frank had
an opportunity to work in car-
pentry and in the lumber industry near Chestertown, at least
in part because of assistance from his brother, Eugene, and so the family
packed up again and traveled the twelve miles by horse-drawn carriage on
a cold autumn day in 1887.[10] One of Frank Oliver's first jobs there captured
his eldest daughter's imagination: he helped to enlarge a hotel in the area,
which involved moving nearby graves. Her father told her stories about his
discomfort over the exhumations, and she wondered if the disturbed souls
would haunt the hotel.

The Olivers lived in various places in the Chestertown area. One residence was known locally as both the "old revolutionary house" and the Braley home, the first because it was standing at the time of the American
Revolution and the latter because the Braleys had been early tenants. This
house was important to Jeanne because of all the lore it held. Her imagination was stimulated when she heard the story of one Braley who was
so overcome by a sermon he heard about King David dancing before the

10. Sometimes JRF identified William as the brother in Chestertown, but Jeanne's cousin,
Adorna Wright, explained in an interview (by RL and JL, 9 September 1998, Warrensburgh,
N.Y.) that William had moved to California, and the brother who helped Frank Oliver was
Eugene. Eugene suffered from tuberculosis.

Ark that he danced all the way home and "never stopped as long as he had life":

> When we lived there one had to step down to enter the bedrooms and the pantry and the summer kitchen. The old beams were in the corners of the rooms and the inside of the front porch was lathed and plastered . . . very quaint. I mentioned the room with the worn floor-boards. We used it for storage for it was the room that had had an iron grill made by the local blacksmith to confine "the dancing man" who danced himself to death. Mother would hardly enter the room.
>
> . . . He was demented of course but he told others he danced for the "glory of God" as King David before the Ark.[11]

Jeanne Foster made it her own story when she created the character of Hezzie Daly in her *Adirondack Portraits* poem "The Dancing Man":

> He danced until his bones showed through his skin;
> Sometimes he danced at night out on the road.
> Finally his folks had the blacksmith come
> And build a cage to keep him in the house
> In the east room—the marks are on the floor.
> (59, lines 30–34)

It was just such ability to imagine and dream that allowed Jeanne to survive difficult situations in her life. She told her friends that when she was a child, she had an encounter with a nasty woman named Hepsy Rising, and that long ago meeting became her "story of inspiration":

> We were forlorn and poor and . . . when Will [*sic*: Eugene] Oliver asked father to come to Chestertown to escape starvation, I could read everything but I had never seen a train nor telegraph wires. These fascinated me. I was

---

11. CP, undated newspaper article sent to Caroline Fish by JRF. The first part of the quotation is from a 6 October 1962 letter to Sara Bowyer O'Connor, repeated in *AP*, 166. The last sentence, also in CP, is attributed to a letter JRF wrote to O'Connor on 27 September 1962.

asleep when I arrived in Chestertown in 1887 on a cold November day, wrapped in a bed quilt on the load of what we had, as I had no coat. . . .

In the morning before nine, I wrapped myself in two scant shawls, one blue, the other brown, and ran away secretly from the house and reached the front platform of Will Remington's store. There, overhead, was a tangle of wires. Due to the cold there was a singing noise on them. I thought this noise was the noise of actual messages flying along over the world. My dress was brown calico; I was cold but I stared in ecstasy and wonder.

Suddenly from a third floor window in the building a woman leaned. She called to Will Remington: "Will, whose brat is that?"

Will Remington looked kindly at me and called back, "I don't know Hepsy. I never saw her before."

Now, in our family the word "brat" was never used but I knew the word. . . . To me it meant a child who did not feed the hens for her father or teach the calves to drink or wash the lamps and polish steel knives for her mother, a lazy, bad child.

I started home, my childish heart filled with grief and rage. I determined to grow up and come back and parade as "somebody" before Hepsy, "that woman." I did not know her name. And I said I would go where the wires went too. I was NOT a brat and nobody should call me one.

Years later, Mary Gould, teaching me fine cleaning when mother was ill, said, "You must learn to clean and wash and cook and someday you may be a nice hired girl."

I was old enough to answer then. I said, "But Mrs. Gould, I'm not going to be a HIRED GIRL. I am going to teach school." This was the second spur.[12]

Only a few years would pass before her teaching career began.

Lumberjacking near Chestertown did not make for an easy life for Frank Oliver. It was difficult, dangerous work, but it paid good wages, and if a man took care with his money, he could find some reasonable success. Because of his lack of "financial sense," prosperity still eluded Frank, but he had other endearing qualities. He was always ready to spend time with his children, and, unlike some of the stern fathers of his time, he was generous in his affection. Some of his daughter's best memories were of the times spent with him, either listening with him to the singers and storytellers or

12. JRF to Caroline Fish, 21 November 1968 (CP).

helping him skid logs out of the wilderness: "His devotion to trees, his deep emotions, love for friends, largely shaped my mind, my life. We were constant companions as long as he lived. We understood the people in the back districts of the mountains" (*AP*, 130).

Yet her father often sent her away to live with relatives because, quite simply, there would be one less mouth to feed. Adorna Wright, a cousin, said that Jeanne enjoyed these adventures with other relatives. At some level, though, it may have been difficult for a young girl to understand that poverty often meant imposed abandonment. Jeanne loved her father, and yet in later life she often talked about his inability to care for his family. It was shocking to her when later her well-to-do husband lost his money on bad investments, and she again needed to deal with financial woes. She had learned at a very early age that she did not want to be in a position to allow others to have control over her, but fate all too often deemed otherwise.

From the ages between eight and twelve, she frequently spent time with the Francis Putnams, whose home was at the base of Crane Mountain. Francis Putnam gave Jeanne his sermons to read aloud to him so that he could memorize them more easily. He had a collection of his old sermons in a barrel, and when he was at a loss for a topic, he would reach in and pull one out randomly, trusting that Providence would guide his hand. Her foster uncle Osmond (1861–1926), Francis Putnam's son, had become a talented photographer and taught Jeanne how to use a camera, a skill that later complemented her journalism and accounts for many of the historic photographs in this volume. She always carried her box camera with her, sometimes taking the picture herself, sometimes giving it to a passerby so that she might be included in the snapshot.

She also spent time living with an uncle, Jacob Davis, a peddler in the North River area. During one winter, 1889–90, she traveled with him to Blue Mountain Lake, expanding her world into other parts of the Adirondacks, and also spent some time with relatives in Indian Lake. On these adventures, she met all the variety of people the Adirondacks held. She didn't know, at the age of ten or eleven, that she was actually doing research, "making a record in my memory," as she put it, of the special characters she observed. In all of these trips, there was fodder for future poetry:

Jacob Davis peddled meat, sausage, buff mittens, socks, yarn, and anything in North River folks had to sell, from North River to Blue Mountain Lake, making the trip every two weeks. We stopped at Indian Lake every trip, and also at Casey's Tavern and "Old Salt's" before we reached there.

The ballad, "The Bound-Out Boy," in my book to be entitled "The Adirondack Trail," described the fate of a member of the Bird family. At that time, the family lived in a poor sort of house between Indian Lake and Blue Mountain Lake.[13]

The bound-out boy is Johnnie Byrd, who was "bound out" to Old Salt, the peg-legged former pirate and owner of a tavern called "The Blue." At the end of the tale, when Johnnie is thrown out in the snow by Old Salt, Jeanne includes some names of friends and relatives, much as the minstrels did when they wandered from town to town in medieval days, inserting names into lyrics to please audiences. Here, she pays tribute to her peddler uncle:

> It was Jacob Davis who came along
> A-sledding up to "The Blue."
> He picked up Johnnie the bound-out boy
> And carried him on through.
>
> He wrapped him in buffalo robes;
> Duane Fuller took him in,
> And kept the bound-out boy well fed
> Till the ice broke up that spring.
> (*AP*, 110–11, stanzas 10–11)

More often than not in the Adirondacks of old, people, sometimes related and sometimes not, had to live together for economic reasons: "Later on, I went to Indian Lake with my great uncle, Duane Fuller, to fish for pickerel. At Blue Mountain Lake, I had the following resident relatives; Duane Fuller, Game Protector and guide boat builder [also known as the man who shot the largest panther ever at "The Blue"]; George Fuller, his son; Clara

13. JRF, quoted in "Author of Book" 1964.

King, née Fuller, wife of Albert King; three King children, and Duane Fuller's youngest daughter, Edith D. Fuller" (AP, 112).[14]

Although these dislocations from her family were necessary, they also provided Jeanne with a closer connection to her clan. There is a sense of adventure tinged with abandonment in these stories. If it was difficult for her to leave her family from time to time, at least the experience gave her an unusual sense of independence for a young girl at the end of the nineteenth century.

The following winter (1890–91) she spent time with another uncle, Erastus Griffin (a Civil War veteran), near the tannery town of Griffin on the east branch of the Sacandaga River about ten miles due east of Lake Pleasant. Jeanne ran wild here with her cousin Lena, both disguised as boys, attending skating parties and going to dances forbidden to them. Her aunt and uncle never discovered their nighttime escapades:

> Expert skaters, we had long blades, not girls' skates, and so we could speed. We borrowed boys' suits and slough hats from the tavern keeper . . . and no one knew we were not male. . . . Uncle Erastus came home weekends; the rest of the time my cousin, Lena, twelve, and I ran wild through the country. We lived in my uncle's log house, with one wood stove for heat. During these years I knew many Adirondack characters my family did not know. (AP, 116)

Jeanne learned that it wasn't much fun to be a girl. There weren't many acceptable ways to assert independence, and the only way for a "good" girl not to displease her elders and yet have some fun was to disguise herself as a boy. Pretending to be a boy in a wild town seemed quite appropriate at the time. She learned very early to wear different masks, depending on the role she was called on—or wanted—to play.

At about the same time that Jeanne visited Griffin, she heard stories about an Adirondack place called "Dogtown" (Baker's Mills), where the men were so wild that they traded wives. The Salvation Army even sent recruits to Dogtown, who prayed and exhorted to drive the devil away, and

---

14. In *Old Houses*, twelve years after the publication of JRF's *Neighbors of Yesterday*, Lucia Oliver tells the story of Duane Fuller and the panther in "Christmas at Malloys" (Oliver 1928, 45).

people began to confess their sins en masse. Such stories excited Jeanne's imagination, and although she didn't quite understand much of the activity in Dogtown, her curiosity about the wild side of life grew as she approached her teenage years. Later, she wrote about similar places in her poems. In one *Neighbors of Yesterday* poem, "Silence Davis," the subject is a young woman who married a man from the notorious "Mormon Hill": "One man traded his wife for a calf and a bridle, / Another for a colt and a halter, / And everybody changed round once in a while" (60, lines 70–72).

In her fourteenth year (1893), Jeanne contracted rheumatic fever. The drug necessary to cure her was so strong that it left her with a permanently damaged right auricle. She took medicine all her life to control this heart defect, but it never slowed her pace to any notable extent. In her years with the Schenectady Municipal Housing Authority, she sat in an overstuffed chair when she felt an imminent "spell": "I would close my eyes until the feeling passed," she said. "My fellow workers thought I was taking a little nap."[15] In the same year during which she suffered from rheumatic fever, she published the first of her many magazine articles. She titled the piece "Autumn Leaves" and sold it to *Vermont Farm and Home*.[16] It was a description of one of her favorite haunts, Chestertown's Panther Mountain, and it was her first byline, kindling a lifelong interest in writing. She also began to write "real" poetry that year ("whereas I had only written jingles before"). She was influenced to do so, she said, by the poetry of one of her mother's elderly cousins, Chloe Weller, who was, as the story has it, the granddaughter of Aaron Burr (the third vice president of the United States) from an illicit liaison.[17]

Jeanne learned early to help with the family chores because survival in the sometimes hostile Adirondack environment was a joint effort. When she was a teenager, she cared for her baby brother so that her mother might be free to do more demanding chores. Elwyn particularly liked his oldest sister to hold him and walk with him, sometimes for hours. She felt a special

15. JRF, interviewed by RL, 15 July 1968.

16. The State of Vermont Department of Libraries and the Vermont Historical Society Library found no record of a newspaper or journal titled *Vermont Farm and Home*. Perhaps it was a small local paper.

17. JRF to Dora Hayes, 7 January 1967 (CL).

sympathy for her brother because he had a physical disability that prevented him from holding his head up and made a normal life impossible.[18] Later in life, when Jeanne was better off and traveling in Europe, she remembered those early years of hardship: "Never during my eight trips abroad—seven with a journalistic or art job—did I slip into a lovely Paris gown or permit myself a small luxury without memories of the *calico* of the Chestertown school; never did I send my mother a gift without thanking God I could—remembering the days when I could *not.*"[19]

In Chestertown, Jeanne helped her father occasionally, driving "Billy," the skidding horse, while Frank Oliver tended to the lumber:

> Billy was a bay gelding, a small, wiry horse. I had bought him from a defunct livery stable at a low price because he was eleven years old.
>      . . . Father's financial judgment had never been good; mother and I feared a loss on the Spruce Mountain job. The skidways were beside the Warrensburg-Chestertown Road, and the logs were skidded from the job that was beyond the old Thomson place. . . . On a Monday, father and I would start at 4:00 A.M. for the job, driving Billy hitched to an old cutter. (*AP*, 133)

Her father enjoyed tracing the roots of stories he heard, knew the songs and folktales of the Adirondacks, and repeated them to his daughter. When work allowed, he would take her to neighboring towns to hear the minstrels. He enjoyed telling her stories about some of the odd characters he had known or heard about in his youth. One was Sabeal, an old Iroquois trapper who was murdered by a lumberman. His ghost still haunts the Adirondacks:

> In the winter when the Northwest wind blows hard,
> Somehow it gets in under the thick ice
> And whistles through each airhole down the lake,

18. Adorna Wright provided details about Elwyn's disability and about JRF's love for her brother (interviewed by RL and JL, 9 September 1998).

19. JRF to Caroline Fish, not dated (CP). Johnsburg Corners was home to one of the first calico-printing mills in the country and was why Frank Oliver came to the area. The mills created industry and thus a demand for grain and other products (*AP*, 64).

And folks will say—unless you pin them down—:
"That's old Sabeal a-crying for his gold."
I'll tell the story—yes, I'll fill my pipe.
("Sabeal," *NOY*, lines 6–11)

When Jeanne was a little girl, she would curl up on her father's lap and listen to him tell such tales and sing the old Adirondack songs in both English and French. It was something he enjoyed with all the children in the clan. Adorna Wright still remembers when she sat on Frank Oliver's lap as a little girl and, like her cousin, was mesmerized by his narratives.

After Jeanne became old enough, she added her own contribution to the family income by serving as a guide for those who wished to explore Panther Mountain near Chestertown or Crane Mountain near Johnsburg when she was staying with the Francis Putnams, the family who had adopted her mother.[20] She knew those mountains as well as she knew her own yard, and she charged hikers the grand sum of twenty-five cents for her services.[21]

Crane was a particularly important mountain for Jeanne. It symbolized the spiritual power and freedom that she wanted, even as a child. The mountain was a "being" with whom she could share her hopes and dreams, her fears and anger. She would "secretly go there and lean against the mountain with out-stretched arms," embracing it until "there seemed to be a strong force passing through me, so untamed and wild and beautiful that there are no words for it." Even beyond her own death, Jeanne felt that she would still be alive "in the intelligence that moves in Crane." She said that while her mother was pregnant with her, Lucia Oliver sat for long hours

20. There is more than one Panther Mountain in the Adirondacks. The one near Chestertown has an elevation of 459 feet. Crane's elevation is 877 feet.

21. JRF sometimes confused her stories in letters to friends. In a letter to Warder Cadbury, 1958, she wrote, "I lived on a remote farm in Essex County, in full view of Whiteface Mountain until I was sixteen. The next two years, I taught in red school houses in different parts of Warren County" (*AP*, 123). JRF lived on the farm in Leonardsville near Olmstedville in Minerva from ages two through eight. Then the family moved to Chestertown. Whiteface is north of Lake Placid, too far to view from Leonardsville or Chestertown. Perhaps she meant Mt. Marcy, the highest peak in New York State at 5,344 feet, which is visible from certain vantage points around Olmstedville (*AP*, 123).

staring at the majesty of the mountain, and in this way Jeanne connected with it even before her birth (Winter 1989, 13).

Almost from the moment that Jeanne learned to control her speech impediment, she showed herself to be exceptional, and her unusual qualities sometimes puzzled her parents. It was as if she possessed knowledge that was almost inexplicable in a child of her age. She had a strong religious sense, but her religion was not the orthodox Protestantism of that mountain community. She refused to be pressed into professing the Sunday-school beliefs that most of the community held. She was not yet able, as a young girl, to articulate this religious eclecticism as well as she would be able to later in her life, but she knew early that the hellfire brand of Protestantism preached in Chestertown and the surrounding communities was not a belief to which she intuitively responded.

Her religion was close to a religion of nature, without the inherent limitations of such a belief. Jeanne rather chose to be inclusive in her approach to life, both in the natural and supernatural planes. She enjoyed the beautiful woods and mountains of her native home, and she also enjoyed the company of the mountain people. In addition, though, she treasured whatever books she could find. Her mother encouraged this inclination, but there was not a great deal of reading available in Chestertown just before the turn of the century. Jeanne studied Latin and developed an extensive vocabulary. She was by far the best scholar in the one-room school she attended; she was so proficient, in fact, that she soon became a candidate for a teacher's position at the age of fifteen, a position that would pay her the substantial sum of five dollars each week. Although she was considerably underage, she had scored so well in the competitive examinations that Roxie Tuttle, the school commissioner for Warren County, decided that the age requirement be waived in view of her performance. Jeanne taught at the Landon Hill District in Chestertown (where Almeron Oliver had once lived, on the road to Pottersville) and at the Spruce Mountain School, sometimes boarding with families nearby.[22] She was following in the footsteps of her mother, who at various times taught both the intermediate and upper grades at the Chestertown school.

22. See also *AP,* 133.

Jeanne's teaching gave her a chance at a future because a woman who was not a teacher usually had the choice of marrying or hiring out as a servant either to wealthier families or, even less appealing, to relatives who could not pay so well. Life then would be filled with caring for the men and children, sewing, weaving, canning, and cooking. After she earned her teaching position, she began to dream seriously of seeing the rest of the world.

But on weekends there was work to be done on the Oliver homestead, and so she would return there to help her father with outside jobs and her mother with the household responsibilities.

One can imagine that teaching school to the first eight grades presented a number of problems to a young girl of fifteen.[23] Some of the students were older than the teacher, and not all of them were as enamored of learning as Jeanne was. Nevertheless, she not only prevailed, but succeeded. She approached the task of making education interesting for those Adirondack children in a determined manner, setting the style for the rest of her life.

By 1896, Frank Oliver had to find other employment and moved his family to Glens Falls, where he worked as a carpenter at the Glens Falls Opera House. The last two decades of the nineteenth century had been especially difficult for the Adirondack lumberjack. In part because of the writings of Verplanck Colvin, who advocated an Adirondack Park to preserve the forests and the water of the area, New York State in 1885 established the State Forest Preserve to protect watershed areas from excessive lumbering (*AP,* 126). That decision, coupled with an unusually large number of devastating forest fires, seriously depressed the lumber industry. Then came the financial collapse of 1893, destroying businesses on a larger scale and leaving the small lumber companies in bankruptcy. Finally, a Forever Wild clause was added to the New York State Constitution to protect forests.

Jeanne's mother was pleased with the move to Glens Falls; now she was in a town that had a growing cultural center. But her daughter didn't stay

23. JRF told RL that she taught these grades (interview, 16 July 1968). She told Laurence Paul Crowley that many of her students "were much larger than myself" (Crowley 1930, 20). She also told several friends that she taught levels or "grades" two and three, which in fact refer to JRF's qualifying levels and not to specific grades she might have taught. Teachers were not so plentiful that they could specialize in one or two grades.

long with her and was not destined to be a schoolmarm. Instead, she married Matlack Foster (1850–1933) in 1897, at the age of eighteen. He was
forty-six.

Matt Foster's family had deep roots in Chestertown; in fact, their homestead was the first erected there. The family was founded by Salmon H.
Foester (the name was later changed to Foster), a Wesleyan Methodist clergyman of Dutch descent. He had attended and supported the Syracuse
Wesleyan Conference, noted for its stand in opposition to slavery. He traveled from city to city with his wife, preaching the gospel and the morality
of slave emancipation. Although he may have considered Chestertown
home, he spoke in many parishes, including Syracuse and, later, Chazy,
where his son Matlack was born and named after a minister Salmon Foster
admired. Old Reverend Foster died in Chestertown when Jeanne was quite
young, and all she remembered of him was that he "looked like Henry
Ward Beecher and, even in old age, had a magnificent voice and preached
magnetically."[24]

Why did Jeanne Oliver marry Matlack Foster? Seventy-two years later,
she explained her choice: "I feared the usual life," she wrote in October
1968. "I did not want it. I married a man older than my father so that I would
be protected from—real—life" (JRF to RL, in LC). In 1970, she wrote to
William M. Murphy that she did not regret her decision: "My amazing marriage—a happy one—was actually an arrangement—to go on living in the
same environment I had lived [in] and—for the privilege of Boston later
on—to go—happily—nursing the family invalids. There are no regrets;
there was no unhappiness. I am grateful life was so ordered" (13 May 1970,
NYPL). These judgments had perhaps been tempered by time.

It seems strange that an ambitious young woman on the verge of following her family to the relative sophistication of Glen Falls should choose instead marriage to a much older man. Stranger still are the circumstances of
that wedding. Instead of in Chestertown or Glens Falls or even Albany, the
couple was married in Philadelphia, Pennsylvania, far from family or
friends. Later in her life, Jeanne told several people that she was only seventeen at the time of the wedding and that she and Matlack Foster were

24. JRF to Caroline Fish, not dated (CP). Henry Ward Beecher (1813–87), American
clergyman, author, and orator.

married in 1896. However, their marriage license from the Clerk of Orphans Court of Philadelphia (no. 95693) is dated 25 August 1897.

After the wedding, Matt and his new bride left on an extended trip to the
western United States and Mexico. Jeanne got her first taste of traveling, a
taste that was never to be sated. While in Utah, she received another tender
of marriage. An elder of the Mormon Church, believing himself to be in-
sufficiently wived, offered to make Jeanne part of his household. (Although
bigamy was illegal at the time, the law was not always honored in Utah.)
Jeanne politely declined, explaining that she was already married to the
gentleman who accompanied her. It may have been the first time that Matlack was mistaken for her father, but it would not be the last.

When the Fosters returned from their honeymoon in the fall of 1897,
they set up residence at 19 East Avenue, Rochester, New York. Jeanne became acquainted with a woman across the street who seemed most interested in Matt Foster's young bride, but it was some time before Jeanne
discovered that this same woman had been one of "Matt's ladies." It was that
experience, she recalled later, that made her aware of her own naïveté; she
was quickly learning that there was considerably more intrigue in the world
of men and women.[25] Sometime during that first year—it is unclear where
or when—Jeanne delivered a stillborn child.

A short story that Jeanne published sixteen years later, in 1913, leads one
to speculate about her relationship with Matlack. "The Reason of the
Cause" tells the tale of young Rachel Sobensky, who becomes pregnant by
her lover. He refuses to meet his obligations and instead pays off an older
man to marry the desperate girl. This friend is "a sponger, an impecunious
hanger-on . . . without a mind . . . simply a lump of clay." Rachel, "at last
worn out with futile rage and passion[,] . . . assented to the disgraceful bargain" (Foster 1913c, 10). Two years before Jeanne published the story, she
wrote about her husband in her diary: "His great failure was that he was not
sufficient unto himself. He leaned, dragged, twined upon others. There
seemed no native energy that gave a robustness of mentality necessary for
attraction" (August 1911, LC). Jeanne had already effectively dismissed
Matlack from her life. Whatever the truth about her marriage, it is clear
that she and her husband were not particularly well matched. Matlack was

25. JRF, interviewed by RL, 14 July 1968.

Matlack Foster, circa 1900. William M. Murphy private
collection.

neither unkind nor cruel, but his age and, more important, his intellect were
against him. Whether from choice or circumstance, there were no more
children. For the rest of Jeanne's life, although she sometimes spoke of the
"baby fever" in her poetry and in her letters to friends, including Dorothy
Pound and W. B. Yeats, her work and her friends became the primary out-
lets for her nurturing.

For several years, Jeanne took care of Mrs. Foster the elder (née Jane
Anne Tripp), who was glad to see her son settled. Until her mother-in-law
died in 1905, Jeanne was her part-time companion. But for a young woman
used to at least two or three jobs, the maintenance of a home simply was
not enough to fill up the time.

Matlack's business was located in the Granite Building in Rochester and
at that time coincidentally needed an extra hand. The office clerk became
ill, and it was apparent that the illness would leave him unfit for business for
some time. Jeanne was only too glad to help Matt with his business, and
one of the barriers to a more efficient office was that there was no one to
type business letters. Matt owned a cumbersome, double-keyboard typewriter, one that almost required, as Jeanne said, "a steamboat pilot's license
to run." He thought that he would have to hire an experienced typist to

handle the business correspondence, but Jeanne practiced in secret until she could manage the machine.

Her purpose in learning to type was strictly utilitarian, but it had other results in addition to helping her be more efficient in the office. Jeanne eschewed the usual keyboard exercises and instead wrote stories and poems on the machine. One of the stories she typed, "Mistress Anne of Glazeal," was later printed in the 5 January 1902 edition of the *Rochester Democrat and Chronicle*. It is a tale about the old Sanders mansion of Scotia, New York, set during the American Revolution.[26]

Anne arranges the escape of her lover, Robert Charbeneau, from Mohawks by claiming that he is a priest, and "priests are wizards, great magicians, medicine men: he will go like smoke and in the morning you will not find him." She plies the Mohawks with liquor, and after they fall asleep, she hides her lover under a hogshead in a cart bound for Albany. In the morning, the Mohawks cannot find him and are convinced of his magic. They are impressed with Anne's knowledge: "The white squaw was wise" (Foster 1902, 5).

In the original local story, set about 1685, there is no bright young woman. Instead, the owner of the mansion, not the daughter, devises a means for a real priest to escape. In Jeanne Foster's adaptation, the leading male figure (Anne's lover) owes his life to his quick-thinking female companion.

In Rochester, Matlack encouraged his wife to continue her studies, and she was only too happy to do so. During her time there, she received a business diploma from the Athenaeum and Mechanics Institute of Rochester, all the while continuing to experiment with writing. The training would serve her well in the near future, when the cities of Boston and New York became almost as important to her as the Adirondacks she had left behind. It was another instance in which her lifelong habit of learning had prepared her to take advantage of whatever befell her. She was always ready to be lucky.

26. The Sanders mansion is currently a well-known restaurant in Scotia, N.Y. One version of the story of the French priest is reprinted and framed on a wall at the mansion.

# 2

# The Harrison Fisher Girl

JEANNE ROBERT FOSTER'S MARRIAGE to Matt Foster and her departure from the Adirondacks were the beginning of a journey that critic Alfred Kazin called a "classic American story of personal migration from the nineteenth to the twentieth century—and the most deeply felt literary portrait I have ever encountered" (*AP*, xi). When she left the mountains, Jeanne could not have imagined what sort of journey lay ahead.

Just before the turn of the century, the Fosters began making periodic visits to New York City. Because of heart trouble that would plague him for the rest of his life, Matlack turned over most of his business affairs to assistants. He felt that he could now leave Rochester for extended periods of time, and he used the opportunity in 1900 to visit with his brother Gardiner, an ophthalmologist, while the latter was taking extended courses in his specialty. Over the next few years, Jeanne and her husband lived in New York for weeks at a time, returning to Rochester to visit Matlack's mother, until her death in 1905.[1] It was a great help to Dr. Foster to have a congenial home, and both Matlack and his wife enjoyed his company and the opportunities that the big city provided. For Jeanne, New York City was a dramatic change from her rural roots, and she loved it from the moment she arrived. Almost immediately she became interested in acting and performed for a year (1900) as ingenue for the American Stock Company, located at Eighth and Forty-second Streets. She played a variety of minor roles, the most important of which was a page in the E. H. Sothern vehicle *Enemy to the King*.[2]

---

1. Sometime between 1900 and 1905, Matlack bought a home in Clyde, New York, where he and JRF lived when they were in the Rochester area.

2. E. H. Sothern (1859—1933), American playwright.

Jeanne related an interesting and rather odd story about her relationship with Matlack during this period. On occasion, he would have to leave her—perhaps to handle some business affairs—but instead of having her stay with her parents or with his brother in New York, Matlack would "abandon her" (her words) at the Saratoga Sacred Heart Dominican Convent. To entertain herself, she strung rosaries. This was all she said about these periodic visits to the convent. It was one of the few times when she sounded irritated at Matlack. She didn't understand why he was not comfortable leaving her to fend for herself in New York City.[3]

On one of their stays with Gardiner, Matlack and Jeanne were out for a stroll in the theatrical section of the city when a man approached them and respectfully suggested that Jeanne might do very well as a model. As a matter of fact, he had just the proposition for them. What did they think of her gracing the inside cover of a cigar box? (The custom of the time was to name a new cigar after a lovely lady, and Jeanne fit the requirements exactly.) Matlack didn't believe that a cigar was the best association for his young wife, but he was amused and flattered by the offer. He had no real objections to her modeling, but he did think that perhaps she could do better than cigars.

Neither Jeanne nor her husband thought too much of the matter until sometime a few months later, in mid-1900, when Gardiner Foster invited a guest for dinner. David Dodge was the editor of *Vanity Fair*, and he was always on the lookout for new talent. When he met Jeanne, he must have thought her beautiful because it wasn't long before her image graced his magazine under the nom de plume Jean Elspeth. Matlack, still a bit uncertain about his wife's new career, thought that the Foster name might be better kept out of it. He suggested Elspeth, from her middle name Elizabeth. Although she occasionally used other aliases, she is most often pictured as Jean or Julie Elspeth. A photograph of her dressed in a riding habit was first published in the *New York Times* fashion page in early 1900; later that same year the photograph was used as the cover of *Spur*.

Two letters, from Street and Smith Publishers (16 October 1900) and from Nicholas Witsch of the American Lithographic Company (23 October 1900), indicate that Jeanne was gaining a reputation very quickly:

3. JRF, interviewed by RL, 11 August 1968.

JRF, circa 1902. Photographer unknown. Londraville private collection.

On the front cover page of Eagle Library we publish the photo of some prominent actress each week. Would you grant us permission to use yours? If so kindly sign enclosed blank and forward it to us with your photo.

Eagle Library is sold everywhere but if you have not seen a copy we would be pleased to forward one of our latest.

Messrs. Eddowes Bros. told me a few days ago that you are in the city again and were willing to pose. Therefore I would ask you whether it would suit your convenience to pose for me next Friday either in the morning or in the afternoon at your own time.

One of the poses will be for a design suitable to use under the title "Pretty Pilot," so in case you have a yachting cap and a nice plain blouse it would come in very handy for the purpose. (LC)

Jeanne's first appearance in *Vanity Fair* was in the December 1900 Christmas issue. The journal wrote: "We . . . herewith present to [our readers], as a Christmas gift, what we consider the most delightsome pictures that have ever appeared in *Vanity Fair,* feeling sure that the delicate beauty of Jean will not fail to receive from them that profound appreciation that is occasionally wanting on the receipt of the most well-meant Christmas gifts." An entire pictorial supplement of the *Sunday Telegraph* was devoted to Jeanne on 9 December 1900, and she was also pictured in the 16 December 1900 issue of the *New York Journal and Advertiser.*

Dodge introduced Jeanne to Harrison Fisher, a contemporary and a

JRF's picture on a cigar box, circa 1910. Londraville private collection.

friendly rival of Charles Dana Gibson, creator of the "Gibson Girl." When Fisher first saw her, he knew that he had found a very special model. He later chose her as the Harrison Fisher Girl of 1903, and his sketch of her sitting on a swing was the October 1903 cover of the *Ladies Home Journal.*[4] Matlack Foster was not averse to her posing for Fisher.[5] The man had a national reputation, and he certainly represented a step above cigar boxes. Ironically, Jeanne's image did eventually find its way to a cigar box, at last with Matlack's approval.

Jeanne often said that Fisher was the favorite of her illustrators. The Harrison Fisher Girl was never trapped by old mores. Illustrations showed her playing tennis or golf, or frolicking at the beach (with no bathing cap, of course, so that the grand locks of hair would never be imprisoned). In one picture for which Jeanne modeled, *A Modern Eve*, a smiling young woman is tempting her man with a freshly picked apple.

Jeanne said that Fisher was "more literary" than Gibson, for whom she also posed. Perhaps she meant that Fisher's figures often portrayed characters from stories and novels (e.g., Jeanne's depiction of Jane Cable in illustrations for George Barr McCutcheon's novel of the same name), or it might

4. JRF wrote to Caroline Fish on 14 January 1966 (CP) about appearing on the cover of the *Ladies Home Journal*. Although she told some friends that Charles Dana Gibson (1867–1944) had done the sketch, she correctly told RL that it was Harrison Fisher (1875–1934).

5. During his busy career, Fisher sketched the famous and the beautiful, including F. Scott and Zelda Fitzgerald, whose portraits by him now hang in the Smithsonian. By the time he died in 1934, he had, according to some estimates, "immortalized more than 15,000 women" (Rinzler 1987, 34; and *New York Times*, 20 January 1934, 15, and 26 July 1934, 15).

JRF as "Jane Cable." Illustration by Harrison Fisher, 1907–8. From *The Harrison Fisher Book* (New York: Charles Scribner's Sons, 1907–8).

be that Fisher's use of symbol and satire attracted her.[6] What R. Armstrong said in his March 1900 article in *The Bookman* may have been what Jeanne meant. "[Fisher] always introduces some symbol into his compositions that relatively suggests the determining meaning. . . . Of the type of person so portrayed, there is never any doubt of his status in life, the quality of caste and the position in society; the reality and the sham one sees at a glance" (53).

Jeanne had practical reasons for wishing to pose. There was really not enough to keep her busy in caring for her brother-in-law's home, and she had always wished that there might be some way in which she could earn money of her own. She also wanted to help her parents purchase a home in Schenectady so that they might have more opportunities than Glens Falls afforded. She did not believe that her husband should share the responsibility that she felt for her family, so she welcomed the opportunity to make some contribution to their welfare. Jeanne Robert Foster was, in 1901, about to become a very busy young woman. Although she would still return for long periods of time to the Rochester area between 1901 and 1905, New York City demanded much of her time.

Jeanne soon had as many modeling jobs as she could handle. Not only Fisher and Gibson but also other artists and photographers of the day

6. The illustrations of JRF are in *The Harrison Fisher Book* (Fisher 1907–8). JRF erroneously identified the book as *The Cup of Tea* (AP, 163). See AP, 163, for a list of the illustrations. George Barr McCutcheon, *Jane Cable* (New York: A. L. Burt, 1906).

JRF as "Jane Cable." Cover illustration of *Jane Cable*, by George Barr McCutcheon (New York: Dodd, Mead, 1906).

wished to have her pose for them. Among them were Philip Boileau and Albert Beck Wenzell. Wenzell titled one of his shots of Jeanne *Enid* and sold the photograph through the Detroit Photographic Co.[7] This picture proved to be most lucrative for her, as it sold nationally for seventeen years. She had other assignments of the same general nature, and for the first decade of the nineteenth century she was one of the most sought after models in the city.

Jeanne was pleased with her success. As Gustav Kobbé wrote in a June 1901 *Cosmopolitan* article entitled "The Artist and His Model," modeling provided young women with the opportunity "to gain artistic association"(1901, 116). Doors opened; opportunities, financial and professional, presented themselves. In September 1902, Jeanne was herself pictured in *Cosmopolitan*.

In a day when models were chosen more for their beautiful faces than for maximum exposure, Jeanne Foster graced calendars from Maine to California. In 1907, when Harrison Fisher paid her his greatest tribute by choosing her image for a number of pages of *The Harrison Fisher Book*, Jeanne knew she had "arrived."

7. JRF, interviewed by RL, 20 July 1967. Philip Boileau (1864–1917), and Albert Beck Wenzell (1864–1917).

JRF in "A Winter Promenade."
Illustration by Harrison Fisher.
From *The Harrison Fisher Book* (New
York: Charles Scribner's Sons,
1907–8).

One especially lovely reminder
of this period in her life hung in
her home until her death: an oil
done by Costin Petrescu, a professor at the Academie de Bucharest.
It shows Jeanne at about twenty-
five, her hair a mass of reds and
golds, her profile Grecian. She
dismissed this work as the "candy"
portrait, but where the sketches
and photographs of the time
tended to minimize her coloring,
Petrescu caught both the exuberant vitality of her youth and the marvelous
tints of her hair and complexion.[8]

Although she was on constant call as a model, sitting still was never
Jeanne Foster's favorite occupation. She decided that acting school might
hone her skills and accordingly enrolled in the Stanhope-Wheatcraft Dramatic School, where she starred in plays at the Madison Square Theatre, including *Rue*, by Eve Brodlique, in which Jeanne, as Julie Elspeth, played the
role of Miss Portia Prattent.[9] She attended the school for about a year, and
although she never had great aspirations to act, she said she used the dramatic academy as her "finishing school." She learned elocution, fencing,

8. The Petrescu painting is in MC.

9. The play was performed on 19 April 1900 but was not reviewed. Eve Brodlique was
primarily known as a Canadian poet. See her "Laudate Dominum" in *Canadian Magazine* (December 1900): 135.

JRF, circa 1905. Portrait by Costin Petrescu. William M. Murphy private collection.

dancing, and general techniques of presenting a dramatic production. She said that her greatest dramatic failure during these years was in the role of Juliet. She realized that as much as she loved Shakespeare, she was simply not a talented enough actress to carry the lead, and, besides, it bothered her to play a role she thought should be acted by someone years younger. Juliet was, after all, a teenager.[10]

Acting was an interesting experience and a welcome change from the static activity of an artist's model, but the stage soon lost its attraction for Jeanne. The productions in which she appeared were enjoyable for her, but they were clearly not of the type to engage her mind. A bit of fluff such as *The Great Ruby*, for example, in which she played a maid, soon lost all its appeal.

Another job Jeanne held in New York City was as assistant to Miss Grace Gould, fashion editor for the William Randolph Hearst papers.[11] Miss Gould often had disagreements with Hearst, who liked to promise ladies of his acquaintance that they could be models in his papers. Unfortunately, he often neglected to inform Miss Gould. Her sense of propriety was frequently outraged by Hearst's choice of models, and some of them had reputations she thought better suited to other, racier sections of the newspaper.

10. JRF, interviewed by RL, 14 July 1968.

11. Grace Margaret Gould (d. 1922) was a fashion editor for *Woman's Home Companion* for nineteen years after she left the Hearst organization. William Randolph Hearst (1863–1951), American newspaper publisher.

Harrison Fisher was by now a good friend of Jeanne Foster and, like Grace Gould, knew of William Randolph Hearst's reputation. He didn't like her being in close proximity to such a womanizer and warned her that Hearst would probably try to seduce her.

But Harrison Fisher didn't have to worry. Miss Gould took good care of her own girls. They stayed at the Model's Club on Fifty-seventh Street in New York—as long as they behaved. If they became too boisterous, they had to leave. After Matlack's brother married, Jeanne didn't want to impose on him, so the Model's Club provided her with a home away from home when Matlack was unable to accompany her to New York City. It was apparent to Matlack that his wife had metamorphosed into an independent and strong-willed career woman. There was no longer any possibility of secreting her in a convent when his business took him elsewhere.

Jeanne's job was to meet the boat from Paris each week to collect the new fashions, to help Miss Gould with the models, and to model herself. This job was Jeanne's first real taste of the hectic activity associated with the newspaper business, and she decided that she liked it. Here was a chance to model *and* to prepare copy, supervise layouts, and have some voice in what finally appeared on the printed page.

During her time working for Grace Gould, Jeanne met Evelyn Nesbit, the "girl on the red velvet swing," whom Stanford White, the architect, supposedly seduced and then abandoned. Nesbit married Harry Thaw, who became so enraged with Nesbit's story of White's betrayal that he shot and killed him. Jeanne said that she believed Nesbit's account of the affair, which claimed that Nesbit had been plied with drink and then awoke to find that White had raped her. Whatever the truth of the tale, Jeanne resolved never to allow herself to be put in such a position.[12]

Although newspaper work was interesting, Jeanne still wished for some activity that could engage her talents more completely. Oddly enough, a family crisis finally enabled her to pursue her interest in writing. In 1905, her sister Francesca became stricken with typhoid while visiting with friends in Boston. Jeanne was summoned to help nurse her sister, whose reaction to the disease required that she be confined to bed for more than a

12. JRF, interviewed by RL, 10 November 1966. Thaw shot Stanford White (1853–1906) while White was attending a theatrical performance. See *New York Times*, 26 June 1906, 1.

year. Fan's illness effectively ended her sister's career as both actress and assistant to Miss Gould, though she continued to model when she was able to take short trips to New York City.

It isn't surprising to anyone who knew Jeanne Foster that the role of nurse was one that did not fully occupy her time. She soon made friends with several people in Boston, among them Mabel Anderson, a schoolteacher. Mabel recognized Jeanne's native intelligence and talent, and suggested that she attend courses at Harvard and Boston University extensions. Matt Foster strongly supported the idea and was more than willing to contribute what he could to Jeanne's future. It seemed a safe enough outlet for his wife's energy. To his credit, he did not oppose most of Jeanne's moves to better herself, and he did finance her education, but it was clear that whatever spousal control he might once have had was gone. She was simply too beautiful, too talented, and too ambitious for an elderly husband to keep reined in.

The more Mabel Anderson encouraged her, the more Jeanne realized that university education offered her exactly what she had missed in her other jobs—a chance to learn something that was beyond popular journalism and entertainment.

Jeanne was particularly fortunate to be taking courses at that time, for the "big five" of Harvard—professors Copeland, James, Royce, Santayana, and Palmer—were then teaching, and she was able to study under each of them.[13] Among the most-lasting impressions were of William James, the philosopher, whom she remembered as a brilliant man who never lost his sense of humanity when dealing with students.

Jeanne's special interest was literature, however, and Charles Townsend Copeland encouraged her to develop her writing talent. In one assignment, he asked his students to write a character sketch of someone they knew. The challenge delighted her, and she chose her formidable instructor. It was Copeland, after all, who unveiled a new world and demanded that she explore it:

13. Charles Townsend Copeland (1860–1952), English-born educator. William James (1842–1910), American psychologist and philosopher. Josiah Royce (1855–1916), American author. George Santayana (1863–1952), American philosopher and essayist. George Herbert Palmer (1842–1933), American scholar and educator.

He had a most vivid and singular personality that stimulated me like a draught of old wine. While he talked or read, I culled enchanted flowers from fields that were doubtless beyond his immediate vision. As there exists in poetry a power to carry thought from the visible to the invisible, to mirror a far off perfection beyond even the poet's comprehension, so there existed a quality in him, a kind of fervor that bore me to realms of dreamy fantasy and ecstasy. (Foster [1906], 3)

In Copeland's class, Jeanne found for the first time a group of people who wanted to understand the nuances of literature. She said that Copeland had literature in his soul, not just in his mind, and that she felt a kinship with him as she had felt with no other human being, except for her own mother:[14]

His lecture platform was a stage, his green-shaded student lamps the foot-lights—his actors the characters of history that materialized, and fiddled, and danced, and shuffled to the music of his voice. He loved hapless Fannie Burney and led us on to undue intimacy with Dr. Johnson; he gave Steele his due and reirained from over-glorifying Addison; he understood Dean Swift and interpreted the "little language" to our great delight. By some legerde-main, some projection of himself into the past, he gave us the feeling that he had been intimate with the characters that chatted or swaggered through the pages of the "Spectator" and the "Tattler"; so that the chronicles of their pages became the happenings of our yesterdays. (4)

In her assignment, Jeanne had to examine Copeland's flaws as well as at-tributes. She wasn't afraid of being bold:

He was indifferent and vain at the same time, a grown-up child who wanted petting and cuddling, which he was much too proud to accept from even his nearest and dearest. His bravery against the flight of time—against the on-coming years of middle age—was pathetic because his heart could never grow old. That was his tragedy—to look perpetually at life with the eyes of unchanging youth and yet be forced to live with his contemporaries. (6)

14. JRF, interviewed by RL, 15 July 1968.

A teacher is, after all, the only person in his or her world who ages; everyone else stays forever a young adult. It is extraordinary, however, when a student is sensitive to that fact. Jeanne explained that Copeland's power as a teacher, his ability to evoke "the Land of Dreams" (as she called it), gave him his place among the immortal poets he so loved: "Death will never overtake his ardent spirit. When the cosmogony of the universe is changed, when we earthlings click our messages to Aldebaran and Alcyone, he will return from the abodes of the deathless gods to tell us 'of those things which neither happened before nor shall be hereafter,' and to clothe once more in vestments of romance the time-blurred records of our yesterdays" (8).[15]

On 9 February 1906, Copeland wrote to Jeanne from Hollis Hall, Cambridge:

> If you did the remarkable sketch of Professor X without knowing any close friend or friends of his, you may be sure that psychological fiction, or psychological fact for that matter—they are so near together in these days—is your vocation. If, on the other hand, you have had help from X's friends, and therefore have not relied solely upon observation and intuition, why then you have at least done something so clever in its structure and expression that you may still think of writing as a probable means of success. . . .
>
> You will receive under another cover everything but the sketch. That I can't be expected to return. The obituary bits in it are too valuable. In due time apply to my executors. (MC)

What student would not be encouraged by such praise from an instructor? From the great "Copey" himself, it was heady stuff. In an interview with Laurence Paul Crowley in Portland, Maine, in 1930, Jeanne remembered her former teacher, whom she called her "personal instructor":

> "Old 'Copey'! Even today after such a lengthy period of time, his influence is still strong. There was a magic in his presence, a compelling charm in his voice, a scorn of the shabby and the second rate in life in his mind that impelled those who came under his influence to attempt to scale the heights."

15. Aldebaran: a brilliant red star in the constellation Taurus. Alcyone: daughter of Aeolus, the brightest star in the Pleiades.

Mrs. Foster's face beamed as she reminisced over her "Boston school days." "One of my chief treasures in my New York home is a tiny casket in which are preserved some tiny violets bestowed on me by 'Copey' at the opening of the football season." (20)

Jeanne wrote to William M. Murphy on 31 December 1958 about her "student-love" for Copeland and enclosed her theme and her teacher's reply. "Keep both the theme and the letter," she told him. "The bunch of faded dried violets, his sole gift to me, will remain in their casket which I will open furtively at times" (MC).

By mid-1906, Francesca Oliver had recovered from typhoid, but Boston had won Jeanne Foster's heart, and she decided to stay. When Matlack arrived on one of his periodic visits from their home in Clyde, "[I] announced to him that I was staying."[16]

While she was attending courses at Harvard and at Boston University, the *Boston-American* offered a prize of fifty dollars in gold for the best student letter criticizing its editorial policy. Jeanne not only won the prize but was also offered a job on the paper. She wrote on 3 June 1970: "The paper sent a special messenger over to my boarding place on Beacon Hill with the shiny gold" (JRF to RL, in LC). She accepted the job and accordingly covered the college news and was assigned to the North Boston and Sculloy Square area (a hangout for sailors) to write feature articles on the problems of housing and employment for the poor, a topic that was to interest her for the rest of her life. She also wrote occasional book reviews, an activity that prompted her to think, as many a reviewer had before and has since, that she could write at least as well as some of the authors she read.

One of her articles for the paper was titled "The Art of Ruth St. Denis" (1909), an attack on a negative review of the dancer's recent performance in Boston. Jeanne connected the dance, as she later did modern art, with the measure of a nation: "The art of a nation images the soul of a nation, and as a nation changes, so must its dance." She asserted that the critic's negative response to St. Denis's work was simply a result of his own ignorance.[17]

16. JRF, interviewed by RL, 10 August 1968.

17. JRF gave RL a copy of the Denis essay (no pages or dates), saying only that it appeared in "the Boston paper" (LC).

From 1905 until 1910, she stayed in Boston, taking college courses, contributing to newspapers in both New York and Boston, and doing occasional modeling. (Matlack moved to Boston as well when he saw that Jeanne was determined to stay.) One of the most famous photographs of her of this period, the "oval plume picture," was published in a Boston paper, and her face became even more famous because now she was a journalist.

Jeanne Foster still had close emotional ties to her mother, who hoped that her daughter had now escaped for good the hard life of an Adirondack woman. Lucia wrote to Jeanne on 1 January 1909:

> I pray for you my dearest—on the eve of this New Year—as I do on all other eves—that your soul may hear a call to some earnest life work. That some heavenly visions may come to your heart, with its dazzling light shutting out all lesser groveling aims. You have talents—you were born to teach—to instruct others—I hope you will find your spiritual wings, and rise out of and above earth's vanities. Why should we who are immortal wear the obsession of things which belong to day. Is a little handful of dust worth so much thought? (LC)

It is a strange admonition to a daughter so successful. Did Lucia think that Jeanne's work until then was unimportant? It is perhaps reasonable that a former teacher would see her daughter as "born to teach," but finding "spiritual wings" and rising "above earth's vanities" would have to take a back seat to material needs for both Jeanne and her family. Jeanne clearly adored and admired her mother and constantly sought her approval. Mrs. Oliver was a woman whose pursuit of "heavenly visions" may have obscured her judgment of her eldest child's accomplishments. Like many a parent, she wanted her daughter to pursue higher goals, and it may be that her reservations were what drove Jeanne always to excel.

Certainly one of earth's vanities, love, was on the horizon for Lucia Oliver's daughter. Although Jeanne Robert Foster would find even more success and fame, her passion for a married man began a long and complicated period in her life.

# 3

# Albert Shaw and the
# American Review of Reviews

THE PARTY HARRISON FISHER GAVE for his friends one night, probably late in 1909, was attended by some of the most notable figures in New York City. One was Albert Shaw, journalist and editor in chief of the *American Review of Reviews*. Also attending was Jeanne Robert Foster, the Harrison Fisher Girl of 1903, who was visiting from Boston. She was now thirty years old. When Shaw, who was fifty-two, met her that night, he was already familiar with her work on the *Boston American*. As they spoke, he discovered a woman of social conscience and intelligence who possessed a special understanding of the Adirondack Mountains, a place whose beauty Shaw found unsurpassed.

Shaw recognized that even though Jeanne Foster had success as a model and actress, she was a capable woman who might enjoy editorial work. Jeanne told him of her interest in writing in general and of the difference her college courses had made in her appreciation of a life well lived. He was working on a series of Civil War books, and Jeanne's insights about the old soldiers who called the Adirondacks their home gave him the idea to have her work with Francis Trevelyan Miller and Dudley H. Miles, who were currently editing *The Photographic History of the Civil War*, a multivolume work featuring photographs by Mathew Brady.[1] Shaw thought that one of the

---

1. The series of ten volumes was published by the Review of Reviews Co. in 1912. It was reissued by Castle Books and Thomas Yoseloff, Inc., in 1957 (see Miller and Miles 1957). Francis Trevelyan Miller (1877–1959), American editor and author. Dudley H. Miles (1881–1954), American editor and author. Mathew Brady (1823–1896), American photographer.

volumes, *Poetry and Eloquence from the Blue and the Gray*, seemed especially suited to Jeanne's talents, although he recognized that it would be risky to hire this Adirondack woman to work with a largely Southern group of men. He suspected that they might make work difficult for her, for it was still very much a man's world, especially in publishing. But he decided to take the chance, and she was hired to collect poetry and songs from the Civil War era. The opportunity came at an important juncture for Jeanne. In 1909, Matt Foster's pension from his insurance business ended, and his investments had not done well. He was too ill and too old to begin a new career.

The job in New York City meant a considerable sacrifice on Jeanne's part, which entailed moving from her beloved Boston and resettling herself and her husband in New York for as long as it would take her to finish her Civil War work. The office she was given was a small, dusty, windowless room. Many of the men refused to speak to her at all; others were curt, barking out directions as if she were the coffee girl. Perhaps she could not have survived if she had been militant about her rights; certainly a less-tolerant woman would have bridled at the reception that the rest of the staff gave her. But Jeanne accepted the conditions without a murmur and set to work with an energy and talent that soon silenced her detractors.

The good old boy network had not seen the likes of Jeanne Foster before. Bit by bit she won their respect. All of them spoke highly of her talent, and those who were not taken with her beauty were easily convinced that her intelligence, "for a woman," was extraordinary.

Jeanne's work on the Civil War project made her think more about the old soldiers she had known in the Adirondacks. When she visited the north country, she spoke with neighbors, listened to stories, and jotted down ideas for poems. One of the central poems of *Neighbors of Yesterday* is "Union Blue," (66–70), the story of a father and son, Ben Hewitt and "Sonny," gone off "to fight the Rebs to make the black men free." Only the father returned. One night he was tortured by robbers when he wouldn't show them where he hid his money, in the pocket of his dead son's Union jacket. He told his story to a neighbor:

> It's mostly tatters now, the pocket tore
> A dozen times; I always mended it.
> I couldn't let those robbers lay their hands

> On Sonny's coat. I'll have it laid at last
> Inside my coffin, when I come to die.
>                     (70, lines 97–101)

A song by Henry Clay Work that Jeanne selected for inclusion in "Songs of the War Days," her section of *Poetry and Eloquence from the Blue and the Gray,* echoes the fate of poor Sonny Hewitt:

> When the boys come home in triumph, brother,
> With the laurels they shall gain;
> When we go to give them welcome, brother,
> We shall look for you in vain.
> We shall wait for your returning, brother,
> You were set forever free;
> For your comrades left you sleeping, brother,
> Underneath a Southern tree.
>                     (Miller and Miles 1957, 344)

Shaw's new writer not only proved she could handle herself in difficult circumstances, but seemed also a kindred soul, one who espoused many of the same ideas he held. He soon saw her value as a regular contributor to the *Review.* She wrote using various pen names, including Jeanne Robert, Robert Foster, and Jeanne Robert Foster.

In 1911, Shaw sent Jeanne to Europe to research a collection of political cartoons about Abraham Lincoln. It was her first trip abroad, and she spent most of that summer in the National Library of Paris. An old friend from Harvard, Frank Cheney Hersey, arranged for her to stay at a private pension near his own temporary residence. The owner was an impoverished baroness who had to board Americans in order to keep her family home in Dordogne.[2] Jeanne also visited Ireland on that trip and spent a few days with Albert Shaw in England.

As the *Review* took more and more of her time, it seemed inevitable that Albert Shaw and Jeanne Foster would become closer. It was as much a commingling of like spirits as it was a romantic liaison. Both loved art and po-

---

2. JRF , interviewed by RL, 11 August 1968.

etry and music. Both loved the wilderness, feared the exploitation of the environment, and admired the strength and fortitude of those who settled the land. Neither Shaw nor Jeanne was unencumbered, a fact they chose to overlook. For possibly the first but certainly not the last time, Jeanne Foster became infatuated with a man other than her husband, whose attractiveness and power had ebbed with failing health and finances. Jeanne was still married to Matlack, and Shaw to Elizabeth. Shaw's biographer, Lloyd Graybar, describes the latter marriage: "[Mrs. Shaw] had no aspirations to write nor any notable concern with the political and social problems that intrigued Shaw. . . . With his wife he had the familiar disagreement over the mountains and the seashore, went mostly to his choice, the Adirondacks, and about every fifth year journeyed as far as Mexico or Europe" (1974, 68–69). Shaw's favorite place to visit in the Adirondacks was Schroon Lake, which was only a few miles from Jeanne's hometown of Chestertown, where she returned as a frequent visitor after she began working in New York City.

Jeanne was alone in New York City much of the time so that she could pursue her modeling and writing careers, while Matlack remained in Schenectady at her parents' home, where he could receive the care he needed for his worsening heart trouble. And so Jeanne Foster's liaison with the handsome and powerful Albert Shaw seemed inevitable.[3]

In 1912, she was sent to Edinburgh to interview George Gray Barnard, a Wellesley professor who was studying wax original models for works of Michelangelo in a forgotten corner of the National Gallery of Scotland. Jeanne photographed the models and wrote an article concerning them for the *Review* ("Romain Rolland's Life of Michael Angelo," Foster 1913d). She and Barnard became lifelong friends.[4] He exhibited six marble sculptures of his own at the Armory Show in 1913, and Jeanne featured one of her favorite pieces, "The Birth," in her review of the exhibition (1913a, 447).

Next, she was off to Ireland, at Shaw's request, "to report on Æ's [George Russell's] economic progress in Ireland as outlined in his *Co-operation and Na-*

---

3. JRF, interviewed by RL, 11 August 1968.

4. George Grey Barnard (1863–1938), American sculptor. Scholars later determined that the models were inferior copies, not originals (De Tolnay 1948, 155).

*tionality.*"[5] The poverty that confronted her at every turn distressed her. In a 1912 letter to her mother, she described a typical accommodation in Ballyshannon:

> We stepped inside a single room of the main body of the house. It was black from smoke from the peat fires. To the left of the door was a table with a couple of mugs on it and a loaf of bread and a steel knife. There was no floor but the hard-trodden dirt. At the right of the fireplace a young woman was stirring a few potatoes that were roasting in the peat fire. The house was cold and damp and cheerless, but neither the man nor the woman seemed to fully appreciate the squalor of their surroundings.[6]

After returning to Edinburgh and Glasgow for several weeks, Jeanne left for New York on the Anchor line, deeply affected by her experiences in Ireland. There is no evidence that she met Shaw in Europe during her 1912 trip.

Jeanne never talked directly about her affair with Albert Shaw. Instead, she said only that in her diaries "R" was Albert Shaw ("R" for *Review of Reviews*) and that the diaries would explain the relationship. What follows is an excerpt from 1914.[7]

August 8, 9 P.M.
  Kew was very lovely today in the soft English twilight. The roses are just past, their prime, but the heather is in bloom and the phlox in its glory.
  In the greenhouses the great lotus buds were lifting from the pools, and the hungry goldfish darting beneath the leaves. The herbaceous gardens are perhaps most satisfying. The benches under the dark trees afford lovely solitude for reflection. I remember sitting here three years ago, when I was waiting for R, my heart torn with pain, my mind bewildered.[8] Yet then I was

5. Æ, George William Russell (1867–1935), Irish writer, painter, economist, and theosophist; author of *Cooperation and Nationality: A Guide for Rural Reformers from this to the Next Generation* (Chicago and New York: The Cooperative League, 1912).
  6. JRF to Lucia Oliver; copy sent from JRF to RL in August 1969 (LC).
  7. Unless otherwise noted, the JRF diaries quoted in this chapter are in LC.
  8. JRF refers to her first trip in 1911, when she also visited France and Ireland.

hopeful for the future. Now, I am resigned. I feel it is almost criminal to be so resigned. Yet life is so short, and the stubborn facts force themselves upon me. R is not young enough to build another life for me against the heavy odds. He has had his children: he is done with certain phases of life. I have no hope. Yet we are inextricably joined together. There can be no other life save his life—or our life together. I do not think much of power, the sense of power in me would revolt. I could send the happiness of a dozen persons smashing down to hell, yet because I could, this I will not.

On 15 August, she added:

I look across the sea into R's mind as into a crystal mirror, and behold the thoughts moving there in. Great thoughts, the survey of past and present, the balance of good and evil, the clear conclusions, the bewilderment, the final mystery.

How brave of men to have any faith at all in the face of events. Have they really any faith or is it a figure of speech? Always when I have penetrated to the depths of men's minds I have not found anything save a noble doubt in great men, and in little men, the devil.

R and I have what men call faith; that is we have courage to trust our barques to the unknown destiny that hurls us onward without fear or regret. At the end I am sure there will be only one value in remembrance, that we have a short span of moments together, that this life has pressed life, and that we have held our love in fine reverence, and lost no moment of possible tenderness.

Flesh is such a marvel, the body, the beautiful eyes, the delicate finger tips, the intricacies of nerve and muscle. Then what wonder, when there is the clear pure light of love, the immortal soul.

In 1916, Jeanne published her poem to Shaw, "The Resurrection: August, 1914," in *Wild Apples* (9):

When the ardor of life is burnt out, and the earth swallowed up in the sea,
When the heavens are shaken with thunders, where then, my Beloved, shall we
Find shelter from storm and confusion, and cover our heads from the blast
That searches the thrones and the kingdoms that were builded up strong from the
    past?

Where then shall we flee from the fury that shall torture the quiet of skies
That have covered us over in solace with purple pavilions of lies?

(lines 1–6)

Jeanne felt certain that no one knew of the affair, even though it was she
and not Elizabeth Bacon Shaw who most often served as hostess at dances
and parties held for the *Review* staff. It was well known that Mrs. Shaw did
not care to involve herself in her husband's business matters, and so perhaps
even this indiscretion would not have raised eyebrows.

One particularly important reception at which Jeanne served as hostess
was for Lady Augusta Gregory when she was visiting America with the
Abbey Players in January 1912. The party was given in conjunction with
the National Arts Club, and Jeanne made all the arrangements, including
hiring a musician to play Irish tunes on a harp and greeting the players and
Lady Gregory as they arrived.[9] In March, Jeanne wrote an article for the
*Review* about Lady Gregory and her efforts to revive the Irish theater, entitled "The Irish Theater as an Exponent of the Irish People."

The love affair brought Albert Shaw and Jeanne Foster equal amounts of
joy and pain, passion and guilt, but neither let it interfere with work. Shaw
had faith in Jeanne's ability as a journalist. Early in their professional relationship, for instance, he learned of her enthusiasm for poetry and for the
arts in general. In 1911, he assigned her to research and write an article on
Julia Ward Howe (1819–1910), the American poet and reformer. The article, titled "Julia Ward Howe as Writer," appeared in the February 1911 issue
of the *Review*. It received a favorable reader reaction, and Jeanne always
treasured some of her first "fan" letters from this work. The article is a brief
biographical sketch of Mrs. Howe, whom, it is obvious, Jeanne much admired. Jeanne had a critic's eye and understood that Howe's work was considered great, but focused on a poem she felt was particularly memorable:

Mrs. Howe's permanent contribution to literature will in all probability be
only a few lyrics of which the popular "Battle Hymn of the Republic" is the
most noteworthy. These fervid lines, sung to the tune of "John Brown's
Body," were written in the spring of 1861, while Mrs. Howe was visiting the

9. Murphy, notes from interviews with JRF, not dated (MC).

scenes of war in the outskirts of Washington. They were first set down on the back of some loose sheets of paper inscribed with the stamp of that patriotic body of men and women, the United States Sanitary Commission. *The Atlantic Monthly* published the poem and it circulated rapidly throughout the country, in camp, in hospital, in prison—wherever men listened to the call of freedom. The popularity of the "Battle Hymn" has only been paralleled by that of Mrs. Harriet Beecher Stowe's *Uncle Tom's Cabin*.[10] It is our "Marseillaise." It sank like a diver into the hearts of men. (Foster 1911c, 252–53)

More and more, Shaw gave Jeanne the responsibility for the literature and art sections of the magazine. In several of the letters she wrote to friends and historians in the 1960s, she verified that she was the literary editor of the *Review* and that it had been her idea to develop the page of poetry criticism and the "New Books" section. Although the magazine was a news and general feature periodical, and although Shaw had his doubts about expanding the section, he had by this time learned to trust Jeanne's judgment. Accordingly, after he agreed to put her in charge of "New Books," it became one of the most popular segments in the magazine. Jeanne took on the assignment with enthusiasm.[11] One of her articles ("Andrew Lang and His Work") focused on the work of poet, historian, and critic Andrew Lang, who had recently died (1844–1912). In two pages, Jeanne gave a short account of the author's life, briefly summarized some of his most influential work in both poetry and history, and examined his virtues as a critic: "[Lang] was not fearful of truth and laid bare faults with a sense of righteousness in so doing, but he did fear and loathe the flippant insincerity that leads straight to a distortion of facts" (Foster 1912b, 375).

Other literary figures and critics whose work Jeanne reviewed included a wide range of talent: Joseph Jastrow (*The Qualities of Men*), Arthur Christopher Benson (*The Silent Isle*), Richard G. Moulton (*World Literature*), Samuel Butler (*Unconscious Memory*), Edwin Bjorkman (*Is There Anything New under the Sun*), T. W. Rolleston (*Myths and Legends of the Celtic Race*), Arnold Bennett (*The*

10. Harriet Elizabeth Beecher Stowe (1811–96), American author and social reformer.

11. In an undated letter to Caroline Fish (CP), JRF explained some of her duties: "I was employed as literary editor, . . .carried eight pages of book notes ('New Books') and wrote all kinds of articles from women's prisons to 'blister pine rust.' "

*Whole Truth about the Author*), John Galsworthy (*The Pigeon*), James Stephens (*The Hill of Vision*), and Edward Gordon Craig (*The Art of the Theatre*). To some she gave a brief review. With others, such as Arnold Bennett and Edward Gordon Craig, she was more engaged.[12] In many such instances, as in the Craig essay, she used her position to argue her own ideas on art:

> To most of us the art of the theater is but cloudily discerned through the great dust of modern scenic effects. The tension of modern life in large cities is so great that we rush in search of any amusement, artistic or inartistic, as a relief for our over-burdened nerves. What we exact from our amusement is not in the main art, but simply respite from thought. It is an open question if very many busy people take the theater seriously or give the art of the theater any reasoned consideration. It does not concern them because they do not know what that art is, nor do they know that it is their duty to be concerned. Now, even to busy persons there comes occasionally a longing for the good old plays and players who acted them, and the question arises, What has gone out of the theater? If art, whither has it gone, and what was it really, after all? Also there comes the realization that the young and the unknowing are accepting the sham for the real, and that since the theater must remain with us or is likely to do so, it had best become a factor in our spiritual and artistic development. (Foster 1912c, 379)

In February 1913, Jeanne heard about a controversial show of contemporary artists held at the Sixty-ninth Regiment Armory and decided to attend. It was sponsored by the Association of American Painters and Sculptors and was financed primarily by the man who gave the opening address at the show, the lawyer and art patron John Quinn. There, as Jeanne wandered the halls of the great building, she saw the work of postimpres-

---

12. Joseph Jastrow (Ignaz Jastrow, 1856–1937), German author of social sciences. Richard Green Moulton (1849–1924), American author and biblical scholar. Samuel Butler (1835–1902), English author. Edwin August Bjorkman (1866–1951), Swedish American novelist and critic, born in Stockholm. Thomas William Hazen Rolleston (1857–1920), Irish author, critic, and historian. Arnold Bennett (1867–1931), English author. John Galsworthy (also John Sinjohn, 1867–1933), English author and dramatist. James Stephens (1882–1950), Irish poet and novelist. Edward Gordon Craig (1872–1966), English stage designer and director.

JRF, circa 1913. Londraville
private collection.

sionists, futurists, pointillists, cubists, and fauvists, and she knew
that much of her reading audience
would be confused, confounded,
and possibly offended by such
work. She, too, had questions
about some of the quality, but she
was captured by the possibilities
and so tried to understand: "The
participants fall naturally into
groups, which differ as to method,
but agree as to the end to be
gained by the so-called Modernist
art, which is the opening of av-
enues leading to regions where
there is more actual reality than
can be found in the objective, visible world. They seek the inner
meaning behind the bodily
form—the divine essence in nature" (Foster 1913a, 442).

She was especially taken with
French artist Paul Cézanne's *The Old Woman with the Rosary*: "It is most intimate and tender in its human appeal. In the cathedral cities of France one
may meet many such old women patiently toiling along the dusty roads to
mass on Sunday. This artist was the boldest of the revolutionists, one who
departed utterly from tradition and sought new fields of expression, but he
remained sane in his 'respect for his design, his surfaces and his mediums' "
(442–43).

When Jeanne wrote about the futurists, she described scenes far removed from realistic art, scenes that challenge the eye to comprehend a new vision:

> [C]omplementary colors are as necessary to painting as blank verse to poetry; that motion and light destroy the concrete aspect of objects; that bodies are not opaque . . . that objects in movement multiply themselves (a runaway horse has not four legs but twenty); that space does not exist (a wet street with puddles of water reflecting the lights and the stars is hollow to the center of the earth). . . . These Futurists are the individualists of art gone mad as it were, in their attempt to make painting motion like music, to create dynamic sensation. While their great imaginative vision makes much of their work interesting and worth attention, they need some common basis of agreement in their interpretations,—a common language that will make their work intelligible. (444–45)

The cubists also challenged Jeanne Foster's traditional sense of art. She was seeing a new world as she looked at Francis Picabia's *La Danse à la Source*, and she gave her readers a sense of her own awakening understanding:[13] "At first glance it is a meaningless jumble of pink and red geometrical forms; but as one gazes hard, it suddenly resolves into two dancing figures audaciously composed of blocks of color, but reproducing with fidelity the planes of light reflected upon dancing bodies" (445).

Even more daring to her was the work of Marcel Duchamp, specifically *Nu descendant un escalier*, No. 2. Satirized in a *New York Times* cartoon as "The Rude Descending the Subway," the painting created some furor, and the old question was heard again, "How can they call that art?"[14] But Jeanne was not willing to dismiss the piece so quickly: "The explanation of the work was not as difficult to understand as it was to catch a glimpse of the lady. Motion multiplies images; there were six sections of the figure partly superimposed upon each other. With the assistance of a moving picture machine to telescope the sections together a single figure could be resolved from the geometric forms" (446).

The Armory Show did not by any means neglect Americans. In fact, it housed the largest collection of contemporary American art until that time.

13. Francis Picabia (1879–1953), French artist and writer in the Dada movement.
14. Marcel Duchamp (1887–1968), French artist.

Works by Arthur Davies, Walt Kuhn, William Glackens, George Bellows, Robert Henri, and Robert Chanler were among the many represented.[15] Among Jeanne's favorites were Chanler's collection of screens: "The 'Leopard and Deer' screen resembles a Beardsley drawing in its mastery of the grotesque; the 'Porcupine screen' is a symphony of dull blues, silver and white; another reveals a scene of tropical deep-sea splendor, corals, devil fish and the beady phosphorescence of trailing sea-weed" (448).

Jeanne began the final paragraph of her article by quoting John Quinn, whom she had not yet met, and ended with her own plea to America to support its young, experimental artists:

> If some of the new art fails it is for the reason that John Quinn has given, "that it is lacking in intellect and there can be no permanently satisfactory substitute for brains." While it is a fine work to preserve that art of bygone ages for future generations, it is even more praiseworthy to appreciate and encourage the art that is of the present. By our loyalty to living art, we measure the ratio of our artistic progression as a nation. We must continue to look upon the "young vision" in matters of art with indulgence, for who can tell when the pattern of life shall change. Every generation has a rhythm of its own art and the succeeding generations will break up this rhythm and form another as surely as age follows age. (448)

Jeanne Foster immersed herself in the artistic climate of New York City, but she did not forget her Adirondack heritage and the hunger, the poor health, and the neglect that some of her neighbors, in particular women and children, still suffered amid the romance of the mountains. She remembered that little assistance had come from government officials who languished in their offices in Albany and Washington. All this became fodder for her *Review* articles, especially when she saw similar problems in Boston and New York.

She attacked legislators for their ignorance, but as quickly rewarded them with praise when they acted for the good of their people. On assignment in the British Isles for three months in 1914, Jeanne used the maga-

15. Arthur Bowen Davies (1862–1928); Walt Kuhn (1880–1949); William James Glackens (1870–1938); George Bellows (1882–1925); Robert Henri (1864–1929); Robert Chanler (1872–1930): all American artists.

zine—noted for its coverage of social conditions, both in the United States and abroad—to expose the harsh living conditions of the poor.[16] She was interested in housing reform as an agent for the betterment of general living conditions, and her ideas were in general agreement with the Fabian socialists.[17] Part of Jeanne's job was to visit and report on housing experiments, an assignment that, coincidentally, was to help her obtain a position a quarter of a century later with the Schenectady Municipal Housing Authority.

In England, Jeanne was given an introduction to a Mr. Peacock, the commissioner of housing. He showed her some of the extensive remodeling and reconstruction that was then going on. More than six hundred obsolete dwellings were being razed in the heart of London to make room for low-cost housing. Her survey also took her to Manchester, Birmingham, Glasgow, and Edinburgh. She was most impressed by Port Sunlight, the attempt by the owners of the Lever factories to make a pleasant and attractive factory town. The houses were solidly constructed of masonry and stone, and were situated in beautiful surroundings. It seemed that more than half a century after Carlyle made his appeal to the captains of industry to take responsibility for the welfare of their workers, something was finally being accomplished. Port Sunlight made the company towns of industrial America look like the slums that they were.[18]

Jeanne's experience with Port Sunlight caused her to consider how little was being done for the poor in general and for women in particular in the United States. She wrote "Woman and the Wage Question" for the April 1912 issue of the *Review*:

> Health is a social question and must be dealt with by government. The regulation of the scale of wages of women by the State is a step toward the preservation of the health of the worker. Those who insist on trying to bolster up the morals of the vast army of working women must first turn their attention

16. During JRF's assignment, Great Britain declared war on Germany. See her diary entries later in this chapter.

17. Fabians were English socialists of the late nineteenth century who proposed change by gradual reform rather than by revolution.

18. Two articles about Port Sunlight published during this period were "Garden Cities in Europe," *American City* 7 (December 1912): 504–5; and "Garden Cities in England," *Scribner's* 52 (July 1912): 13–16. JRF did not write an article about Port Sunlight.

to the physical welfare of these women. Mary Ann must have before her the ideal of pure womanhood, but Mary Ann must eat and be warm and have a roof over her head in order to protect that womanhood. Nor must she become a mother who is a beast of burden, a weary, bedraggled servant of a parasitic trade. Two children out of every four or five die before the age of five years. If the mothers can be given a little more comfort and a very little more leisure, she shall not find it necessary to raise the cry of race suicide in the streets. (Foster 1912f, 441)

Jeanne understood that poverty made people desperate. In an earlier piece, "The Care of Women in State Prisons" (July 1911), she had touched on this theme. A free-market economy may work for a Bounderby, but when it came to the poor, to women and children, to the old and sick, laissez-faire was a failure. The article stimulated reaction and was reprinted as far away as Manitoba, in the *Winnipeg Tribune* (Tuesday, 12 March 1912):

It has often been said that the barometer of crime rises as that of prosperity falls, and this is particularly true as regards the crimes of women. The thousands of women factory workers in every manufacturing city are never more than a few days from actual want. Given a period of overproduction or a depression in trade and the women's prisons fill with these despairing, idle workers. In New England, when the factories are running with a full force of operatives, there is a decided slump in the prison population, for all goes well with even these weaker spirits so long as they earn enough to eat every day and have a place to sleep every night. (Foster 1911a, 83)

Jeanne's ideas about women's rights were an integral part of her writing, and she voiced her concerns whenever possible. In her article "Ideas about Women" (April 1911), she reviewed a satirical novel (Marian Cox's *The Crowds and the Veiled Woman*, 1910) and an essay (J. Laurence Laughlin's "Women and Wealth") that attacked society's treatment of women (JRF scrapbook, LC).[19] Both authors feared that weak moral fiber was developing in the modern woman of the time, and, in a piece that hints at some of her own difficulties in a man's world, Jeanne agreed with them: "The Amer-

19. Laughlin's article appears in *Scribner's* 49 (February 1911): 199–206. (J. Laurence Laughlin, 1850–1933; Marian Metcalf Cox, 1882–?).

ican man of wealth . . . has abundantly looked after the physical need of
the American woman, but he has left her mind and soul to take care of
themselves. If she preys upon man with her false standards of vanity, extravagance and foolish emulation, it is man who must shoulder part of the
blame, for he has instilled into her shallow, childlike mind these same
predatory instincts." Jeanne asked that her readers help women develop a
"tenderness of conscience and humility of spirit" and reminded each
woman reading that she had the power for herself to decide what her character would be and whether or not she would be responsible for her own
destiny.

Her concern for women encompassed all facets of American society.
Whether women were rich or poor, in New York City or San Francisco or
prison, Jeanne's point was simply this: the government must provide them
with opportunities for education and success.

Jeanne Foster was particularly interested in the education of immigrants.
With a conviction that anticipated a later movement to multiculturalism,
she believed that there was a great deal to be learned from new cultures
brought to America. She saw immigration as revitalization, an "enduring
asset of American citizenship" (Foster 1917, 73). In "The Vitalization of
City Schools," Jeanne praised the work of an Italian immigrant who had become a principal at School No. 45 in the Bronx. Angelo Patri had come to
the United States from Naples as a young boy and had learned firsthand
about the inability of the American educational system to handle immigrants:[20] "He continually felt the great social gulf between the American
children and the foreign-born. The curriculum was taught, nothing more.
There seemed no desire on the part of the teachers to enter into his life or
assist in solving his problems. As he passed from lower to higher grades he
felt himself slipping away from his parents, undervaluing them, and cher-
ishing a kind of shame because they did not look or talk like Americans"
(Foster 1917, 73).

After Patri graduated from college and ultimately became a school principal, he worked on reforms that would better suit his student body:

20. Angelo Patri (1876–1965), Italian American author and educator, born in Italy.

He brought into the school curriculum gardening, dramatics, cookery, sculpture, and music, arranged out-of-door classes for anemic children, special classes for special needs, special teachers for defectives, social-settlement work with clubs and classes in music at the settlement house, obtained children's departments at the dispensary and a provision for a kindly woman who as "school visitor" investigated and adjusted the friction between the school and the home. The school became a living organism, a healthy, life-giving stimulus to the community. (74)

Jeanne's own view of education combined the study of citizenship, trades, the traditional "three Rs," love of the land, and the arts. The arts held a notable place in her scheme because literature, music, painting, and sculpture, in her view, touched and raised the soul, and it was this soul of the people that would ultimately be the measure of a nation. In Patri's school, she found the beginnings of her ideal:

Beside the school building a large new brick structure for shops is in the course of erection. Opposite the school are the gardens with carefully weeded plots of vegetables, enclosed by a border of flowering shrubs and plants. In the garden is a practical greenhouse built by the boys of the school. Beyond the garden is a spacious playground filled from morning until night with divisions of happy children. The school proposes . . . to build a Greek theater in the playground and enclose the plot in a wall decorated with bits of sculpture made by the children and their parents. (75)

In New York City, young immigrant children were learning new ideas and a new language, while their parents were struggling to put food on the table. Even though these parents were laborers and were not well versed in American ways, they still had valuable skills and talents. For Jeanne Foster, the family was the best hope for this nation, and it had to be fortified by the entire community:

The child who learns a new language and different habits from the neatly dressed teacher and goes back to a home where the parents do not speak English and cling to slovenly ways of living, soon tends to drift away from parental love and the family feeling unless corrective influences are brought to bear in the school. The children of foreign peasants and artisans are shown in the new schools how much better their parents can do certain kinds of work than the smart teacher. Antonio's father can raise more vegetables on a plot than the school gardener. Victor's father, who makes the replicas of classical sculpture, can do better than the teacher at modeling. Aida's mother can make more beautiful lace and embroider better than the sewing teacher.

    . . . I believe that statistics show that a large percentage of our younger criminals in States prisons are recruited from the children of foreigners who have drifted away from home influence and parental love and guidance. (76)

Schools needed to be community centers because in most cases they offered the only chance for escape from poverty and hunger at worst and from drudgery and mediocrity at best: "Bring the work of the community to the school and then give the work of the school to the community" (77).

Although Patri's program was a success, it was only one success among many failures. What would happen to those already lost, to the young beggars and criminals roaming the street? There had to be other institutions to deal with their reality, but were prisons the only answer? In Freeville, New York, not far from Cornell University, Jeanne found another alternative and wrote about it for the *Review*. It was called George Junior Republic, established by "Daddy" William R. George. In her article ("A Republic for Boys and Girls—After Twenty Years,") she attacked an American society that would allow its young people to be lost to the squalor of city slums and to be educated, if at all, by a Gradgrind system of schools:

[The youth] were nurtured on a dry-dust educational diet consisting almost entirely of memorized facts. They were carefully kept from any knowledge of the concrete workings of their book-learned theories. And—because of their aggregation in large schools—they were afforded too little part in helping to apply the principles of economics that lay about them. Mr. George's experience during a summer spent in caring for "Fresh Air" children recruited from the slums, thoroughly convinced him that the boy who struggled with difficult conditions in life (conditions that gave nutriment to temptation and that aroused by their very exigencies the impulse to crime) could not become a normal and useful citizen under the existing system of education.

This boy must be taught a political creed not based upon the "spoils system." His mind must be made fertile and the seed of democracy sown therein during the tender years of his life. (Foster 1910, 705–6).

Jeanne reported that although George Junior Republic was once investigated by the Department of Public Charities when rumors about mismanagement circulated, no evidence had been found of impropriety.[21] She was so certain about the value of George Junior that readers were swept along by her enthusiasm and her hope:

The Junior Republic is as thoroughly organized as the Greater Republic. The Town Meeting is a substitute for the Legislature, and voting citizens are those between the ages of sixteen and twenty-one. . . . There is a Bar Association, and in order to be admitted to the Bar, the aspiring boy must pass an examination before the Judge and three members of the Association. . . .

The citizens live in cottages that are presided over by an adult helper called the housemother. . . . The accommodations at the various cottages differ in quality and in price. A boy who is industrious may afford to live at the cottage that is called "The Waldorf" because of its superior fittings and food. If he is lazy he will be compelled to put up with a room at the "Beanery," where the rooms are plain and the food of the simplest.

. . . Many of the Republic boys have entered Cornell, Harvard, Columbia, University of Pennsylvania and other colleges, where they make a particularly good showing in logic and economics. A Republic boy won an important prize at Harvard this year. (708)

Because of her interest in prison reform, Jeanne was particularly interested to discover that the community had its own jail and that prisoners were sentenced by the community's own justice program, overseen by trustees but administered by the boys and girls:

21. In *The William R. George and George Junior Republic Papers* (housed at Cornell University, not paginated), Douglas A. Bakken writes: "George and the Republic had weathered an investigation in 1897 by the New York State Board of Charities. The Board, 'shocked perhaps, by the non-institutional untidiness and independence of the "citizens," issued an adverse report on the Republic.'"

[The jail] is a small building somewhat resembling a chapel in its style of architecture. Within, two-thirds of the space is taken up by ten steel cages containing bunks for the prisoners.

"How do they treat a boy in jail?" I asked the boy keeper.

"Oh, good enough, the same as the rest of us, except he doesn't get pie or cake and he has to work where the keeper says, and he can't get his own clothes until he gets out. There are books in there he can read if he wants to when he isn't working."

The girls' prison is a small cottage at the farther end of the grounds. The girl prisoners wear a uniform of brown, but there are no steel cages in this building,—simply bare walls, cot beds and tables covered with oilcloth. No prisoner, either boy or girl, is debarred from school privileges by his imprisonment, as there is a separate school kept for the prisoners. (709–10)

Modern readers may judge Jeanne Foster's obviously sympathetic treatment of George Junior Republic as advocacy, but if Jeanne lost some objectivity because of her passion for reform, at least her optimism was prophetic. She would be delighted to know that in 1995 George Junior Republic celebrated its centenary and continues its work with young people today.

Jeanne was frequently out of New York on special assignments for the *Review* and was on such an assignment in 1914 in London when the British declared war on Germany. On 2 January 1969, she wrote about her experience: "I landed in England three days before war was declared, on the next trip in 1914. I remained in England mostly but managed to get to Scotch Arran and tour that interesting island but failed to get to Ireland.[22] I spent much time with the Straus American Committee in London and managed, with my credentials, to see the troop movements on the Salisbury Plain, ride troop trains about, and send many pictures back to New York" (JRF to RL, in LC). Her diary entry for 5 August 1914, midnight, reads:

War declared upon Germany at 11:30 P.M. Hearing the commotion in the streets I drove down Piccadilly in a cab to see the crowd. It was gay—one might have thought a holiday declared instead of war. Processions marched singing the "Marseilles" and "God Save the King." Flags were sold by the

22. Scotch Arran is an island in the Firth of Clyde, southwest of Glasgow.

hawkers. French people shouted "Vive le Belge." Presently the crowd tore away to Buckingham palace and after a brief wait King George and Queen Mary came out on the balcony of an upper window and bowed in answer to the cheers.

Jeanne was aware that she was in the midst of an important historical event, and, as all good reporters do, she took extensive notes of the hectic days that followed the declaration. The next day she wrote: "The excitement continues. John Bull offers a startling poster—'To Hell with Serbia.' Soldiers march hither and thither. The Scotch Territorials came down the Strand to the skirling of bagpipes. Men are rapidly enlisting. The service force of the hotel is depleted, so many French and German waiters have returned to enlist" (diary, 6 August 1914).

While in London, Jeanne found herself caught up in the general excitement of "the war to end all wars." But she still arranged visits to the Tate Gallery and to Salisbury Cathedral. She formed the habit of noting her impressions of works of art, and these impressions were a written reminder by which she could summon up the original experience. Of the Salisbury Cathedral sculptures she wrote in part: "Around the walls of the chapter house run curious miniature sculptures giving the main incidents of Bible history down to Moses receiving the law" (diary, 14 August 1914).

Although she continued her note taking at cathedrals and art museums, she was struck by the contrast of the energy that man had put into his art and the energy he was now expending for destruction. Still in Salisbury, she wrote: "It is raining, down on old Sarum, down on ancient Stonehenge, down on the British battalions encamped on Salisbury plain on the white winged airships and the black guns. Military law has been proclaimed. All stations are in charge of the British Territorials. One seemed before to live outside history: suddenly history is in the making everywhere" (diary, 15 August 1914).

Jeanne Foster was seldom outside of history from that point on. Her position with the magazine gave her access to information that an ordinary citizen, especially a foreigner, would not otherwise have. During her three months' stay, she took a great many pictures of England's mobilization, which she sent to her magazine. She had earlier resigned her position on the *Review*, believing that she should stay in England to help as well as she could with the war effort. Shaw of course refused her resignation and instead told her to do as she wished, but to send whatever copy and photographs she could.

Accordingly, Jeanne remained for the most part in London, but she used her press pass to go where most women were not allowed. At one time, when train space was almost nonexistent, she settled for a wild ride on the top of a railroad car to Cambridge, which included harrowing moments rounding curves and estimating clearances under trestles. There was little that could get in her way once she sensed a good story, and the inconveniences of wartime England posed no insurmountable problem for a woman with her grit. Her propensity for being in the right place at the right time resulted in many stories and photographs for the *Review.* She was in London, for example, when the first Zeppelin was shot down. It came down at Euston, directly on a school for poor children, killing many of them.

One of Jeanne's most arresting memories of the war concerned her interviews with the London Rifles. Several British regiments were bivouacked in Hyde Park before their eventual overseas assignments. While she was interviewing the young men who comprised this particular regiment, they noticed that she carried a camera and asked if she would take pictures of them in their uniforms, so they might send them home. Jeanne was glad to do so and arranged for copies to be sent to them at the front. All of the packages of prints she sent to France were returned. None of the men whose pictures she took survived the first battle of Marne.

Jeanne was to have one more adventure before she left England for the United States. In the early days of the war, when she thought that she no longer had a job on the magazine, she decided that she must economize to make her money last as long as possible. She therefore sold her return passage on an American steamship. There was a general terror of the German submarines, and passage on an American line was at a premium because American shipping was at this point still exempt from U-boat attacks. Soon all the available space was taken, and those who would sell their passage could name their own price.

Jeanne decided to use the extra money from the sale of her passage for expenses while in London. When she finally did leave Britain, there were still no passages available on American ships, so she booked on the *Columbia,* a Scottish ship. At first, she had been inclined to discount the stories

JRF's photograph of soldiers from the London Rifles, Hyde Park, 1914.
William M. Murphy private collection.

told of submarine terror, but she confessed to some fear when shortly before her departure she heard that the passenger ship *S. S. Belgray* had sailed
from New York for a secret destination with war supplies. The conflict was
heating up. She was apprehensive when she saw that the British battleship
*Tiger* was to accompany the *Columbia* for the first five hundred miles of the
crossing, but, except for one periscope sighting, the trip went as smoothly
as could be expected.[23]

Jeanne continued to write occasional articles for the *Review* until the
early 1930s, although during the later years she did not contribute as often
because so many other demands were being made on her time. When exactly her relationship with Albert Shaw ended is unclear, but even after she
met John Quinn in 1918, there was still affection between Jeanne Foster
and her editor. He wrote to her on 17 June 1919 about her piece on "the
*beautiful* Roosevelt poetry feature, that will be so much liked, and that will so
help our July no. to have success."[24] He spoke of his disappointment over
not being able to see her and of flowers—"poor little dewy pink roses"—

23. JRF, interviewed by RL, 15 July 1968. See *New York Times*, 31 October 1914, 3, for the
Belgray incident.
24. Shaw refers to Foster 1919b.

that he had sent her. He ended, sadly, "I have a piece of gold in my pocket but sorrow in my heart because I needed to see you today" (NYPL). Some years later, after John Quinn had died and Jeanne had returned to Schenectady, she received several letters from Shaw, who was by this time spending much of his time in Winter Park, Florida. From there, on 7 March 1932, he wrote to Jeanne about a gathering he had been invited to at writer Irving Bacheller's home to honor writers Clinton Scollard and Jessie Rittenhouse.[25] "I should like it tremendously if you would write one of your charming little tributes, and send it to me so that I may read it, as from you, next Sunday night" (NYPL). On the evening of the party, Shaw read a short piece about Dorothy Parker and then read "your poem impressively, with everybody in the room listening with attention and approval, and giving ample applause."[26]

In June of the same year, Shaw was in New York City, where he arranged to meet Jeanne, who made the journey from her home in Schenectady. "It was wonderful to see you," he wrote after she left on 16 June. "You were looking amazingly well, in view of all that you have been through. I wish you were here. . . . I shall expect to see you soon" (NYPL). The strain of her brother's death in May that year must have shown. Fifteen months after her day with Shaw in New York City, Jeanne informed him of Matlack's passing. Shaw wrote to her on 9 September 1933: "Mr. Foster was fortunate, thro' long years of inactivity and invalidism, in your devoted care of him, and in your courageous example, as you were fighting the battles of life so resolutely. We shall go at our appointed time, one and all, and words about it may help a little, but not much. You would know that you have such sympathy as I can give" (NYPL).

This is the last letter from Albert Shaw to Jeanne Robert Foster, and there are no more from her to him. If she continued to have any kind of relationship with him, no documentation exists. Shaw's own wife of thirty-eight years, Bessie Bacon Shaw, had died two years earlier, in 1931. His magazine was losing readership and finally merged with the *Literary Digest*. His time with the *Review of Reviews* was ending. Shortly before he received

25. Irving Bacheller (1859–1950), American author. Clinton Scollard (1860–1932), American poet. Jessie Rittenhouse (1869–1948), American author, critic, and editor.

26. Shaw to JRF, NYPL. The letter is dated only 1932.

Jeanne's letter about her husband's death, Shaw remarried. It was another example of Jeanne's remarkably bad luck with men. Whether or not she and Shaw might have married and shared the last years of their lives together we will never know. Instead, he wed Virginia McCall, his secretary, twenty-two years old. They seemed from all reports to have had a comfortable marriage. He was able to continue to spend most of his summers in the Adirondack Mountains he so loved, but escaped the cold to winter in Florida (Graybar 1974, 195).

Albert Shaw died in New York City on 25 June 1947, one month shy of his ninetieth birthday, and was buried at Sleepy Hollow Cemetery in North Tarrytown, New York. Jeanne never mentioned how his death affected her.

No matter how painful their relationship might have been for her, Jeanne was forever grateful to Shaw for her position with the magazine. The job changed her life in immeasurable ways, and living in New York City provided her with fresh opportunities to meet important people. One such occasion presented itself shortly after she began working for the *Review*, when she took dinner at the Petitpas restaurant, locally celebrated because of one of its patrons, Irish portrait artist John Butler Yeats.

# 4

# "The Father of All the Yeatssssss"

ON A SEPTEMBER EVENING IN 1992, in the Adirondack village of Saranac Lake, New York, an audience of teachers, writers, woodsmen, and historians gathered to learn more about one of their local literary figures. On that night the topic was Jeanne Robert Foster's connection to the Yeats family, for she was primarily known to them as a regional poet. When they discovered that Jeanne was buried next to Yeats's father[1] in the cemetery in Chestertown, only a short trip from Saranac, they were intrigued. In a memorial poem about her friend, Jeanne once described the setting of his grave:

> He sleeps in foreign soil but in an earth
> Not alien to the Sligo that he knew.
> The grass a duller green and washed by rains
> Slanting upon the headstone that records
> "Painter and writer," words that his son wrote
> To be incised above his father's sleep.
> The mists move slowly in the ancient trees
> Above the circled cross and the birds sing
> As long ago, piercing the elegy He did not hear.
> Now each one listening,
> Doubting his senses, hears an overtone
> As of a voice that still threads ancient dreams
> Upon a silver chain. It may be sound
> Or other script and the incredulous eye.
> See iridescence quivering on the mound.[2]

1. "Yeatssssss" is Ezra Pound's tag for Yeats père, quoted in *MFNY*, 15.
2. JRF, quoted in Fish 1970, 42.

How did the father of the great Irish poet come to be, as Jeanne said, "the one artist to whom I felt the most gratitude and friendship"? What is the story of these two "improbable neighbors in death"?[3]

While Jeanne Foster was making preparations for her and Matlack to move to New York City for her job on the *Review of Reviews*, one of her friends told her that if she must leave Boston, then she should at least take advantage of what culture there was "in the provinces." The best show in town was not on Broadway but in the Petitpas restaurant on 317 West Twenty-ninth Street, where John Butler Yeats took his meals:

> I met a young man, John Weare, a proctor of one of the Harvard Dormitories. . . .[4]
>
> After I had written myself into a job in New York with the *Review of Reviews*, John gave me advice.
>
> "Go to Europe as soon as you can and go alone and after that trip get a job there if you can, but go.
>
> "When you reach New York, do not wait. Go directly for your first dinner to Petitpas restaurant, West 28th St. John Butler Yeats is there. He presides over a long table. I am sure you will meet him." (Foster n.d.a)

JBY, who had a "rakishly paternal benevolence to young writers and artists" (Alfred Kazin in *AP*, xi), was the doyen of a group that included most of the important young literary and artistic figures of New York City, among them John Sloan and Van Wyck Brooks.[5]

One evening in early 1911 Jeanne decided to follow John Weare's advice and take her dinner at Petitpas, quite honestly hoping to catch a glimpse of JBY and perhaps to overhear some of his famed talk. She took a table removed from the central board where JBY and his friends were eating and talking, and was soon enthralled by the conversation. She was not so spell-

3. JRF, interviewed by RL, 11 August 1968, and Frank 1984, H-1.

4. John Weare was a descendant of Meshech Weare (1713–86), who graduated from Harvard in 1735 and was the first president of New Hampshire (1784–85) and a distinguished jurist.

5. John French Sloan (1871–1951), American painter, etcher, and illustrator who gained fame as a member of "The Eight" or "Ashcan" school in New York. Van Wyck Brooks (1886–1963), American critic and writer. See Brooks 1927.

bound that she forgot to take notes, however—a habit she had refined in her college classes and one that would catch JBY's attention. He once said, "Some of us learn by talking, but the wise men, the fine men, learn by listening" ("John Butler Yeats" 1962, 10). Jeanne was a beautiful woman, and JBY seldom ignored beauty. Intrigued by Jeanne's presence, he asked her to join them for dinner. She told the story in a 1970 letter:

> I went to Petitpas and sat down at one of the small square tables and ordered dinner (meanwhile I was taking notes as I listened to JBY talking to his friends). Before I could be served one of the Petitpas sisters came to me and said: "Mr. John Butler Yeats, the gentleman at the long table, requests that you will have dinner at his table." She took me over and the white bearded JBY greeted me and gave me the seat immediately at his right. He most graciously asked me if—when I came to Petitpas, I would occupy the same seat.
>
> From the first, I took JBY to the Poetry Society and National Arts Club dinners. All the rest you know: the posing, the care, the [resting place] in the Adirondacks—all from JBY's calling a strange girl to his table. (JRF to RL, in LC)

Thus began a friendship that was to endure until the painter's death in 1922. For his part, JBY gained the respect and admiration of a beautiful, talented woman; for hers, she found a mentor whose wit and humanity shaped her life and her art. The old man liked it when Jeanne Foster escorted him to friends for an evening of conversation, and he developed a bit of a crush on her, writing on 27 December 1921, "I wish I was forty. I wish I saw you oftener. I wish I had lovely blue eyes and a silken moustache, and that I could make clever rhymes—" (MC). Through him, Jeanne became acquainted with people such as Padraic Colum, Eamon de Valera, Douglas Hyde, and other Irish notables who were looking for their pots of gold in America.[6] All liked to have John Butler Yeats at their tables. Like Co-

---

6. Padraic Colum (1881–1972), Irish poet and playwright, a leader of the Irish literary revival. Eamon de Valera (1882–1975), Irish statesman, born in Brooklyn but raised in County Limerick. He served as head of state from 1959 to 1973. Douglas Hyde (1860–1949), Irish scholar and writer, leader of the movement to revive Irish language and literature, and one of the founders of the Abbey Theatre. He was the first president of the Republic of Ireland (1938–45).

leridge's, some of his best ideas may have spent themselves in conversation. Fortunately, enough of his genius is preserved in his letters, especially those to Jeanne, that we retain a glimmer of his remarkable critical insight. Jeanne once wrote about him:

> John Butler Yeats, more perhaps than any other man living in his time, was able to instantly penetrate the hearts and minds of friends and acquaintances with understanding and sympathy and view their problems from the angle of each individual cosmos. He was a good listener. . . . But withal he was the best talker that ever came to our shores, a master of the lost art of conversation. He was perhaps a greater personality than an artist but both his art and his personality will live. (Foster n.d.b, 1)

After one of her first dinners at the Petitpas restaurant, Jeanne returned to her apartment and recorded part of the conversation:

> I went to Petitpas last night. Mlle. placed me at an empty seat near the head of the table. I saw an empty envelope lying on the next plate. It was addressed to Mr. J. B. Yeats. Presently a fine old man came. . . . His beard was white and his eyes looked brown under the shadow of his white eyebrows. He addressed me and we talked of Ireland and then we drifted to W. B. Yeats of whom I had been writing in the last Review and on to the Irish Players. I said that I had seen The Countess Cathleen that week. "I told my son," said J. B., "that he should write a prologue for that play. One is lifted into an atmosphere of miracle and wonder without due preparation. People listen and do not understand until the play is over and then they do not know whether they like it or not." I agreed and then we talked more about Ireland and I told him some stories of my inspection of the tenements of Glasgow and the regulations there about babies that they should not be fed fish and hard food before they were a year old. J. B. was delighted and shouted to Mrs. Chapman.[7] "Do you know Mrs. Chapman that in Glasgow if one feeds a baby fish before it is a year old the mother is hauled before a magistrate?" Then turning to

7. Mrs. Chapman was wife of picture dealer Frederick Chapman. JBY did not care for either of them, describing the husband as having "the manner and ways of the Englishman of the type Tristie Ellis, only without the intellect." He considered Mrs. Chapman "haughty" (PF, 390, 619, note 65).

me—"And what about the Irish babies?" "They were very dirty in Derry," I
answered, "outside the walls on the north side of the down, dirty but sturdy,
rosy rascals. Ireland is kind. Her soft winds comfort the children and the
faeries give them health in spite of the dirt." "But we have the model Guinness tenements at Dublin," he hastened to say.[8] "Yes," I answered, "but one is
never interested in model tenements. There's nothing to do there. I always
had that fear about Heaven. If I succeeded in getting there, I'm sure its perfection would bore me." (Foster n.d.b, n.p.)

In spite of his susceptibility to their charms, JBY had very strong opinions on American women, which he outlined in "The Modern Woman":
"Self-improvement is her passion; improvement in what direction? You will
ask. She herself does not know. Meantime she insists on absolute personal
liberty—moral, physical, mental, and also political. That she may be free
she places a ban on the senses and upon sex; either of these would put her
back under subjugation" (1969, 264). Feminists would find little with which
to agree in JBY's attitudes regarding women and literature, but Jeanne, as
she did with many other men in her life, dismissed or ignored the negative
aspects of JBY's advice and concentrated on what was useful to her. Whatever his feelings about the deficiencies of American women, it is clear that
he exempted Jeanne from his judgments.

Over the years Jeanne affected the painter's life in ways no one could
have predicted. B. L. Reid tells one humorous story about a sketch JBY
made of Jeanne: "On the headlong emotionality of the French J. B. Yeats
had just had a demonstration from the Petitpas sisters. They had been so
pleased with his drawing of the beautiful young matron Mrs. Jeanne Robert
Foster that they had enthusiastically set alight the house furnace, cold for
weeks, and smoked him out of his room" (*MFNY*, 313).

And on another occasion, JBY showed the sisters a particularly beautiful
photograph of Jeanne. Again, warmth pervaded, for a short time at least: "I
showed the photo to the Petitpas and they liked it so much that they im-

8. For information on the Guinness firm's welfare work, see John Frederick Halterman,
*Industrial Relations Policy: Arthur Guinness, Son & Co. Ltd., St. James's Gate Brewery, Dublin, Eire,
1914–1937* (N.p.: n.p., 1940); and J. Lumsden, *An Investigation into the Income and Expenditure of 17
Brewery Families and a Study of Their Diets Being a Report Made to . . . A. Guinness, Son & Co Ltd., St.
James's Gate, Dublin* (Edinburgh: Morrison and Gibb, 1905).

mediately kindled the furnace and gave me a pleasant afternoon in a warm room—the emotion of an impressionable race. Alas! It did not endure—the next morning things were as before, and the furnace was cold" (7 May 1917, NYPL).

Jeanne Foster intrigued JBY for several reasons. When she spoke to him, he discovered that she had a quick mind as well as a beautiful face. He had read some of her work in the *Review* and some of her poetry. Here was a young woman who could grace his table with more than beauty, one that could hold her own with the spirited group that had gathered around him.

Although Jeanne had already been to Ireland, JBY encouraged her to go again:

> I should like you to meet my daughters and thro them become acquainted with Æ and Susan Mitchell and all the literary people of Dublin.[9] If you thought of going there, I would write to all these people, and you need not be afraid of "putting them out." We are all too delightfully poor and happy, to be put out by anything—we are just awfully glad to see a genial stranger, and want him or her to tell us things and hear about our things. It is all conversation and a sprinkling of tea cups but lots of conversation. (letter, 10 August 1913, MC)

He delighted in telling tales of his country and soon had Jeanne eager to visit, armed with JBY's directions and suggestions. She already felt that she knew Ireland, at least in part—not from her previous trip, but by virtue of her upbringing in the Adirondacks, where many of her neighbors had immigrated from the old country. JBY thought that in spite of Jeanne's family name, he detected strong Irish qualities in her. She had the "speckled" hazel eyes and the complexion of a colleen. The more he talked, the more she was determined to see "his" Ireland.

The opportunity arose on her next assignment for the *Review*. She first stopped in Edinburgh to work on her Michelangelo article and then crossed the Irish Sea: "Finding that I was with the *Review of Reviews* pleased [JBY], also that I was devoted to W. B.'s work. In 1912, with his encouragement, and an assignment from the *Review*, I went to Dublin. W. B. was not

9. Susan Langstaff Mitchell (1866–1926), Irish poet and editor.

there then nor Jack but I covered the Cuala Shop, met Susan Mitchell and Æ." Jeanne also met Lily and Lollie Yeats, JBY's daughters, and she and the Yeats sisters immediately liked each other and remained friends for as long as the latter lived, exchanging presents and letters until the end.[10] Some of these first presents from the Yeats girls were proof sheets and working copy from the Cuala Press.

On the same trip, Jeanne performed what she described as "an act of abject cowardice" that prevented her meeting George Moore.[11] She had just finished an examination of his *Hail and Farewell* for the March issue of the *Review* and wanted very much to speak with him. She wrote in her review: "One arrives at the conclusion after reading *Hail and Farewell* that either we do not care to be saved, or that Puritanism has triumphed over paganism, or that George Moore has grown a trifle garrulous and a bit uncertain of the righteousness of his creeds." But she added: "He has the knack of being interesting no matter what he writes about, and the fascination of his style is as wonderful as ever" (Foster 1912d, 380.) She went so far as to walk up to his door, but lost her nerve at that point. She had heard tales of his womanizing; in short, she was afraid. She resolved from that day never again to let fear prevent her from those experiences she needed to be a journalist and a poet.

JBY was disappointed that Jeanne had missed his son Willie on her trip. He wrote to WBY about her on 10 May 1914, shortly before the poet visited the United States. JBY would make certain they would meet:[12]

A young lady with me at the time who writes (and writes well) all the poetical criticism in the *Review of Reviews*, told me that you were the only poet of any account, and that of course she agreed with me. She is a Mrs. Foster and extraordinarily pretty and clever—and tho' her husband is old and an invalid

10. Lollie Yeats assisted Evelyn Gleeson when the latter founded Dun Emer Press. Ms. Yeats eventually took charge of the publishing house.

11. JRF, interviewed by RL, 16 August 1969. George Augustus Moore (1852–1933), Irish writer. In his trilogy *Hail and Farewell* (1911–14), he wrote about his associates in Ireland, sometimes maliciously.

12. JRF wrote to RL in June 1969, "Later on, in 1913, in New York accompanied by his father, I met W. B." (LC). From JBY's letter, we can assume that JRF had forgotten the exact date.

the most malicious tongue has nothing to say. . . . She says that since she was a child she has been interested in white magic and wants very much to know something of black magic. She comes from very poor people in the Adirondacks—her husband educated her and she married him. Then he lost his money and became an invalid and has only enough to support himself in a hospital.[13] I first met her here, everyone likes her. It is rare to find so much really strong intellect with kindness and affection. (J. B. Yeats 1946, 259)

When Jeanne Foster first saw William Butler Yeats, only a few days after he had received this letter from his father, he stood before an almost reverent audience in New York. It was a moment she never forgot. Jeanne had expected to be impressed, but the effect of Yeats's reading seemed to her a synthesis of man and art. WBY was forty-nine at the time, in full command of the force of his poetry and masculinity. It appeared to Jeanne that he had achieved his desire of being one with the ancient bards of Ireland. On 31 December 1968, she wrote about that night: "He seemed to me the most beautiful human being I had ever seen—tall, dark haired with beautiful eyes and with so much music in his voice as he read that I could only recall a description of Tir-na-Og, where soul was 'music glittering in the air' " (JRF to RL, in LC).

Jeanne Foster met William Butler Yeats after his lecture, and then returned with John Butler Yeats to the latter's room at the Petitpas boardinghouse. In the course of the evening, they discussed some of the differences between WBY's earlier work and his current poetry. JBY suddenly got up and began to rummage in his papers. At length, he drew out two pieces of manuscript. "Here's something Willie did when he was a lad," he said. "You can see the difference in the imagery and technique."

What he brought forth was an early version of "The Cap and Bells," which was titled "The Queen and the Jester." When he was finished using the poem as an illustration, he gave it to Jeanne. This characteristic generosity of the older Yeats was to account for many of the items in her collection. She wrote on 3 June 1968: " 'The Queen and the Jester' was given to me by

13. Matlack Foster's illness did not prevent him from taking a train trip across Canada and around the western and southern United States with his wife the following year (1915). JRF's interest in black magic was instrumental in her attraction to Aleister Crowley when she met him in 1915 (see chapter 6).

William Butler Yeats, drawn by
John Butler Yeats, 1903.
Londraville private collection.

John Butler Yeats after W. B.'s
lecture in 1914 at the National
Arts Club, Grammercy Park. It
had been enclosed in a letter to
him by W. B., his father said. (I
judge that is why it lacks his signature.) JBY said, 'Willie asked
me to give him my opinion of a
poem.' JBY did not refer to an
earlier version and said he
thought I would 'like to have a
poem of Willie's written in his own hand' " (JRF to RL, in LC).[14]

JBY always seemed to have treasures lying about. He had a habit of carrying a small copybook with him, which he used to illustrate points with
sketches and sometimes to write some of his thoughts on aesthetics. He
was careless with these copybooks, however, and when he had filled one,
he usually threw it away. Jeanne was horrified when she saw him do this,
and she asked if she might rescue them from the dustbin. He agreed, more
to humor her than for any other reason. He was a perfectionist who threw
away most things that he did not consider his best, and the sketches and
paintings that remain today are only a small part of his total output.

Some of the less dramatic but most interesting parts of JBY's work that do
remain are the notebooks that Jeanne saved. They comprise a unique
record of those nights at the Petitpas restaurant. There are sketches of his
friends, explanatory drawings that JBY could use to describe someone's fea-
tures more easily than he could recount them, interesting faces and scenes
that he saw from his vantage point at the head of the table, and many notes

14. The manuscript is now in LC.

in his almost undecipherable hand. Jeanne's vigilance in preserving these notebooks and her own transcripts of conversations with JBY have provided scholars with an otherwise unobtainable view of the Petitpas group.

A part of JBY's talent less well known than his painting was his remarkable critical sense. His ear was excellent, and he had a gift for recognizing and excising the sentimental. When he helped Jeanne Foster with her work, he suggested many of the same techniques that he had employed with his son. He wanted her to write her ideas first in prose, for example, and he encouraged her to make her poetry dramatic. Above all, he pleaded with her to rewrite and not to believe that her first impulse was necessarily her best. He also enlisted her in conversations about other poets, so that by teaching her about them he would encourage her to think more about the flaws and attributes of her own work. In JBY's letters, there is ample evidence to support Jeanne's contention that he was a "teacher of writers." On 17 August 1916, he wrote to her about his poetic discourse with WBY. Both he and his son were saddened by the tragedy of the Easter Rising in Ireland a few months earlier:

> I have lately been maintaining with my son the thesis that the poet's serious mind is to be found in his metre and his cadences and his rhymes and that the rest, the contents of his verse, is a levity. The levity of tragedy or of comedy. What is "Romeo and Juliet" but a wild levity and a monstrous dream, enclosed and incased in sorrowful metre and that to my mind is the test of true poetry. Because of the metre, we tremble and deliciously believe. I think that the poor innocents whom the English shot had the heroic levity. But their metre failed them. They had not worked over it long enough and so they failed. Then the English came and convicted the verses and even their levity is flawlessly expressed in marmorean verse. And Ireland stands up with all the world their friend. The shooting of these martyrs is Ireland's natal day. (NYPL)

JBY was not reluctant to attack writers Jeanne Foster knew and admired. One of her favorite newcomers was Kahlil Gibran.[15] His mysticism appealed to her, but JBY saw through Gibran's sentimentality. Seldom has a writer been skewered with such good humor.

15. Kahlil Gibran (1883–1931), Syrian symbolist poet and artist.

Last Monday . . . amidst all the noise and enthusiasm . . . sat a quiet man, charming, tactful and modest amidst the general homage—your Syrian, the artist of "The Madman"—a man endlessly clever and practical, that is to say where art is concerned *quite insincere*—and all the time I kept wondering how Mrs. Foster could take this man for a genius. Except in organizing a practical success, cleverness is always insincere in poetry as in Religion, because cleverness aims at *external* success—whereas genius belongs to the inner world of conviction and idea and mood, and vision. I am sure that he is a nice fellow enough and perhaps he believes that he believes. (letter, 6 February 1919, NYPL; see also *PF,* 500)

By using Gibran as example, JBY identified a quality of Jeanne's judgment that characterizes much of her lesser poetry. She had a tendency to be mawkish, and that fault never improved her verse. JBY was concerned that her poems were too maudlin, especially some that were to appear in the *Wild Apples* collection in 1916. He wrote to her about one of the poems on 3 June 1915:[16]

A personal confession . . . is something ragged and repellent. Transmute it into music and dream, and it begins to throb with something that is akin to the harmony of the spheres.

My advice is to keep that poem longer—for months even—on the anvil. You have got a good thing—such as comes to one only once or twice in a lifetime. Don't let it slip from you till you have conquered it—like Jacob wrestling with the angel. Women are often bad artists—they find that with their personal charms they can get people to listen to their confessions. Men are better artists, because their personal charms count for nothing with male critics. (NYPL)

He accused her of not thinking hard enough, when he wrote on 4 July 1915: "I was at once interested in your 'wife to a husband.'[17] You write best when you think hard about something which interests you so much that

16. One typescript of this letter is in MC and is dated 3 June 1915. Another typescript of the same letter is in NYPL but dated 2 June.

17. *WA,* 31. The poem's actual title is "The Second Wife Speaks."

you are compelled to think hard. The basis of every good poem is a prose thought born in a poetical mind" (NYPL).

A few weeks later, she sent him another verse, "Come Thou with Me" (WA, 26). He did not spare her feelings:

> As to your poem—I will be frank—always in everything you write, there is intensity, and intensity is so rare—hardly ever do I see it anywhere—in other words, there is so seldom a real human being behind the technique—and now comes a curious thing—intensity is the best friend to technique and so often its enemy, especially in woman's work. A woman is so impatient for a result, an achievement, that she won't wait—won't let the "intensity" be long in her mind and heart. The gestation of a poem is like the gestation of some antediluvian monster—in this I do not put things too extravagantly. For one thing the intensity must be kept far remote—it must be there, but so subtly that we feel it rather than see it. (letter, 28 July 1915, MC)[18]

Seven months later, still explaining and teaching, JBY gave Jeanne Foster the same advice he gave to his poet son:

> My theory is that every poem should first of all be written in prose. Not a word admitted which is not to the accurate truth—just as God Almighty first of all constructed the skeleton with every bone accurately adjusted—utility the only purpose—afterwards adding in a kind of transport the bloom and the loveliness of flesh—so the poet should work—and when anything has been put down in the strictness of severe thought, let him add the beauty— slowly as the heather catches fire will come the metre and the music and all the imagery. . . . In nothing does the major differ from the minor poet so much from each other as in the quality of strong thinking. Aeschylus in his "Furies" has said everything that can be said on punishment for criminals. To the prose man it is a profound treatise on criminology.
>
> Oscar Wilde's theory that one should begin with the music is all right for certain moods and certain minds, but for the thinker poet, among whom I unhesitatingly place you and also my son, my theory is the right one. (letter, 16 March 1916, NYPL)

18. JRF took JBY's advice and revised her work.

However trenchant his criticism, it was an honor for Jeanne to be mentioned in the same sentence as William Butler Yeats. On 24 March 1916, JBY told her that even though she had flaws as a poet, there was something about her verse that captured him. Perhaps he felt as if he might have written a bit harshly in his previous letter: "The real thing that most matters is that the poet be a natural singer—you are a natural singer—logical or illogical you sing—and it is your singing quality that finds its way to the marrow of my bones" (NYPL).

JBY didn't want Jeanne to listen only to him and so sought out friends who might be able to offer useful comments. One was Van Wyck Brooks. When JBY first submitted some of Jeanne's work for Brooks's judgment, the verdict was less than enthusiastic. On one occasion, JBY sent a report: " 'Well,' [Brooks said], 'it is quite queer,' and after a pause, 'extraordinarily interesting, but it is not poetry.' I drew his attention to several sentences. Such he acknowledged to be true poetry. And why are these sentences poetry? Because they are musical" (letter, 3 June 1915, MC).

Jeanne used these comments to improve her work. By May 1916, Brooks had read more of her poetry. JBY reported the positive results: "The other day when Van Wyck Brooks was here I read to him several of your poems, without telling him anything of their author, without any preliminary whatever, and he was enthusiastic in his praise—and I assure he is not at all disposed to accept the people I praise—very much the contrary—he is a stern and competent critic" (letter, 19 May 1916, MC).

JBY warned her against calling her collection *Wild Apples*, "a title which makes me grind my teeth. You must live it down," and, in a letter two months later, again cautioned her about what he saw as one of her poetic flaws: "The little poem you send is a rough draft, a very rough draft of what may become a good thing—there is in it a something sombre which promises well—but it has the fault rather characteristic of woman's work—it needs artistry. That is, you have not worked over it long enough—it is without shape, and it is without music—yet there is in it the seed—the good seed" (17 August 1916, MC).

Even as late as 1921, he did not want her to forget the weaknesses he saw in her work. Some of her verses were still compromised by sentimentality. She had to fight the impulse to write "personal" verse. He felt so strongly that he wrote her two letters on the same day (26 February 1921):

[Letter 1] Some time ago I took up "Wild Apples" and at once found it so in-teresting—interesting is the word I would always apply to it—yet it has faults—you don't think hard enough. . . . in you I find more of the *materials* of art and poetry than in any one else, a sort of tumultuous richness and music also—broken music, but still music. Only there is disorder and worst of all monotony in thought—the love motive overworked. For instance, in one of your poems, you seem to summon all your ancestors and you say you are welded with them by love. Were all my ancestors to come together and we could look into each other's eyes, the tenderness with which I and they would regard each other asks for another word—a word much more definite and precise than that overworked word "Love." What is the word?—Hard thinking would find it and achieve a triumph.[19]

T. S. Eliot says [William] Blake had an extraordinary gift of language—*so have you.* I suppose it is because your life is so busy that you don't think hard enough. If only you would think hard what jewels, what pearls, and dia-monds you would fetch for us—out of the vastly deep of a sound logical se-quence.

It is illustrative to read how appropriate JBY's advice was, especially for a young poet impatient to share her feelings. Paradoxically, JBY's problem was exactly the opposite. He could not bear to abandon a piece and deem it finished.

[Letter 2] There is plenty of genius in your poetry, indeed for that matter there is plenty in America—but where is the artist? There are no artists be-cause there are no critics—the critic does the analysis, scientifically and coldly—and then the artist discovers himself, comes to birth in the man of genius. For instance in your poem about your ancestors—the critic in his careful prose-way would have analysed "the situation"—and the feeling— and then the man of genius having with his awakened artistic conscience lis-tened long is inspired and names the feeling which the other described, and that name is a note of poetical music.

Love should never be overworked. Love is the emotion of the Beautiful, and must not be turned into a maid of all work.[20]

19. The poem is probably "The Yellow Rose."

20. One typescript of letter 1, in MC, is dated 26 February 1921. The other, in NYPL, is dated 28 February. Letter 2 is in MC.

"The love motif overworked," "because your life is so busy." These two fragments reveal a great deal about Jeanne Foster's poetry. Her love relationships were at least disappointing, yet she was young enough to dream of meeting someone, and this unfulfilled yearning permeates her verse.

Jeanne said that she understood and tried to use JBY's criticism, but with limited success. If she had time to keep some of her weaker poetry "on the anvil," it might have improved, but it was difficult to separate her emotional life from her work.[21]

JBY's most appropriate advice that Jeanne was able to use in writing her poetry was his suggestion to dramatize her work. In a dramatic monologue, there would be no place for Jeanne's personality; she had to assume the mask of the speaker and use only that voice. That is why *Neighbors of Yesterday* is a better book than *Wild Apples*. In the former, she is forced to be the dispassionate teller of a tale.

When *Neighbors of Yesterday* was published in the autumn of 1916, Jeanne gave a copy to JBY, and in that collection he found what he considered to be her true poetic voice. He was an admirer of Robert Browning's dramatic monologues (Browning, he said "most sharply and pleasantly titillates the *surface* of my soul" [letter fromn JBY to JRF, 27 December 1921, NYPL]), and he had encouraged his son in the dramatic when Willie was just a boy, suggesting that "all must be an idealisation of speech, and at some moment of passionate action or somnambulistic reverie" (W. B. Yeats 1965, 42–43). Now, with Jeanne's second book, JBY saw her finally becoming the artist he knew she could be:

> I have just read your book at a sitting. I don't know why I like it so much, why it carries me along, and I shall often read it. I think it is just *because you have something to say*—tho what this something is I can't say—it is an essence indefinable. *The something to say that is the test* of eloquence and of poetry and art— only it must be an *essence indefinable*. I wish so much that I had made a drawing of you to be put in as frontispiece—when the next edition comes out, let me put into it a drawing of you. Knowing your book I think I could do a good one. It would help the appreciation of the book. But photos are horrors. In

21. JRF, interviewed by RL, 10 August 1968.

this case the photos of Adirondacks scenes etc. are justified by the fact that it is all a picture of the Adirondacks—but don't let anyone persuade you to put a photo of yourself. I don't know why photos strike such a chill but they do. They are always bad company among the dreams of art and poetry. . . . I am enthusiastic over your book—it set my heart beating, it is *vital.* (letter, 21 December 1916, MC)

Three months later, JBY was still singing praises:

Accidentally I picked up your little book of Adirondack stories and have read nothing else yesterday and today.

"Break their wills, break their wills, teach them to kiss the rod with tears," wrote the genial John Wesley about the bringing up of children.[22] Yet fine literature is to me like John Wesley's rod—and so is your little book—I love the *words* in your book, they are perfection every time, and you know so much. Where did you get it all? The specific gravity is weighty in every line and when you like to be abstract you have a fine set of the grandest words—and there is music, heaps of it, and such *common sense,* which is the substance of poetry, and in consequence no straining after pathos, or sentiment or "Beauty." It is as natural as baby talk—and we know how startling and wise that can be. (letter, 2 March 1917, MC)

It is remarkable praise, especially in light of his previous reservations, and the reader can appreciate JBY's sense of discovery. There was little in Jeanne Foster's earlier work that foretold the breakthrough in *Neighbors.* The book renewed his desire to paint her, for although they had become very close, it is possible, Jeanne said, that JBY's enchantment with her Adirondack book made its author more enchanting as well. He became excited and frustrated. His room had to be made exactly right for her to sit. If it could not, he would have to find another, for, as he wrote to her, "Portraits of handsome women who also are poets must run no risks" (7 May 1917).[23]

On 11 March 1920, he elaborated on her verse and his idea of the great poet:

22. John Wesley (1703–91), English founder of Methodism.
23. JRF, interviewed by RL, 10 November 1966; and JRF to JBY (MC).

I am constantly from time to time reading your poetry and *getting into them* deeper and deeper and repent me that I said you were a rebel. Or if it is rebellion it is constantly *arranged by innumerable pictures.* You have this in common with the great poets. The constant surprise of felicitous expression.

I think a poet is always a solitary. Yet under conditions, he is a solitary explaining himself anxiously, pleadingly, asking for friends and listeners. Every *poem is a social act done in solitary.* Hence comes so much of that elaborate ceremony of art, so delightfully apparent in the manner of the great poets. He is a sublime courtier who finds himself in a king's court and because of the delicacy of his spirit he has a supreme courtesy. Let others rave and shout and defy the world. This cannot be his way. He is too much of a stranger in a strange world, too timid. The social men who are not and cannot be solitary, the creator and the writer of prose, they can do these things. They are to the manner born. They are a robust crowd of noisy fighters who uplift and sentimentalize, with the ease and freedom of a people who know their friends too well to be afraid of them. (letter, NYPL)

In another letter written two months later, JBY reiterated that Jeanne needed to move away from the sentimental and conventional that he saw as the weakness in *Wild Apples.* She needed always to concentrate on dramatic forms: "I have discovered—or I think I have—that you are at your best, strike your real note, send out your clear bell note when you are dramatic. Drama is your pole star—sail for it always, and your wild apples will no longer be wild. It is your serious side—all this came over me some time ago in a flash, and I said to myself she is a dramatic poet. How can I get her to see it?" (28 May 1920, MC).

He warned her on 7 June 1920 that she had an audience now, and they would expect much from her. She could not return to her less-mature work, or her following would be lost: "I want to impress on you the fact, that tho a real poet and a solitary, you have an audience who will not forgive you if in your advance towards them you make some one slip—they must be flattered and coaxed and cajoled, above all they must not be *bored*—any extravagance or exaggeration bores them and vehemence offends them" (letter, MC). JBY had told her only a month earlier that her work suffered from these flaws and that she had to battle them as his son had battled them: "Your work has one fault against which [WBY] is always contending—*extravagance* and that is what I mean by saying that it needs more work—'all art is simplification' " (letter, 10 May 1920, NYPL).

Unfortunately, Jeanne did not heed his advice and returned to largely conventional poetic forms in *Rock Flower* (1923), and although the collection contains some good verse, as a whole it falls far short of her Adirondack work. She fell again into the trap against which JBY had cautioned her. Later in life she successfully returned to her dramatic work and to the Adirondacks for her subject. She didn't fully assimilate JBY's advice until long after he was gone, when she was "old and gray . . . and nodding by the fire," when she could slowly read and think about the words he had written to her long ago.[24]

24. JRF, interviewed by RL, 10 August 1968.

# 5

# John Butler Yeats
## The Last Years

JEANNE ROBERT FOSTER had not thought about being a caregiver to
John Butler Yeats during the first few years of their acquaintance, but on
several occasions when he needed help she provided both comfort and
care. One day in 1915, JBY, never a careful pedestrian, was crossing the
street when he was hit by "a cart carrying goods for Greenhut and Company" on Sixth Avenue and Forty-sixth Street (PF, 432). He received a
"stunning blow" and found himself "crumpled up in the mud" (PF, 433).[1]
While he was recuperating, he drew a sketch of himself sitting in a chair by
a window, arm resting on a table, pipe in mouth, and sent it to Jeanne with
the inscription: "I ought to have answered your note sooner, but—I have
been making bad weather against adverse winds. I have been taking my
ship with all her tackle torn into port. She is now safe at anchor, and I am
sitting ensconced in my favorite inn from the window of which I can see
her sleeping on her shadow, a glass of warm punch at my elbow, while I am
filling the room with peaceful tobacco smoke. There I am a picture of
happy somnolence, relaxed to my finger tips" (PF, 434–35).

He accepted her invitation to accompany her on a picnic with the Un-
termeyers (26 April 1915), but, for all his assurances and efforts, JBY never
completely recovered from his accident.[2] If he had been on the financial
edge before, he was now beyond it. He thought he would be able to make
enough to be self-sufficient, but he did not. William Butler Yeats paid a

---

1. JBY to Lollie Yeats, 22 Jan 1915.
2. Louis Untermeyer (1885–1977) and Jean Starr Untermeyer (1886–1970), American
writers and editors.

number of his father's bills during his recovery and sent him money; and even though JBY knew that WBY could ill afford the additional expense, he had no choice but to accept the gift. He wrote to Jeanne on 30 July 1915 that WBY "is his family's constant aid & help & mine also. It is done in such a way that one is left to think he is not himself conscious that he is doing anything" (PF, 455).

Without financial help from John Quinn and WBY, JBY would have seen difficult times. He wrote to Jeanne, "I wish I could avoid getting more money from WBY and I am doing my best, but still I can't neglect the portrait." [3] Over the years, even she occasionally gave him money. He thanked her for her donations of ten and twenty-five dollars respectively in letters dated 28 July 1915 and 22 June 1919 (MC). Jeanne never said exactly how much she gave the old man; she said only that she "occasionally" sent him a little money. These contributions were not payments toward various portraits he was doing of her. Indeed, he pursued her on that matter and even wrote, "I shall ask no payment except the pride of painting you. Every decent artist will envy me my luck" (22 November 1916, NYPL). [4] Financial aid was something Jeanne Foster could ill afford to give, but her generous nature made it difficult for her not to extend help to a friend in need.

Still ensconced in the Petitpas boardinghouse in 1918, a place with little ventilation and warmth, JBY began to plan his trip back to Ireland. The price of dinner had been increased ten cents, and every penny put more strain on the old man. He wrote to his daughter Lily that he might go home in the autumn, but fate decided to take another turn. Continuing to plan his departure, JBY wrote again to Lily on 30 October that one of the house guests at Petitpas had caught the flu. Ten days later, he fell victim himself. When John Quinn found out, he ordered his own doctor to visit JBY to try to convince him to go to the hospital. JBY refused. Quinn visited him once but was so worried about his own health that he dared not return. He had gone through a major surgery earlier in the year and did not trust his constitution. He castigated the doctor for failing to convince JBY to go to hospital, and as a compromise a nurse was hired, one Miss Finch-Smith. Quinn

3. JBY to JRF, 30 October 1911, NYPL. The JBY work was a self-portrait, *Myself seen through a glass darkly*, for John Quinn.
4. Many JBY sketches of JRF are in MC.

wrote to Jeanne Foster, whom he still had not met, to ask her to manage the "medical outpost" (*PF,* 487–88).

The flu progressed to pneumonia. JBY survived when thousands in the country died in the epidemic that year, but this illness was the second blow to his system. The accident had weakened him; the flu damaged his heart and lungs. Quinn wrote, quite accurately, to JBY's daughter Lily, "I have had a devil of a time with your father."[5]

The man who was to have the most profound effect on Jeanne Foster's life introduced himself first by telephone. In the early days of JBY's illness, Jeanne kept Quinn informed about JBY's health mostly by letter, and he was grateful to have someone calm and competent to watch over his friend. He was startled when he finally saw her; she was not some wrinkled old lady friend of JBY, but was instead an intelligent and beautiful young woman. JBY reported Quinn's reaction in a letter to her on 29 December 1918: "J. Quinn called yesterday morning and as he looked at the book of Russian tales [which JRF had given JBY]—he murmured over to himself, 'She is an awful nice woman,' saying the words twice over—and I repeated them again to myself. . . . When Quinn is happy he is an angel of light" (NYPL).

Two years later, in the spring of 1920, about the same time that WBY and his wife, George (1892–1968), were visiting New York City, Cuala Press published an edition of the collected letters of JBY, which undoubtedly pleased the old man.[6] Quinn bought six copies and inscribed one to Jeanne: "To J. J. O. [Jean Julie Oliver] These letters of an old friend of hers from a friend of both. J. Q. April 16, 1920." Jeanne was delighted and took the book to JBY, who sketched in it a self-portrait and signed it: "I write my name with pleasure at Mrs. Foster's request. J. B. Yeats" (MC).

Jeanne Foster and the young Mrs. William Butler Yeats got along well when they met, the latter finding Jeanne to be an intelligent and amiable new friend. On 29 January 1920, Jeanne had a memorable evening with the Yeatses when she attended a dinner given by the Poetry Society in New York City in honor of WBY and sat with JBY at table number 21. Mrs. Yeats's notes about the evening include a number of pointed remarks about

5. John Quinn to Lily Yeats, 20 Nov. 1918 (*PF,* 488).

6. Cuala Press, formerly Dun Emer Press, was the publishing house of Dun Emer Industries. The Cuala Shop, another division, employed Irish girls to work in arts and crafts.

some of the ladies attending: "a dreadful woman," "a ghastly bore," "another dreadful woman." But she was impressed by her father-in-law's friend and told Lily Yeats that "of all the women in America only Jeanne Foster was able to carry on a conversation properly."[7] Although Jeanne liked Mrs. Yeats, she did not think George had completely replaced Maud Gonne in the poet's heart. She remembered what JBY had told her in 1914: "I don't think Willie will marry. He has always been devoted to Maud Gonne. She didn't care for him! Maud Gonne could not love a poet. She would only love a man of action. She is a fine woman—a handsome woman—but doubtless she never looked at a line of Willie's verse. Besides Willie has no money. It was better he did not marry Maud Gonne; his unsatisfied love has made many fine poems" (PF, 422). On 10 May 1920, JBY suggested that Jeanne send Mrs. Yeats a copy of *Wild Apples*: "[WBY's] wife tells me how much she likes you and how much she admires you. She did not know that you were a poet" (letter, NYPL).

As the months wore on, Jeanne continued to watch over JBY, knowing that he was failing. He seemed tired, even of conversation: "I am supposed to see every evening a throng of poets and wits and be master of them all—bosh!" (letter, 21 February 1921, MC). By 17 May 1921, he may have felt better because he asked Jeanne for another sitting: "I will be disappointed beyond words—if you do not give me another sitting—all I ask is one sitting—my mind is full of this subject" (NYPL). He was never satisfied. Two years earlier he had shown one of his sketches of Jeanne to Matlack Foster, from whom, interestingly, he had received a mixed review. That response had only motivated him to rework and redo: "Mr. Foster has a quick mind . . . and he condemned the sketch, altho he wanted to carry it off, and besides in its present state being unmounted, he could not take it with copy and drawing, so I got his leave to keep it a few days longer. I shall then but 'carry the drawing farther,' as Turner used to say, and . . . afterwards send it to whatever address you like. Or I can take it back here and keep it for you—this last plan would please me best—for reasons" (letter, 1 September 1919, MC). Perhaps he did not want Matt Foster to have the sketch of Jeanne after all.

---

7. JBY to Lily Yeats, 10 June 1920 (PF, 507). See also PF, 642, note 7.

Any improvement in JBY's health was short-lived. In June 1921, John Quinn and Jeanne Foster, now in love and wishing to escape New York City for a time, left on a trip to Europe. Before their departure, Quinn brought JBY to his apartment for a quiet lunch. The lawyer did not deal well with illness—it frightened him and reminded him of his own mortality, especially now that his health was failing. What happened at the luncheon upset him so much that he did not tell the Yeats children about it until after their father died:

> While I was talking on the telephone he [JBY] passed down the corridor to the end of the hall and into my bath-room. Just as I had finished talking I met him in the hallway coming back. His lips were red. I thought that he had a fever, then I got the odor of creosote which I realized that he had taken.[8] . . . He said, "Well, Quinn, I think I will be going now."
> . . . When I came back to my bathroom afterwards I found traces of blood on the toilet seat. He had wiped most of it off but there were traces of a hemorrhage. It was a tragic thing and very brave of him not to speak of it. I knew what that hemorrhage meant. (*PF,* 527)

It was too late for Quinn to change his travel plans. When he returned from Europe, he decided to arrange for JBY's passage back to Ireland, but the old man was stubborn and wrote to Jeanne in late November, "I have told [Quinn] I won't go, defying every principle of good behavior and affronting his kindness."[9] Jeanne knew the end was not far away for the old Irishman. He tried to keep working, as if the attempt to fulfill his duties would keep him alive. On 12 January 1922, he pleaded to Jeanne to let him work more on her portrait: "Give me another chance to save my soul, and your face. Both are for eternity. . . . Come here and let me do half a dozen of you all in one sitting till I get the right angles. I *did not know your face as I now do*—don't disappoint me—besides if I fail with those six—the other remains—when I did that other I did not know as I do now how to draw the *outside contours* of any face—do you know what I mean?" (*PF,* 534).

---

8. Creosote was at the time used for indigestion and other intestinal discomfort.
9. JBY to JRF, November 1921, postmarked 28 November (MC).

While he sketched, they chatted.[10] Once, JBY asked Jeanne about death:

One day when I was sitting for Mr. Yeats for a pencil sketch he asked me about W. T. Stead and his belief in spiritualism. Then he asked me if I had read "Letters from Raymond."[11]

J. B. "Do you think one could know what was going on about one so soon afterwards?" (meaning after death)

Mrs. F. "I don't know if I think about it at all. I feel that I shall know."

J. B. "Willie would have a good deal to say about it I daresay. . ."

Mrs. F. "Why?"

J. B. "Because I should enjoy going to my own funeral."

Mrs. F. "You would."

J. B. (with great animation) "Yes, I'd enjoy seeing all the strangeness . . . looking at myself, watching the people, hearing what they said. I'd like to go through it all with my sketchbook. Think of what a sketchbook a man would have—sketches of his friends at his own funeral. And I'd have such a curiosity about everything. By Jove, I would be interested. I might even do a sketch of myself."

Had he known "what was going on" at his burial in Chestertown, old Yeats might have been disappointed in the attendance at his service. There were few faces to sketch.[12]

On 27 January 1922, John Quinn took Jeanne Foster and John Butler Yeats out shopping, and they stopped to see a showing of the Kelekian Collection pictures.[13] Quinn later wrote: "Five or six beautiful Cézannes hung on the walls.[14] I said, 'There are some fine Courbets. I imagine you prefer them to the Cézannes.' To my surprise he said, 'No, Quinn, I do not. I like

10. The "transcription" of this discussion is in MC. Murphy also includes portions of the JBY-JRF discussions in PF.

11. JBY refers to Sir Walter Scott's Letters on Demonology and Witchcraft . . . by Raymond Lamont Brown (London: G. Routledge and Sons, 1884).

12. Even though there were few people at the burial in Chestertown, the service for JBY in Ireland was well attended.

13. The DiKran Kan Kelekian art sale is reviewed in the New York Times, 1 February 1922: 23: 1.

14. Paul Cézanne (1839–1906), French artist.

Cézanne very much. I do not think that everything by Cézanne is great, but I think he was a very great artist' " (Hone 1965, 365).

On 3 February, at 6:50 in the morning, John Butler Yeats took his final breath. Jeanne was the one by his side much of the time during the last few days. On 1 February, he had written to his daughter Lily that he had done two more pencil sketches of Mrs. Foster, but he had felt tired and ill, thinking that he was once again fighting flu: "I must stop and go and see that Doctor," he wrote to her. "How I hate N York and its winter!" (*PF*, 537).

These were his final written words. The pain increased that evening, and Jeanne was called to his side again. She arranged, with Quinn's help, for morphine shots and promised her friend that the pain would not return (*PF*, 536–38). The last time she saw him he spoke to her with all the wit and charm he had always displayed. It was difficult, she said, to think that he was so near the end.[15] As soon as she returned home that evening, she recorded much of this final conversation with him:

JBY: I think those doctors should have told me that that horrible pain I had last night would not last long. Here I was in the midst of it fearful that it couldn't be stopped and thinking that I must go on suffering and then I went to sleep and when I woke up it was gone. By Jove I went to sleep in hell and woke up in heaven. And you tell me that it won't come back. That is a relief. You're sure they (the doctors) can stop it if it should?

JRF: I'm sure. Don't worry about it. The doctors could have stopped it at once if they had been here. You won't have to suffer any more.

. . . Later in the day he had me tell him about the prices and the buyers at the sale of the Kelekian collection paintings held at the Hotel Plaza. I had been at the sale both evenings and I remembered incidents of the bidding and the name of some of the buyers and the prices. He listened with eagerness and asked questions. He has seen the paintings twice while they were at the American Art galleries and remembered many of them distinctly. He was pleased that the big Cézanne still life, which he admired, had been sold to Miss Lizzie Bliss for $21,000.00. He was glad that the Detroit Museum had bought the Van Gogh self portrait which he admired, but he laughed aloud when I told him that the Brooklyn Museum had bought the Degas nude, a back view of a coarse fleshy figure, "one of Degas's washerwomen," John But-

15. JRF, interviewed by RL, 10 November 1966.

ler said, and then he told me a story of the waggish son of some professor of Greek he had known long ago.[16] The professor was very forgetful and also very prudish. He was unable to endure any stories or any kind of jesting that bordered on pruriency. His son was studying Greek. In one of the books he was reading in Greek this phrase occurred—John Butler gave the Greek, then translated—"the Venus of the beautiful buttocks."[17] About once in three months the son would go to the father with the book open in his hand and say, "Father I cannot quite make out this phrase. Will you translate it for me?" The professor would take the volume, scrutinize the passage gravely and then say "That phrase my son, is in translation 'the Venus of the beautiful buttocks.'" After which he promptly forgot the matter and in about three months the same comedy of translation was gone over again. It's very amusing that the Brooklyn Museum should have selected out of all those lovely paintings this Degas washerwoman of the "buttocks" for the edification and education of the Brooklyn high school boys and girls. (Foster n.d.b, 1–4).

A sketch of Jeanne Foster lay on one of JBY's drawing boards. The unfinished self-portrait of JBY sat on his easel. He asked her, shortly before she left, "Did you see Quinn looking at my portrait?" She answered in the affirmative (Hone 1965, 364, and *PF,* 538).[18] A few hours later, John Butler Yeats was dead.

The day following JBY's death, Albert Shaw stopped by to pay his respects. Jeanne recorded his visit in her notebook so that she could later reproduce it for JBY's family:

Dr. Albert Shaw sent a large box of white Kilarney roses and lilies of the valley to the house—Petitpas—Friday morning. On Saturday morning, he called and asked if he might go up to Mr. Yeats's room. When he came down he was profoundly moved. He said, "I have seen many persons after they had passed out. I remember my mother, that there was beauty and peace in her face, but I have never seen such dignity and nobility as I saw just now. He re-

16. JBY's opinion of Degas's work was a taste that WBY shared. In the prologue to *The Death of Cuchulain,* the Old Man says, "I spit upon those dancers painted by Degas . . . above all upon that chambermaid face." Edgar Degas (1834–1917), French artist.

17. Venus Callipygia.

18. The portrait of JBY is in the private collection of Michael B. Yeats.

minded me of one of the old Greeks—as I imagined one of their great artists or poets would look. I wanted to find something—some line that would be fitting. I could only think of 'Here lies our master, gracious calm and dead.' " (Foster n.d.b, 6)[19]

JBY's funeral was on 5 February, Sunday, at the Church of the Holy Apostle, in Ireland. The Yeats family could not afford to transport the body of their patriarch back to Ireland, and so for that winter JBY rested in the Wood-lawn Cemetery vault in Westchester, New York.

Jeanne Foster and Lily Yeats wrote to one another frequently during the next month, both expressing their love for old Yeats. Lily told Jeanne about her dreams: "I dream constantly of my father and he is always in the highest spirits, two nights running last week I dreamed of him. The first night he said to me 'You builded better than you knew' and on the second night he gave me a very ornate gold key—it was so vivid I thought the key was in my hand when I awoke. What the dreams mean I don't know, but they remain with me still as something very pleasant" (3 May 1922, NYPL).

Jeanne offered to have JBY buried in her family plot in Chestertown, New York, and William Butler Yeats accepted: "I have been able to see all my family and all are most grateful for your offer of a burial place for my fa-ther. It is most kind and generous of you. We of course accept" (29 March 1922, NYPL). Because of the winter, JBY was not buried until late July. Jeanne wrote on 10 December 1968 about the service:

I took JBY to Chestertown and placed him in my plot in the Chestertown Rural Cemetery. The Sloans were to be there, Colum and Gregg and others. Quinn was too ill to come, but when Mr. Fred Mundy, the friend in charge of the funeral parlor in Chestertown met the train at Riverside to bring them over, and also the casket, no one had come, so with the Leggett Grave dig-gers and the Methodist Dominie, we laid John Butler Yeats away, the leaves of the white birches trembling in the breeze, the songs of the birds wreath-ing through the service of the Methodist parson.

Later on, I wrote the Irish Senate to please send a battle ship to take John Butler Yeats to Sligo. I have their reply. They said: "a member of the family

19. The reference is to Browning's "Grammarian's Funeral": "This is our master, famous calm and dead, / Borne on our shoulders" (lines 27–28).

must make the request and that no request had come from the family and that the great old man must remain where he was." (LC)[20]

For her friend's final resting place, Jeanne chose a stone made from Vermont marble, with a Celtic cross cut in the top. The inscription ("In remembrance of John Butler Yeats of Dublin, Ireland. Painter and Writer. Born in Ireland Mar. 16, 1839. Died in N. Y. City Feb. 3, 1922) was written by his eldest son, the poet. William Butler Yeats wrote to his sister Lollie on the day following his father's death: "If he had lived longer, he would have grown helpless and known that he was helpless. He had his hopes and ambitions to the last, constantly writing that he was painting his masterpiece. . . . An American publisher who came to see me a few weeks ago had promised to sit for him on his return to New York. He lived in hope and I think the past hardly existed for him, and his hopes filled his life" (Donoghue 1976, 269).

In 1967, with William M. Murphy and Jeanne Robert Foster by his side, Senator Michael Yeats, son of the poet, visited Chestertown and the grave of his grandfather, who had once written to Jeanne, "To be with you is to come home after weary alien sojourning" (letter, not dated, NYPL). She never forgot his place in her life.

From "John Butler Yeats: 'Alas, for the wonderful yew forest!' ":[21]

> We shall remember him
> As a man who had a little in him of the men of all time.
> We shall remember him—
> This tall, lean-shouldered, witty Irishman,
> Master of the art of conversation,
> Jesting with us in his high-pitched Irish voice,
> That lilted to a delicate string
> Beyond our hearing.
>
> (lines 1–9)

20. JBY was Protestant—hence, the Methodist parson.

21. This poem was published in William Stanley Braithwaite's edition of the *Anthology of Magazine Verse for 1922;* in the *New York Times* on 6 February 1922; in *Current Opinion* 7 (22 April 1922): 535; and in *RF,* 3–4.

# 6

# The Occult
## W. B. Yeats and Aleister Crowley

JEANNE ROBERT FOSTER'S FIRST venture into the supernatural occurred when she was a small child living in Leonardsville, New York. Her
great-aunt, Joanna Lavery, let Frank Oliver and his family move into a
home she owned after she evicted a local man, Joseph Burteau, because he
had stopped paying his mortgage. Burteau "stood outside the house and
cursed the place with black curses." Jeanne's mother told her the story when
she was only a few years old, and she never forgot it: "I felt because of his
curses we should never be happy there."[1]

Because her mother was also interested in the supernatural, it was reasonable for the daughter to study it as well. When a child, Jeanne found a
book about the teachings of the compassionate Buddha on a dusty Adirondack road. Even at such a young age she had already felt some of the con-
strictions of her Calvinistic heritage (see the "Deacon's Wife," *NOY*,
43–44), and she considered the book to be given to her by a spiritual messenger.[2] She explained her early interest in alternative religions to Aline
Saarinen: "I escaped set religious belief at fourteen. My father was one of
the trustees of a prominent church, and a deacon, but my mother had at first
followed the transcendentalists and later became immersed in the cosmog-
raphy of the Vedantists whose system is a part of the Indian gospels"
(NYPL, 1962).

Later, in New York City in the early 1900s, Jeanne became interested in
theosophy. In 1906, at twenty-seven years of age, she formally joined the

1. JRF to Caroline Fish, not dated (CP).
2. JRF, interviewed by RL, 16 July 1968.

New York Theosophical Society, and in early August 1909, when Annie Besant was in New York City, Jeanne heard her speak.[3] She was impressed with the Englishwoman, who was head of the Theosophical Society, then headquartered at Adyar, India: "She was the finest woman orator I have ever heard."[4] Jeanne also had conversations with Colonel Henry Steel Olcott prior to his death in February 1907 and proudly wrote on a copy of the *American Theosophist* magazine (1907), "I am perhaps the only living person whose papers bear Colonel Olcott's signature."[5] She was attracted to Olcott's emphasis on education—not just from books but from rich cultural heritage. He established more than one hundred schools in the Ananda area of India, where there had been only two before. Olcott was friends with Madame Blavatsky, who went to India to assist him for a time.[6]

Like her mother before her, Jeanne also became friends with Vedantic disciples. She knew the famous Swami Vivekananda and followed his teachings.[7] The Vedantic system appealed to her because she shared the belief that great men from time to time seem to appear in civilization in groups. She felt that she had been born into the middle of one of those groups—Shaw, the Yeatses, Quinn, Pound, Eliot, Brancusi, Picasso, etc.: "I came to accept reincarnation as truth and—as life went on and the mountain girl met—seemingly through special dispensation—great men and women, and when life gave me opportunities I could not have earned in this life, I felt that I had returned to that group" (letter to Aline Saarinen, c. 1962, NYPL).

Jeanne Foster's choices in life had not always resulted in happiness, but the Vedantic system at least gave "purpose" to those choices: "It teaches that a great genius is built up by many incarnations, that his mind is never lost any more than the Atman, the soul, and that—as love binds—one may

3. JRF often took five or six years off her age when speaking or writing of it. She said she was twenty-one when she joined the Theosophical Society, but her certificate of membership to the society is dated 7 November 1906, signed by Henry Steel Olcott, which would have made her twenty-seven. Annie Wood Besant (1847–1933), English social reformer, theosophist author.

4. JRF to Aline Saarinen, not dated, ca. 1962, NYPL.

5. Henry Steel Olcott (1832–1907), American author and theosophist.

6. Madame Helena Petrovna Blavatsky (1831–91), Russian-born theosophist.

7. Swami Vivekananda (1863–1902), Indian mystic.

hope to return with that mind, somewhere sometime—and on the heights of our human powers—even make some kind of contact with that mind wherever it may be, while here" (letter to Saarinen, c. 1962, NYPL).

By 1911, when they first met, John Butler Yeats seemed attracted to Jeanne's fascination with the supernatural, which was unusual considering his skepticism about his eldest son's forays into the occult. JBY said to her, "Let me look at your hands":

> "There is not much there." I answered, "Let me see yours."
>
> "Ah, you too are a palmist?"
>
> "I have studied hands and ears," I answered. "If you know one, it is hardly necessary to know the other; but it is difficult to learn either one."
>
> "You cannot learn it from books," said J. B. Y., poring over the lines in my palm.
>
> . . . J. B. was still examining the lines in my hands. He announced, "It is fortunate that you have courage and self-control, otherwise you would die of acute melancholia before you were many years older. You have personality and perhaps destiny; you have fought, I see, many battles. One rarely finds such courage in a woman." (Murphy 1971, 5)

JBY's skepticism intensified when Jeanne became attracted to occultist Aleister Crowley (1875–1947). Crowley had been embroiled in a power struggle in an occult organization at the turn of the twentieth century, the Order of the Golden Dawn, one of W. B. Yeats's main interests of the time. When Yeats launched an investigation of MacGregor Mathers, the group's leader, Mathers reacted and appointed Crowley (who at that time thought Mathers was James IV reincarnated) to take possession of the property and the papers of the Isis and Urania Temple of the order.[8] Crowley later wrote a pamphlet about the affair called *The Rosicrucian Scandal* (1911). Although the author of the pamphlet is given as Leo Vincy, Jeanne said that Vincy was a pseudonym and that Crowley was the actual author.

In the United States, Crowley used his personal magnetism and devious charm to arouse the interest of those he met. Near the end of 1914, he visited John Quinn, the latter not yet personally known to Jeanne, to convince

8. Samuel Liddell MacGregor Mathers (1854–1918), English author and member of the Order of the Golden Dawn.

Quinn to buy some of his manuscripts and books. Quinn wrote to WBY on 24 April 1915: "He is a perfect misfit here of course. . . . His writings have no popular appeal. One hears awful things about him but beyond a big capacity for strong drink I have seen nothing crooked about him" (PF, 438).

Jeanne Foster first met Aleister Crowley in New York City through the circle of friends that included Albert Shaw. In fact, she was introduced, she said, through a "journalist friend," who may very well have been Shaw himself. Jeanne was at a difficult point in her personal relationships. Only a few months earlier, the entries she had written in her diary detailed the pain and guilt she felt about her affair with Shaw. Her marriage to the elderly Matlack Foster, always problematic, did not satisfy her yearning for a more traditional role as muse and helpmate to a powerful intellect. Crowley, with his dark, brooding looks and his preoccupation with the occult, seemed at first a likely candidate. In addition, there was an aura of the sinister about him that Jeanne found difficult to resist.

Crowley was an enigma to some, a devil to others, and the latest flavor to sophisticated New Yorkers. Traveling in the circles she did, Jeanne was bound to meet him. Her studies in the occult and in theosophy made her naturally curious about this strange and intriguing man. Her dear and devoted friend, J. B. Yeats, was to "watch in horrified fascination as his son's old enemy proceeded to captivate the sensitive and vulnerable 'loveliest of women'" (PF, 431).

Crowley found Jeanne, whom he alternately called "Cat" and "Hilarion," a woman of many talents. He wrote that she "possessed a unique atmosphere. I can only describe it as 'sweetness long drawn out'" (A. Crowley 1969, 767). She could also write and was an experienced editor; he was in need of her professional talents. She said that in 1915 (probably early summer) Crowley asked her to quit her job with the Review and go to work for him as a ghostwriter. She did not think it economically feasible, though the offer may have tempted her because of her difficult personal situation with Albert Shaw. She told Crowley she would consider it. William M. Murphy writes: "For a time he succeeded in duping Jeanne Foster, who was betrayed by his ugly good looks, his charisma, his position as leader of a magical cult, and his reputation as poet. She was disturbed and fascinated by him, alternately attracted and repelled" (PF, 438). In early summer 1915, when Jeanne finally asked her friend John Butler Yeats for his opinion about Crowley, he

replied judiciously on 4 July, "Learn magic by all means, but be careful
of the magician. They that sup with the devil must have a long spoon"
(*PF,* 440).

But she didn't heed her friend's advice. By September 1915, Jeanne's relationship with Crowley had become more complicated. William M. Murphy describes one version of events:

> Suddenly Mrs. Foster and Crowley disappeared from New York. . . . JBY ei-
> ther did not know the details of her adventures or chose not to speak about
> them. Crowley had persuaded her to accompany him to California, and even
> to bring her invalid husband along. . . . Crowley describes the curious he-
> gira, during which Mrs. Foster presented herself to him at intervals. One
> time he met her "in the dusk just beyond the town limits" at Santa Cruz; at
> another time in Los Angeles she spent two hours with him during the morn-
> ing. His innate cruelty soon destroyed her illusions. He was vicious of
> tongue, constantly berating people he considered his inferiors, and the pres-
> sure became too great for Mrs. Foster, a kindly and idealistic person, to bear.
> To Crowley's fury, she left him and with her husband returned to New York.
> (*PF,* 440)

Jeanne didn't mention Crowley in her 1915 diary, at least not directly, as
she did Albert Shaw in her 1914 notebooks. Crowley did not literally accompany the Fosters on the trip to California but left New York on 6 October, three weeks after Jeanne and Matlack Foster's 13 September departure.
In his hagiography, Crowley claims that Jeanne ran away from New York
after they had shared a night of lovemaking:

> We consecrated ourselves . . . to [Love's] service. But though the Cat had
> given herself thus simply and straightforwardly, she enjoyed the exercise
> of her power over me by tormenting me with doubts of her truth. She
> pretended to be disgusted by the sexual side of love and in a thousand
> ways kept me on pins and needles. Not many days elapsed before she sud-
> denly left the city without leaving word for me. She had driven me to such
> desperation that I nearly lost control of myself when I heard that she had
> gone. (1969, 799)

Crowley then explains his own departure:

On October 6th, I left New York for a trip round the coast. I wanted to see the San Francisco exhibition, and I wanted to get first-hand facts about the attitude of the people, outside the Wall Street machine, to the war. With this I combined a honeymoon with Hilarion; though the sky was cloudy and windy, she popped in and out all the time, having decided to spice the romance and adventure by taking her husband in tow. (1969, 768)

Crowley first went to Detroit and then to Chicago. He visited San Francisco but was eager to leave so that he might meet Jeanne on her trip through Santa Cruz:

I hurried south, stopping off at Santa Cruz, to see the famous big trees. . . . My sweetheart was waiting for me in the dusk just beyond the town limits. "How glad I am you have come," she whispered. "Let us walk together to the grove. You shall sleep on my bosom all night, beneath the shadow of the giant sentinel whose spear points salute the stars." My sweetheart wove herself about me, an intoxicating ambiance. Drunk with delight I strode through the silence. (1969, 770–71)

He reports that in the morning he awoke refreshed, but Jeanne Foster was gone. His tribute to the experience is a poem called "At Big Trees, Santa Cruz":

> Night fell. I travelled through the cloven chasm
> To where the redwood's cloistered giant grove
> Sprung gothic and priapic. . . .
> . . . . . . . . . . . . . .
> . . . I found the treasure trove
> Of Fire, and consecrated all to love,
> Smiting my soul within the protoplasm.
>
> (1969, 771)

Jeanne probably met Crowley in Santa Cruz, but her diary is filled only with descriptions of the cities and countryside she and Matt were passing: "long ledges of rock running into the sea from a forest of gnarled cypress and cedar. Wild crags, covered with sea fowl, and lazy seals" (5 November

1915, LC). With her husband nearby, Jeanne might have decided not to record extramarital excursions.

On 6 November, the Fosters traveled to Santa Barbara through the Salinas Valley. In her diary, Jeanne commented on the ranch land and farms. On 7 November, she wrote from Santa Barbara, penning extensive notes about her trip, detailing again the beautiful sights of nature and the character of the towns through which she and Matt Foster traveled. There is no hint of Aleister Crowley.

Crowley claims that his "outward journey ended at San Diego" (Crowley 1969, 774). Jeanne arrived in that city on 10 November, where she visited the San Diego Exhibition. She recorded many details about the collection of treasures from the Mayan culture. Catching her journalistic attention was the Welfare Exhibit, "an exhibit to show what child-labor really means" (LC). Again, wisely, there is no mention of Crowley.

There are a few intriguing pieces in Jeanne's diary of that adventurous trip in 1915, which may be references to Crowley. From Victoria in September, she wrote this short thought:

> —Night—
> Moonlight on
> water black?
> lying hills —A.
> (LC)

And beneath it, two words: "White nights—." The initial A at the end of "hills" was her camouflage for Crowley. The "vanity of vanities" entry follows:

> Oh the vanity of vanities that is called love. Oh the worms that creep in the flesh and the venom that lurks in the blood. The sacrifice . . . the spirit-mad seeker—how desperately must they strive against this most potent spell, this princely hallucination. It is a fever which runs its course—a disease that renders the victim weaker after each successive attack.
>
> To love God—and God alone—to be consumed with His passion and His glory—to know the companionship of the Holy Guardian Angel, this is the only love that is not profanation and abomination.

Deliver me from the snare of the flesh. Deliver me from its sharp delights. Deliver me from its lures and its tender secrets.

If it be in God's will that I shall find the love of God mirrored in a human being and that he loving God shall be God mirrored in me—then verily— holily we may love and even fearfully . . . love each other and forget God. (LC)

There are other entries in her diary, not quite so passionate as this one, that speak of God and various battles in life. Under an entry that she titled "Beauty," for example, she wrote: "Hail to Thee most Holy, most Blessed Beauty. Thou are the restorer of my soul: Thou art the Light of the universe: Thou art All Good. Those who know thee not live in the darkness: they are the children of Evil: they are the abomination of the earth, the fruit of adultery and of fornication."[9] Jeanne crossed out these words, as she did in several other entries, including bits of poems she had written. She may have rejected them editorially, or she may have changed her mind for other reasons about which we can only speculate.

The contents of these entries smack of lover's remorse. If, as Crowley suggested, Jeanne was disgusted by the physical side of love, one can hardly blame her. From her stillborn child to her entanglement with Shaw to her episode with Crowley, her adventures with sex had rarely been positive. She had certainly learned that, no matter what her heart told her, there was little to be gained from giving herself to a man, especially the successful and predatory males she knew. Whatever currency her beauty and charm had was often diminished for such a man after sexual conquest.

Back in New York, Crowley became a frequent contributor to *Vanity Fair*, and a number of his published sonnets were written for Jeanne Foster. One of these poems, "In the Red Room of Rose Croix," commemorates his meeting with her in California:

> Ah then, what grace within our girdle glows,
> To garb thy glee-gilt heart, Hilarion,
> An Alpenbluehn on our star-crested snows.

9. In JRF's diary, this piece follows the entries about the San Diego Exhibition (LC).

O scarlet flower, smear honey on the thigh
Of this shy bee, that sucks thy sweetness dry.
(1969, 767)

Crowley returned to his rented studio at Carnegie Hall, where he made plans for Jeanne to do writing "far more meaningful than any writing you might do for a magazine." She was not interested when she found that most of the help he wanted was clerical; he particularly wanted her to clean up his grammar and diction. Her refusal made Crowley incensed at her impertinence. Finally, he shouted, "If you refuse my orders, I will kill your mother. She is with you now, and I will kill her before your eyes." [10]

This outburst startled Jeanne, both for its vehemence and irrationality. She was used to managing ill-tempered men with her charm, but Crowley's anger frightened her. At that time, her mother was visiting at Jeanne's apartment in New York, and Jeanne had no inkling as to whether Crowley had heard of this visit through ordinary channels or had utilized his supernatural contacts. She returned home that night, understandably troubled by this bizarre conversation. She did not mention Crowley's threat to her mother, who was also a believer in the occult and therefore might be frightened if she knew. That night the two women retired to the same bed, for Jeanne had an intuition that "something might happen."

They were awakened about midnight by the appearance of a hideous apparition perched at the foot of the bed. Jeanne did not panic, but recited a white-magic spell that, she said, caused the demon to disappear. She then explained the circumstances to her shaken mother, who chastised her daughter for her involvement with such a depraved magician.

Jeanne had trouble getting rid of Crowley. She said that he bothered her incessantly. William M. Murphy writes that when Jeanne returned to New York after the western trip, she was "badly shaken." Several events tested her mettle. Murphy explains the first: "Crowley had wanted to have a child by her, and when his hopes were dashed, he deluded himself into believing that by a series of magical acts he had begotten with her on the 'celebration of the autumnal equinox' a mystical child who was born 'on a plane other than the material,' and who proved to be in the flesh one of Crowley's fol-

10. JRF, interviewed by RL, 31 July 1969.

lowers, C. Stansfeld Jones, already a grown man but now mystically reborn during the summer solstice of 1916" *(PF,* 440).[11]

This mystical child didn't seem to be enough for Crowley. He wrote letters to Matt Foster—anonymously—warning him that Jeanne was plotting to poison him and that she was "living with a wealthy lawyer" *(PF,* 440). (Perhaps he meant Shaw, who was not a lawyer; perhaps he made up the story. Jeanne would not meet John Quinn for another two years.) Once Crowley threatened her with a "curious looking knife" after she emerged from work one day in midtown Manhattan. John Butler Yeats wrote to Quinn on 14 March 1916:

> He [Crowley] boasts that he is not afraid because John Quinn will always find bail for him and protect him. She [JRF] thinks he is a cocaine fiend. At the very start I had warned her, so that she has never let him get so much as a letter from her. He has some girl with him, and he sent this girl to her with a message to say that she [JRF] must help him or he would destroy her. The girl wept all the time while giving the message. Mrs. Foster told her politely to go to the devil. *The Government here* and the *English government* are both busy watching him with detectives. The English authorities say he is a spy and that he has been to Canada. *(PF,* 629)[12]

Finally—it isn't quite clear when, but probably early 1917—Crowley faded out of Jeanne's life.

William Butler Yeats, Crowley's old enemy, was a strong force in Jeanne Foster's attraction to the occult. They had shared many stories about experiences. Shortly after JBY died, on 29 March 1922, WBY wrote to her about a strange experience he had with a medium:

> We [WBY and his wife] took care that this medium should not know our name. She was a medium for what is called "the direct voice."
>
> A contact was made with someone called "John B," who explained he was "a lost little dog—black and white—brown—run over 3 doors up road." When I saw my sister I learned that a neighbor's dog black & white with some

---

11. See Crowley 1969, 769, 801. Crowley called Jones a "Babe of the Abyss."

12. Crowley wrote, "I had by this time been enlightened as to the falseness of the Cat; it therefore became my duty to slay her" (1969, 805).

brown spots had been run over a few days before I saw the medium. The dog was run over three doors up from my sisters. (NYPL)

Jeanne treasured these narratives from the poet, and they confirmed for her the existence of a mysterious otherworld. A special occult treasure Yeats gave Jeanne, now in William M. Murphy's private collection, was *Per Amica Silentia Lunae*, which he autographed, "Mrs. Foster, from W. B. Yeats because she is like this book which, in the writing of it, set my own mind in order March 26 1920." Years later, Michael Yeats, WBY's son, signed the book when he stopped by to visit Jeanne on one of his American trips.

On 15 November 1968, she wrote about a "visit" WBY had paid her two days earlier:

I thought I was awake about 2 A.M.

Sarah came to my room—or I thought she came—and told me, despite the hour, that there was a "gentleman to see me in the living room."[13]

As I prepared to go in to meet him and to find out the reason of his being here at that hour, I was aware of what I would call blobs or small concentrations of deeper darkness in the rooms that seemed to move.

As I entered the adjacent room, the dining room with the wide archway, the moving darkness became more animated and deeper, but it did not obscure a figure standing under the archway. A glance showed me the figure was William Butler Yeats, young, as he looked in 1913. He would have been about forty-eight then, his hair dark and beautiful, his eyes brilliant, his smile reassuring.

To my astonishment, he placed his arms around me, around my shoulders, and said: "I have come to thank you about John Quinn; he did so much for me. I know I never gave him sufficient appreciation, but now I know how much he deserved."

Trembling with joy and worship, I stood by him listening when suddenly the black wheels of darkness closed in and he was not there, at least I could not see him or hear his voice. Then I *did* awaken. All was still.

I did not sleep again until daylight or perhaps not at all. He was so real, flesh and blood. This is the first time W. B. Yeats ever appeared to me. (JRF to RL, in LC)

---

13. Sarah Washington, a servant of the Foster household for nearly fifty years.

Richard Londraville with JRF in Schenectady, 1968.

In a letter dated 2 February 1969, Jeanne wrote again of WBY. She missed him deeply—and all of her friends from the old days. Now she was looking to newer, younger friends:

> There is so much to be dreamed, conjectured, and determined. In my own experiences, I found of course that W. B. Y. was beyond the comprehension of most of the occultists that I knew. . . .
>
> The first summer, three years ago, when you [RL] came to me and showed me part of the copy for one of your Yeats papers, I had the sudden swift comprehension of your being allied with him, of having something in your mind that was of W. B. That was one of the reasons I suggested "Evocation" if your need of him came. I felt sure that he would reply and also that as long as you lived, you would have, as Quinn had when he was alive, an actual contact—this in spite of the fact that W. B. might not be on this plane. (JRF to RL, in LC)

Later that same year, on 6 October 1969, she wrote about Yeats as the "great occultist":

> I feel sure that Yeats did not believe in the Sufi Tree at the end of the Road where forgiveness drops from regions to an individual outside—where one can be freed from attachment. I sincerely believe that . . . that there is no

"waki" to help a soul from one incarnation to the next. The Eastern teachers, Jinarajadas and Vivekananda—I have a rare manual of Vivekananda before me as I write—believed that the individual Self must depend upon that Self for freedom, for the dropping of the load.[14]

Yeats—openly—to his close friends and to his father, consulted his "daemon," his "waki" was a part of himself, or so I believe.

Yeats, the great occultist, will sometime come to light. (JRF to RL, in LC)

On 22 October, Jeanne wrote again: "As far as one human being can worship another, a worship possessed me that has never ended. . . . I was acutely aware of the fact that he [WBY] did not belong wholly to our type of creation, the earth type, and the old continuing worship filled me, thrilled me as it had over the years" (JRF to RL, in LC).

In Jeanne's later life, belief in palmistry, astrological signs, numerology, and the occult remained just as strong, but she did not often have such opportunities to share her ideas. She had many friends who loved her dearly, but she was concerned that they would not like her perception of the supernatural. When she met radio and television personality Aline Saarinen in the mid-1950s, she was delighted to find a kindred spirit. After Saarinen's husband, the renowned architect Eero Saarinen, died in September 1961, Jeanne wrote to comfort her friend:

> The law of Karma, cause and effect, and the belief in reincarnation color all that I do, all that I think and feel but I do not talk about these things nor do my friends here know that I am not orthodox. The service work I have done and still do makes me a follower of that great spirit, the Christos, the Logos of the last two thousand years.
>
> I believe that your Eero's mind is not lost. It will return and you will surely be with that mind again.[15]

14. Curuppumullage Jinarajadas (1875–1953), Indian mystic.

15. JRF to Aline Saarinen, not dated, c. late 1961, NYPL. JRF, with WBY, subscribed to the theory of alternative two-thousand-year cycles as proposed by Giambattista Vico (1670–1744). See his *New Science (Scienzia nuova)*, 1725. Aline Saarinen (1914–72), American art critic and author. Eero Saarinen (1910–61), Finnish architect.

Jeanne postulated that a great mind such as Eero Saarinen's could not simply cease to be, and she was always prepared to receive any kind of contact. On 2 July 1966, she wrote:

I was violently—psychically—pulled back into a period when I had been a Buddhist, moved into a life of great beauty.

This life seemed to be in Japan.

The existence of this past life is somewhat confirmed by my present incarnation.

Now with these memories—very real to me—this was because the impress of lost beauty was so overpowering, beauty in the past—so that I did not want the present. (JRF to RL, in LC)

On 15 July 1968, she wrote about Mrs. Carmichael, a psychic friend of hers:

She is starting for the Vale of Cashmere, Accra, Mongolia, and Iran—where she will be entertained by the Shah. Our conversation:

Mrs. Carmichael:

"Your house is different; there is something here that was never here before."

(Moving around, fingering books.) "It is here on the books; your house will never be the same again. What is the young professor like who has been working with you?"

Mrs. Foster describes you [RL] and speaks of your work and ambitions.

Mrs. Carmichael:

"And you will never be quite the same again. What is this I feel?"

Mrs. Foster:

"One thing might be what is called his 'energy field.' This field is strong."

Mrs. Carmichael:

"Where does he come from? I mean in the past. He must have made one full circle." (Manvantara.)

Mrs. Foster:

"I do not know, but I believe old Japan. He teaches Japanese. But there must have been a Celtic incarnation between that time and the present. He also teaches Yeats and Joyce" (etc.).

More remarks from Mrs. Carmichael relative to her impression of forces left in the house and her opinion, feeling them, that all I might do in the future would be colored by the powerful psychic energy field, my phrase, you had left there.

I believe that the appearance to me of certain things of the far past was brought about by knowing you and your being a part of that far past. I have been confronted with a glimpse of my Mask. If now I could go on living for a long time, I might be given more than a glimpse. (JRF to RL, in LC)

In a note written on 20 April 1970—only a few months before her death—Jeanne Foster remained firm in her belief: "To those who do not or cannot believe that we reincarnate, I will seem quite mad. But personally, I have had so much proof that I have belonged to a certain group. This belief has been my life" (JRF to RL, in LC).

# 7

# Vachel Lindsay, Marya Zaturenska, and Salomón de la Selva

IN 1914, JEANNE ROBERT FOSTER decided that it was time to promote in the *Review* the work of a young poet she admired. She had read a
few of his poems when they appeared in one journal or another over the
years, but his work had never won the acclaim she thought it deserved.
Then, in 1913, Mitchell Kennerley published *General Booth Enters Heaven and
Other Poems,* and Jeanne felt that at last Vachel Lindsay's importance as a
poet would be more formally recognized.[1] She gave his book a leading notice in her feature "New Volumes of Verse: Poems of Lindsay" in the February 1914 issue of the *Review*:

> Nicholas Vachel Lindsay's book of verse, just published, bears the title, *Gen-
> eral Booth Enters Heaven, and Other Poems.* The "other poems" do not make the
> universal appeal of the title poem, but they are in many respects equally re-
> markable. They give a new twist to familiar scenes and common points of
> view. Sometimes the telescope is reversed, and that which appeared as a
> mountain is revealed as a gnat. Sometimes a giant hand sweeps the mists
> from our vision for a moment and we see "face to face." . . . He glories in full-
> blooded asceticism and sings its raptures and rewards in the teeth of a mate-
> rialistic age that clamors for complete expression at any cost. His
> arraignment of Americans is that we lack the imagination to conceive that
> which we might be. (Foster 1914, 245)

1. Mitchell Kennerley (1878–1950), English-born American publisher. Nicholas Vachel
Lindsay (1879–1931), American poet.

Such a notice in one of the most widely read magazines at the time helped to bolster Lindsay's reputation. *The Little Review* was the next to recognize his work when later that same year Eunice Tietjens wrote, "It is not too much to say that many of us are watching Vachel Lindsay with the undisguised hope in our hearts that he may yet prove to be the 'Great American Poet' " (qtd. in Masa 1970, 12). Even Ezra Pound was intrigued: "I wish Lindsay all possible luck, but we're not really pulling the same way, though we both pull against entrenched senility" (qtd. in Masa 1970, 12).

Both Lindsay and Jeanne were members of the New York Poetry Society. They became good friends, and she often attended the poetry receptions Lindsay and his wife hosted. One anecdote she shared was that Amy Lowell attended these fetes on occasion and apparently paid too much attention to the handsome young Vachel. Mrs. Lindsay finally refused Miss Lowell any further invitations.[2]

It was with great sadness that Jeanne Foster watched Vachel Lindsay become lost in "the City of his Discontent."[3] His popularity as a kind of social entertainer dismayed her as she saw his poetry dissolve into mediocrity. She was not alone in her observations; the once-admiring Ezra Pound wrote later of Lindsay's work, "Believe me, one can write it by the hour as fast as one scribbles" (qtd. in Masa 1970, 12). Like many of the critics of her time, Jeanne was disappointed that Lindsay was never able to find again the extraordinary tone of "General Booth." Still, her personal affection for the man did not waver. Unfortunately, only one letter survives from their correspondence, written by Lindsay on 22 March 1920 while he was on a trip to the western United States. It captures his disappointment in himself and foreshadows darker days to come:

My Dear Mrs. Jeanne Robert Foster:
    I am in the sandstorm and alkali-lake region of eastern New Mexico, on the way to Albuquerque, and the wind rocks the Pullman.

2. JRF, interviewed by RL, 10 November 1966. Amy Lowell (1874–1925), American poet and critic.

3. Lindsay wrote in his poem "Springfield Magical," "In this, the City of my Discontent, / Sometimes there comes a whisper from the grass, / 'Romance; Romance—is here' " (Lindsay 1963, 76, lines 1–3).

We pass a few dry farms, with the furrows never ploughed, yet with sand and dust blowing into them.

This is just south of the country where I lost my nerve in 1912, and I never forgave myself for it. It is the first time I have been in the region since. We are just about 84 miles east of Albuquerque and about that far south of Wagon Mound, where as I may say, speaking in figures, I met the Devil in Red.

Yet I have always felt I would find something better in the desert, having lost a deal here, and having quit all the Rules of the Road at Wagon Mound about Sept. 15, 1912, and having never taken them up since, I should find them waiting for me again here, somewhere in the shadow of a small cactus.

Have you noted—or perhaps I told you—that what you said in "The Review of Reviews" is now the only thing quoted on the present Booth jacket.

. . . I walked through 200 miles of desert between Pueblo and Trinidad in 1912 and always found lodging at nightfall, in some sudden gulch where the hollow spread out into a tiny ranch.

In the little adobe houses, like these I am passing now, the dry farmers gave me as jolly and intelligent a welcome as I ever had at a university and my heart warms the same way to think of it.

The dry farms are now so thick it is really no desert at all just now.

But I know on and on and on it is desert.

Be good to my literary daughter Marya, and teach her:

(1) To walk.

(2) To walk toward God. (NYPL)


Lindsay's "literary daughter" was Marya Zaturenska (1902–82), the Russian-born American lyric poet who would win the Pulitzer Prize for her book of poetry *Cold Morning Sky* in 1938. Zaturenska was eighteen years old when Lindsay wrote his letter to Jeanne in 1920, and she had already become an important part of Jeanne's life. In fact, Jeanne had discovered Zaturenska while working in New York City with the Sing Sing Social Service Bureau and as a "lady on the block," a volunteer social worker, during the second decade of the twentieth century. Jeanne recognized at once an exceptional but lonely child (only eleven years old when they first met), and the two soon became friends. Jeanne discovered that Marya liked poetry, and she encouraged the little girl to write. Zaturenska's early attempts were much like those of any youngster, but in 1922, when she was only twenty, she won the John Reed Memorial Award from *Poetry*. Later, she developed into one of America's finest women poets of the 1930s generation, publishing her first collection of poetry with Macmillan (*Threshold and Hearth*) in 1933. She won the Shelley Memorial Award in 1935 and the Guarantor's Award (again from *Poetry*) in 1937, followed by the Pulitzer in 1938.

In 1912, shortly before she met Jeanne Foster, Marya Zaturenska had to quit school to go to work to help her father. Her mother had died, and the family was trying to survive. She earned some money using the embroidery skills her mother had taught her, but Jeanne saw only a black future ahead in such a profession. In her 8 June 1913 *New York Call* story, "The Reason of the Cause," she described a young seamstress: "She entered the house by a basement door and toiled up a dark flight of stairs to a back room where several slatternly women sewed under the rays of sickly gas jets. In this room, vitiated of wholesome air, [the girl] pulled bastings and made herself generally useful. Sometimes she was sent out to carry home finished work. This girl was now thirteen, badly nourished, with a lanky body and thin limbs" (Foster 1913c, 10). But Marya Zaturenska's life took a different turn from the story's young girl when, a few years later, Jeanne arranged for her to work at Brentano's Bookstore while taking night school courses to finish her high school education.

In an undated letter (circa 1916), Zaturenska sent Jeanne a picture of herself, which she signed, "To my fairy godmother, Mrs. Jeanne R. Foster, With love—Marya Alexandrine Zaturensky."[4] (Her actual middle name was Alexandrovna, and she later changed the ending of her last name from "sky" to "ska.") Enclosed with the picture and letter was a poem entitled "To Jeanne"—a thank you for a picture of Jeanne, a youthful expression of love and gratitude from a young woman to someone she considered her mentor:

> There where the waters kiss the hungry rocks
> Where grey sea birds and helméd ships hold sway
> Your brave, sweet eyes a muted language speak
> Lighting despair to hope ineffable
> They too have known the sorrows of the world.
>
> (lines 7–11, LC)

4. The Zaturenska letters to JRF are in LC.

Zaturenska's own mother was gone; now Marya had found a surrogate:

This morning was the kind of a morning for good wishes. I sent mine all a' twinkle (like a baby's eyes opening all dewy) out over the world via Julie Foster—of course I loved 'em and kissed 'em before I let them go and I guess you found them in the sunshine—'twas more like May sunshine today—a sky that was blue from the beginning—Precious so—so precious when you called today, your voice so sweet with love in it—. That moment you give to me of your voice, your heart, your love may mean as much to me as a year of you to some one else—yes even a lifetime—that moment reveals such beauty of soul—. All my life points to the fact that I must learn to stay by myself—I must learn to be alone—I feel the ecstasy of joy and pain so exquisitely that I am not conscious of the constant bleeding of my heart—An indescribable sadness fills my whole being but I am keenly aware of true enjoyment in all life gives me of you.

I am your little child soul.

In 1918, when Zaturenska was only sixteen years old, largely through Jeanne's encouragement, she began to submit her poetry to magazines. She wrote to Jeanne on 8 December: "I sometimes feel if I do not see you often that you may lose touch with me and that would make me dreadfully unhappy. I wonder when I could see you and spend a real whole Sunday with you." She told Jeanne about a recent visit to a Poetry Society meeting in New York City, where Jeanne had first introduced her: "Mr. Padraic Colum and Clement Wood had an awful fight in the society. There was almost a fist fight and Clement Wood caused lots of excitement by making a fiery speech denouncing everything and everybody."[5] Zaturenska was thrilled, like any young poet would be in those days, to be moving in such company. She told Jeanne an interesting anecdote about their mutual friend, Nicaraguan American poet Salomón de la Selva (1893–1959):

Mr. Kreymborg introduced me to Muna Lee, a Russian Jewish poetess . . . who said that Salomón was engaged to her for three blissful months but

5. Clement Wood (1888–1950), American poet and editor.

failed to turn up at the time appointed for the wedding.[6] I think he left her waiting on the steps of City Hall! She was quite unreserved about her disappointment! Did you ever hear of another such lady-killer as our Sal! I have lost all my respect for him, though my affection for him is as strong as ever. Besides he was always good, and sweet, and a brother to *me*. So I am going to stick by him if everybody else in the world leaves him.

The relationship between Selva and Zaturenska was complicated, and Jeanne Foster served as a go-between to placate two passionate personalities. Selva wrote to Jeanne from England on 7 October 1918 in an attempt to explain his manic disposition: "I enjoyed suffering, and it always was of my own choosing. I have preferred to be carefree, and to have to give no one thanks for anything; and also, I have liked always, for the mastering of my sinful pride, to humble myself."[7] A soldier in the Third Battery Loyal North Lancashire Regiment in World War I, he felt damaged by the chaotic world: "I have changed my mind about becoming a drunkard when the war is over: I'll engage a full orchestra to play for me at all hours; for there is no intoxication comparable to music."

Selva, young and handsome, was fascinated by the youthful and vibrant Zaturenska. Jeanne was concerned and perhaps jealous. Zaturenska was only sixteen years old at the time, and Selva was a charming and talented but dangerous man. Like Vachel Lindsay, he wanted to take Zaturenska under his wing and "nurture" her, but Jeanne, for reasons we can only speculate, subtly kept the two apart as much as possible, and Selva considered it rejection. He did not care for those who did not love him:

> You have been very kind to the little Russian. I daresay it will be hard to keep it up. I wish I had a whole heart to give away to every one that is as unhappy and as hungry for affection as she. I do not think her pretty at all. And I wish she could take better care of her teeth and fingers and hair than she does. And what has she told you of my "sufferings"?

6. Alfred Kreymborg (1883–1966), American playwright and poet, founder of avant-garde poetry journal *Others*. Muna Lee (later Muna de Muñoz Marín, 1895–1965), American writer and diplomat.

7. All the letters from Salomón de la Selva to JRF are in the Foster-Murphy Collection, NYPL.

Jeanne's affection for Zaturenska did not waver, no matter what Selva predicted. She continued to promote Zaturenska's career and to introduce her to important people. One evening at Jeanne's apartment at 300 West Forty-ninth Street, for instance, Zaturenska met Eamon de Valera, who in a few years would be the president of Ireland. "I was too young and unin-formed to find him interesting," Zaturenska said in an interview in 1977, but she never forgot that night; she met most of the New York Irish group (John Butler Yeats, Padraic Colum, and so on) through Jeanne (Phillips 1978, 36).

By 1920, Zaturenska was eighteen years old, independent, and well es-tablished among the literati of New York, but Jeanne was still worried that the young Marya might not have judgment mature enough to make the best decisions for herself. She was particularly concerned that Zaturenska might fall in love with someone who would be more destructive than help-ful. When Selva enclosed a letter to Zaturenska in a letter to Jeanne (March 1920), she paused to consider. She gave the letter to Zaturenska with reser-vations and advised her not to reply. Selva wrote that he was getting mar-ried to "a Central American woman," but his peculiar passion worried Jeanne:

> I thought now I have never kissed you, Marya; and was a little sorry, a little happy, thinking also that should either of us die, there would be that one dear thing that never was to remember of the dead: a memory somehow like a lovely cup—empty! For when I was a soldier you wrote me promising me a kiss, and I dreamed much of it, so wrought a bright pure chalice of desire. I still have that cup of longing. . . .
>
> I shall not kiss you yet, but hold you warm and close to my breast and feed you so, and do you gurgle when you have had your fill, and do you go to sleep and to your dreams: I will watch over you.

Jeanne Foster had placed herself in an odd position. She was protective of her protégée and did not want to relinquish control over her. Why? Per-haps she saw a talent in Zaturenska that made her both envious and appre-ciative. Her influence over the girl and Zaturenska's devotion gave Jeanne a special sense of power. She may have enjoyed the role and perhaps didn't recognize that in some ways she was as dangerous to her young friend as was Selva. In any case, Selva became less of a concern to Jeanne when he permanently left New York City, shortly after publisher Alfred Kreymborg had authorities issue a warrant for his arrest for a debt of sixty-five dollars.

By 1923, Zaturenska had met many powerful literary people, including Willa Cather, who secured a fellowship for her at Valpariso University. A short time later, Harriet Monroe helped her get a Zona Gale Scholarship at the University of Wisconsin, where she studied "everything [she] could" (Phillips 1978, 36), including poetry and music. Jeanne by now had either relinquished or lost control. In 1924, when Zaturenska was twenty-two, she married twenty-six-year-old poet, critic, and editor Horace Gregory, whom she had met in New York through Kenneth Fearing, another poet and editor.[8] Four decades later, in interviews and letters, Jeanne was happy to acknowledge the union as "one of the bright moments" in a dark year. Gregory's intelligence, his good sense, and his kind heart made him a suitable match for her "spiritual" daughter. The fifty-seven-year marriage was by all accounts happy and successful. Zaturenska and Gregory had two children, Joanna and Patrick, and were devoted to each other until their deaths.

It isn't clear if Zaturenska and Jeanne ever completely lost contact. In 1934, when Zaturenska was at Yaddo, the writer's colony in Saratoga Springs, New York, she visited Jeanne at her home in Schenectady. The last letter in the correspondence between them is from Zaturenska, postmarked from New York City, and dated 5 June 1936, but others were probably written and lost. The erotic undercurrents suggest that the two were still very close, even though they saw each other infrequently. In 1936, Zaturenska was thirty-four years old. In two years, she would be awarded the Pulitzer Prize for poetry:

Tonight you are very near to me. There is the design of a rose on my bedspread with layers and layers of petals and somehow I see your face everywhere that I look. I am down here in Edgewater N. J. My [step]mother is very low and they sent for me about 2 wks ago. Please Julie Julie I miss you so ter-

8. Willa Cather (1873–1947), American writer. Harriet Monroe (1860–1936), American poet and editor, founder and editor of *Poetry*. Horace Victor Gregory (1898–1982), American poet, editor, and journalist. Kenneth Flexner Fearing (1902–61), American poet and editor.

ribly. Could you write me a little note. I love you so. I could stand it better when I was in the same city but now the distance seems cruel and it seems your thought doesn't reach me. I want to know how you are.

Marya Zaturenska died in January 1982. We can never know the full nature of her relationship with Jeanne, but from the moment they met they shared a lifelong bond of mutual admiration, love, and respect.

Jeanne had her own history with the intriguing Salomón de la Selva, but her experience allowed her to handle his manic moods with gentle grace. Early on, he professed his undying love and wrote many poems declaring his devotion. Certainly Selva cared for Jeanne, but he was not exclusive in his devotion. In one undated letter (circa 1915), he told her that if she withheld her pledge of eternal love, she would be doing "a great wrong" to another woman who did love him: "If you do not love me truly, and if you do not intend to love me *forever,* you are doing Amanda a great wrong keeping me from her. But if you jilt me, I will die. Poor Amanda! Either way she cannot have me." Jeanne was his muse, he told her in another undated letter. For the great good she had done him, "God will translate your beauty, untouched, to immortality":

Because of you, I conceive life not seriously, not ponderously—but holily; and love not mad, not thoughtless, but serene and full, with a comely gravity like that the Virgin wears in the loveliest pictures of Her of Raphael's. And poetry, too, is now to me so heavenly. I have always loved it; I have respected my gift, cherished it and given it all my heart; but it was only for its own sake, which means "partly for my vanity." Now, it is infinitely more precious: it is to sing for you.

Once, Jeanne refused to accompany him to a party, but did so with such gentleness that he could only tease her in return: "Your not coming makes a great difference, but if it is best for you to be home, please don't even regret being away from us. I shall take no girl with me, but will flirt with all the girls my friends bring" (letter, n.d.).

From England during the final days of World War I, he wrote passionate letters to Jeanne (beginning with "My Darling"), tinged with his own brand of humor. In one, he wrote about a friend ("Mike") who had fallen in love with one of Jeanne's pictures: "It may please your darling vanity to learn that you are his measure of desired loveliness. He looks at your picture . . . and quite imprudently asks me to will you to him should I be killed. I tell him that if I die you cannot fail to take a short cut to our meeting place in the next life." But later in the letter, he added, "You can love Mike, if you want to, when I am gone" (4 October 1918).

Selva tried to maintain his sense of humor, but he also wanted to shock Jeanne:

> I wish it were possible to have a picture of me in full equipment taken before I go to France. I feel all laced up in it, and would myself like to know what I look like. And I would like also to see myself making a point with the bayonet. We practice it every single day, and I like it lots better than pressing triggers and pulling bolts up and down. I shan't be satisfied until I have felt the clean blade—it's so beautiful, straight, and keen, and bright in the sun!—run through flesh and bone. I have run it into wooden boards, but the creak of wood is not terrible. I want to hear a mad dying shriek and feel the despairing gasp of a done-for foe on my rifle. The bayonet is the most expressive of all weapons, and I love it. (letter, n.d.)

This letter was written from the comparative safety of a posting in Britain; although such sentiments may not be that unusual for a soldier before he experiences combat, blood lust is rare for those who have been in a firefight.

Even in the last dark days of the war, the correspondence between Selva and Jeanne was often about poets and poetry. Jeanne had written to Selva about their friend American poet Joyce Kilmer (1886–1918), informing him of Kilmer's death. For Jeanne, a dramatic death somehow added value to an artist's work, and this sentiment at times altered her judgment. Selva, too, had lost a friend, but in his reply he reserved judgment on the poetry:

> You may be right about Joyce; but I somehow can't sum him up at all. When I first read "Trees" and Other Poems [1914] I thought him the best of the young poets of America. There was fine promise in "Martin" and in the poem to a poet who had committed suicide. I daresay he thought of suicide too often, though he once told me that he had intended that poem for Seaumus

O'Sheel—another blasted morning glory.—I have been trying to write about Joyce; but I don't know what to say.[9]

Always, in the letters from England, the war intruded. Jeanne said that Selva wanted sympathy and affection from her and most of all understanding of his fear. She remembered her time in England during the early days of the war, of the soldiers who died at Marne, and so she provided Selva with the tenderness he sought. He tried to shock her at times with an insouciant tone, but she said she knew that, like so many young men facing battle, he was frightened.

In spite of his forebodings of death in combat, Selva returned to New York unharmed. On 16 June (circa 1923), he again pledged his love ("The golden thread of you is all so rich, it is cloth of gold I am wearing") and told Jeanne that he had translated a sonnet of hers that he was going to publish, with her picture, in the August issue of *La revista de Indias*. This gesture was, Jeanne said, Selva's kindest tribute.

The last letter in the existing correspondence between Selva and Jeanne was written by Selva on 10 June 1925. He "never [forgot] her" and heard from friends that she was "as beautiful as a triumph." He called her "the most beautiful thing God made ever" and asked her to take care of Dr. Luis H. DeBayle (Rubén Daríos's friend) when he arrived in New York.[10] Although Jeanne never saw Selva after he left New York City because of the Kreymborg suit, she was happy to introduce his friends to the Poetry Society and, as always, to promote those she felt worthy of attention. Luis DeBayle, scientist, surgeon, poet, and a member of the famous Nicaraguan DeBayle family, was someone she felt certainly deserved her time.[11]

Whether or not there was ever a physical romance between Jeanne Foster and "S de la S," as she often called Selva, is impossible to say. He wrote to her sometimes as if he were in love, but later in her life she never offered

9. The letter is not dated but because of its subject must be 1918. Seaumus (also Shaemas) O'Sheel (1886–1954), Irish American (born in New York City) historian, journalist, and poet.

10. Dr. Luis H. DeBayle (1865–1938), trained in Paris. Rubén Darío (pen name of Felix Rubén García Sarmiento, 1867–1916), Nicaraguan-born journalist, diplomat, and poet.

11. JRF, interviewed by RL, 10 November 1966.

to share any intimate details about their relationship. When prodded a bit about their friendship, all she said was, "He was my contribution to the war effort." [12]

Although Jeanne kept her apartment in New York City until 1933, her focus after 1924 had turned to her family in Schenectady. Trips to New York City became less frequent, and she wrote letters to friends less often. Marya Zaturenska was married and busy raising a family, as she continued to work on her own literary projects. Salomón de la Selva was in Nicaragua pursuing his journalism career. Sadly, Vachel Lindsay committed suicide in 1931.

As the days of the Great Depression wore on, it seemed to Jeanne Foster that the world had gone mad. Even her beloved Czechoslovakia, with its "new flag of freedom upon the streets" of "Golden Praha," was beginning to show signs of strain.

12. JRF, interviewed by RL, 10 February 1967.

# 8

# Karel Pergler and the Masaryks
# of Czechoslovakia

ONE OF THE MOST INTRIGUING and least-known chapters in
Jeanne Robert Foster's life was her involvement in the Czech nationalist
movement headed by Tomáš Masaryk and Edvard Benes. In 1915 at a dinner in New York City given in Masaryk's honor by Department of Labor
deputy R. J. Caldwell, Jeanne met Masaryk and his fellow patriot Karel Pergler. She soon became friends with Masaryk's American wife, Charlotte,
and with his son and daughter, Jan and Alice.[1]

Always interested in political movements, Jeanne was attracted to
Masaryk's desire to liberate those oppressed by the Austro-Hungarian Empire. When Pergler became head of the Slav Press Bureau in 1918, he was
particularly concerned with promoting the Bohemian cause in American
papers and magazines, one of which was the *Review of Reviews*. No doubt the
Masaryks and Pergler thought that some good for their republic might
grow from their friendship with Jeanne Foster. They saw her as a representative of her nation and as a journalist whose words might very well catch
the attention of those who were in a political position to help their country,
including President Woodrow Wilson himself.

---

1. Tomáš Garrigue Masaryk (1850–1937), leader of the Czechoslovakian independence
movement and the first president of the Czechoslovakian Republic. Edvard Benes
(1884–1948), Czech statesman. Charlotte Masaryk (1850–1923). Karel Pergler
(1882–1954), Czech lawyer and diplomat, and a leader in the Czech independence movement. R. J. Caldwell (1875–1951), American diplomat. Jan Masaryk (1886–1948), Czechoslovakian diplomat and statesman. Alice Masaryk (1879–1966), director of the
Czechoslovakian Red Cross.

Their interest in Jeanne paid off in 1918 and 1919, when she wrote several articles for the *Review* about the newly formed Czechoslovakian Republic. In an August 1918 article, "The Czecho-Slovaks," Jeanne positively reviewed Lewis B. Namier's (1888–1960) pamphlet *The Czecho-Slovaks, an Oppressed Nationality*: "The real difference between Czech and Slovak is neither racial or linguistic; it is historic. While the Czechs of Bohemia, Moravia, and Silesia, numbering six and a half millions at the present day, have fought for a thousand years against German aggression and suffered from German tyranny, the two and a half million Slovaks who live in northeastern Hungary have had their bitterest enemies in the Magyars" (Foster 1918a, 197).

Whether Jeanne's synthesis of hundreds of years of complicated history into a few sentences was naïve or calculated, her purpose was to promote the Czechoslovakian cause for her friends. She continued: "They know that liberty is not possible for them or cannot prove durable without the liberty of other sister nations and foremost of the Jugo-Slavs and Poles, but where they themselves hold the line they have decided to hold it with united forces" (197). Jeanne answered questions raised about the Czechoslovakian Republic's attitude toward other groups within its own borders, in particular the Magyars. The republic hoped for the liberty of all people, but practicality had to intervene at some point. Reasonable controls were needed until people could learn to live together.

Jeanne's piece in the October 1918 issue of the *Review*, "The Czecho-Slovaks in Russia," was another positive review, this time of Jules Chapin's article in an unidentified number of *La Revue de Paris*. She wrote: "Czechs of Austria and Slovaks of Hungary, they are deadly foes of the Dual Monarchy and mean to fight it at all hazards. Unable to do so in Maximalist Russia, they have resolved to gain the distant port in Asia, Vladivostok, in order to join the armies of the Entente in the West" (Foster 1918b, 421). They were "valiant troops seeking to come to the aid of their Russian brethren—repulsed as they were by the Czar's Government. . . . The number of Germans and Austrians bunched against them increases daily, obliging them to guard the road which they have conquered but cannot use. It is in order to escape from this painful situation that these Slavs, become our allies, appeal to the Entente" (421–22).

Woodrow Wilson, in a press release on 3 August 1918, voiced U.S. support for the Czech legion and stated that military intervention in Russia would be permissible to help the legion against attacks by Austrians and Germans. By the middle of September, a month before Jeanne published her article, the military force fighting the Czech soldiers was collapsing (Wilson 1968–89, 49: 495).

After their return from Vladivostok, some of these soldiers arrived in the United States for a celebration provided by American Czecho-Slovak groups. Jeanne received an invitation to the event, which several dignitaries from the new republic, including Karel Pergler, attended.

Her ideas about democracy and the responsibility of government so clearly portrayed in her *Review* articles—from educational policy for immigrant children to proper training and care for women prisoners, from the right to earn a decent wage to the right of self-determination—all show why she would have been attracted to Masaryk's ideas. He was concerned that too many of his people, in particular the wealthy, idealized the past and refused to see the coming modern age. They didn't understand that a new Czechoslovakia could be formed only by all its people working together for better health, education, and technological progress. A new society would not be possible without ending the exploitation of the lower classes and without enlisting their cooperation, a lesson the czar of Russia refused to learn, with tragic consequences for his country and his family.

Jeanne Foster and Tomáš Masaryk enjoyed talking about their philosophies of education, and on a number of points they agreed.[2] Masaryk believed, she said, that all people, including the poor, needed to be educated for his country to move into the twentieth century. He thought that the state—and thus the educational system—should be completely separated from the church. In this way, both the moral and the intellectual parts of a person could develop unfettered, so to speak, by either church or state. The Czech must not sit back and resign himself to his lot in life. He must work with any tool he could: hands, brains, or machines.

Jeanne agreed. In one of her *Neighbors of Yesterday* poems, "Peleg Skinner" (47–48), about a man doomed to live for years in the poorhouse because of his lack of training and his inability to get a job, Jeanne wrote that "it's a disease that's catching" and can just as easily destroy a man as a woman:

2. JRF, interviewed by RL, 10 August 1969.

Maybe if my rheumatism gets better
I can leave this Fall and go to farming
And look out for myself. But I'm afraid,
Because I talk with the other paupers
And they're afraid. So we keep on staying.
It's a disease that's catching. . . .

(lines 13–18)

The poorhouse has taught Peleg to be poor forever; he has become a ward of the welfare state. For Jeanne, a government's responsibility was to free people by training them for occupations suitable to their limitations (farming for the arthritic Peleg was not practical) and by providing the young with tools to reach beyond the difficulties that would surely confront them.

By 1920, Jeanne was well established as both political ally and friend of the Masaryks, and consequently she was invited to be their guest for two weeks in Czechoslovakia. Already in Paris on business for John Quinn, she felt she could not pass up the opportunity to see a new country, and so set off on the Orient Express in November with a naïveté that was perhaps shared by American politicians involved in the remapping of a war-torn Europe. She was dedicated to an ideal for which Tomáš Masaryk was a most articulate spokesman: the right of national self-determination. The result was the creation of several small nations torn from the Austro-Hungarian Empire.

But Jeanne's eye was not only on Czechoslovakia; she had not forgotten Ireland. A few years earlier she had hoped that Woodrow Wilson's doctrine of self-determination would commit him to support a free and unified Ireland. In Wilson's address to the Senate on 22 January 1917, he said: "No nation should seek to extend its polity over any other nation or people, but that every people should be left free to determine its own polity, its own way of development, unhindered, unthreatened, unafraid, the little along with the great and powerful" (Wilson 1968–89, 40: 539). By working for the Czech nationalist movement, Jeanne felt that she was also working for Irish independence. If the Czechoslovakian plan succeeded, perhaps the international community would give attention to a similar experiment for an Irish republic. But Wilson ultimately refused to speak for Ireland.

In 1920, undaunted by her disappointment with her own government's inaction, Jeanne set off for Prague:[3]

> Two years after the liberation, when I was doing some special work in Paris, I received an invitation from the Masaryks to spend a fortnight in Prague as their guest. If I accepted the invitation, there was one stipulation. Jan Masaryk asked me not to write up my trip at any time after my return. He said my visit was to be an intimate friendly one, almost a family affair. Of course I gave my assent immediately. That is the reason this story has not been written heretofore.
>
> I left Paris on the Orient Express, November 11, 1920. A few days previously I had received as an enclosure in a letter from Jan Masaryk, a letter from the president of the Czechoslovak Republic, Tomás Garrigue Masaryk. When I started for Prague, I carried this letter with me, and you will find a little later on in my story how important a part in my escape was played by this letter.

Jeanne must have known that central Europe in the 1920s could be a dangerous place. To get to her friends in Prague she had to travel through Germany, a confused country whose military was generally opposed to the Weimar government. The much debated Treaty of Versailles, signed on 28 June 1919, went into effect on 10 January 1920, and Germany had to cede acquired territories to France, Belgium, Poland, Denmark, and Czechoslovakia. By March, General Freiherr von Lüttwitz, Berlin's commander, forced the Reich government to leave the city and installed as administrator Wolfgang Kapp, a man who had during the war advocated "extravagant German annexations."[4] The Erhardt Brigade, run by Captain Hermann Erhardt, supported the Kapp putsch. His command had recently been ordered to disband, but he had no intention of complying. In retaliation for

3. JRF gave the typescript of her Czechoslovakian experience to RL in 1968, and it is now in LC. It is unclear when she wrote it.

4. Wolfgang Kapp (1858–1922), German statesman. The bourgeois wanted to remove "the Noske-Scheidemann-Ebert government. On 13 March 1920, 12,000 troops . . . under General Lüttwitz entered Berlin to establish a military dictatorship and declare . . . Kapp . . . the new Chancellor." See "The Kapp Putsch," at http://www.marxist.com/germany/chapter4.html (27 March 2001).

the Kapp putsch, the government called for a general strike. Germany was
in chaos. Ultimately, the putsch failed, but the desperate, conflicted feelings of the military seethed beneath the surface. Pamphlets condemning
the government and the Versailles Treaty circulated. Many of the demobi-
lized soldiers remained armed and became members of the "Free Corps."
Their Germany was gone; their honor was gone; and their jobs were gone.
The elements that caused this pain had to be eliminated (Dill 1961,
279–85). This was the Germany whose border Jeanne Foster crossed on the
night of 11 November 1920:

> My trip was comfortable and uneventful until we had passed Strasbourg
> where the German officials came on the train to examine our passports. I was
> sharing a compartment with a little French dressmaker who was going to
> Turkey. She introduced herself but we will have to call her Madame X. as the
> extraordinary events of that night completely blotted out my remembrance
> of her name, which I heard only once. We had undressed and were in our
> berths when the Germans came on the train. I have always thought my
> guardian angel, if I have one, must have whispered to me when I was taking
> off my clothes. I suddenly remembered the letter I was carrying from Presi-
> dent Masaryk. I removed it from my leather shoulder bag in which I carried
> my money, passport, and other identifying papers and credentials and
> pinned it securely inside the shoulder of my night robe.
>
>   There was a knock on the door of the compartment and a call: "Passports."
> Madame X and I left our berths, slipped hastily into dressing gowns and
> opened the door. A stout short blond German in an official uniform came
> into the compartment and demanded our passports. When he looked at
> mine he flew into a rage and bellowed at me in German. The conductor of
> the Express finally came and explained, because I did not speak German. By
> that time, the inspector had looked at Madame X's passport and was shouting
> at her. The conductor explained that I did not have a visa for Germany. I had
> received the wrong information from an employee at the American Legation
> in Paris. Since I was passing through Germany without a stop-over, bound
> for another country, I had been told that it was not necessary to have a visa
> for Germany. I was not the only one who lacked a proper visa. It turned out
> that there were seven passengers in the same boat: myself, Madame X, an En-
> glishman, and four Americans with commercial interests in Eastern Europe.
> The German official ordered the express stopped at the next station so that

he might consult his superiors. This was done and as we did not have time to dress, as the next station was within sight, we were ordered off the train and into a frigid station. I was not quite fast enough to suit the official—whom I dubbed "Moustache" because of his immense walrus-like moustache—and he took me by the arm. Luckily, I had a fur coat which I slipped on over my dressing gown. As I stepped out of the compartment, I saw the other visa-less passengers coming down the aisle.

"Moustache" had gone behind a glass partition to use the telephone. While he apparently consulted his boss, the station master came out from behind the partition and talked with us. He spoke French and English as well as his native German. After he heard our story, he actually wrung his hands.

"How wrong," he said. "It could all have been arranged. You meant no harm. The war is over. It is just stupid, stupid. My poor country. When will she ever learn?"

It was fully three quarters of an hour before "Moustache" came out from behind the partition and ordered us all on the train again. I wondered if the Express had waited for us, but, God bless the French, the train had waited and there was an indignant meeting in our car in the aisle over the way we had been treated.

"Moustache" told us that we would all be taken off the train at Karlsruhe and interned until we could take up the matter with our respective governments. He said that our passports were now the property of the German government.

We did not try to go back to our berths for there was no more sleep for us that night. Two of the seven passengers consigned to internment by "Moustache" were in the same car with me: Madame X, who was sharing my compartment, and Major Thomas Russell of the Grenadier Guards—"Major Tommy," as I found later on that he preferred to be called.

Major Russell said that he would resist being taken off the train and advised us to do the same.

"After all," he said, "the war is over and I don't think they will dare take us off by force. Hang on to your seats. The train crew will not permit violence."

When we reached Karlsruhe, two uniformed men came on the train and joined "Moustache." They ordered us to leave the train with them. Major Russell refused to leave, and I refused, but Madame X and the four American men (one was a commercial traveler from St. Louis) filed meekly off the train, herded by "Moustache" and the two men in uniform. As they left, "Moustache" jeered at the Major and myself.

"See how far you get in Europe without a passport," he said (the Major translating for me). "You can't cross the border into Czechoslovakia. I'll have you back in Karlsruhe very soon."

After the train was on its way again, the Major and I looked at each other wondering what we would do next. I had asked him to sit down with me in my compartment.

"Well," he said, "here we are and just how we are to get across the border without passports I don't know. I wonder if the Czechs will listen to our story and pass us along when we get to Eger. I'll make a try for it. I've been in several tight places during the war. Maybe we can squeeze out of this one."

I moved nervously and apprehensively. Then I remembered something that I had forgotten in all the excitement and confusion—President Masaryk's letter, which I had removed from my night robe and pinned inside my blouse when I dressed. A warm glow almost like an electric shock raced over my body. I reached for my letter, unpinned it, and took it out of the envelope.

"Major Russell," I said, "we may be able to get over the border into Czechoslovakia. Read this letter. I've been so excited that I completely forgot that I had it."

We read together the letter written on the stationery of the President of the Czech Republic, signed Tomás Garrigue Masaryk, giving Mrs. Jeanne Robert Foster and her party safe conduct to Prague. Major Russell looked at me, and I looked at him. For a moment we could say nothing.

Then he said almost incredulously, "You managed to keep this letter. It wasn't with your passport."

I explained that I had a hunch to conceal it in my clothing and separated it from the rest of my papers after I boarded the Express.

When we reached Eger, I jubilantly offered President Masaryk's letter to the Czechs when they asked to examine our passports, and together Major Russell and I told our story, which was corroborated by the conductor of our train. We were triumphantly passed over the border and a wire was sent to Prague to ensure our welcome at the Prague railway station.

The thrill of the letter was lost in the greater thrill of our arrival in Prague. (I still love to call that city by its Czech name, Praha.) Before I walked down out of the Orient Express, I heard a voice calling, "Pani Foster . . . Pani Foster." A Czech, in a soldier's uniform, was running up and down the platform shouting my name. I walked over to the man in uniform and made myself known and introduced Major Russell. A little to one side of the station was

President Masaryk's beautiful sleek limousine waiting for me, flying the flags of the Czech Republic and the United States. It was the thrill of a lifetime. An orderly who was chauffeuring the car handed me a note from Jan Masaryk, which said that it had been impossible for him to meet me on account of official business but that he would see me later at the Hradzin, the ancient palace that was now the residence of the President. I explained to the orderly how we had lost our passports and had been passed over the border by the President's letter. I asked him to drop Major Russell off at the British Legations before he took me to the Hradzin.

Jeanne always kept the note from Jan Masaryk, and it is now located in the Foster Murphy Collection at the New York Public Library, along with one other from him, which begins, "Sweet Lady—."[5]
Her story continued:

Looking back on the events of the ten days following my arrival in Prague, they still have all the glamour that they had then—of a dream too wonderful to be true. The city was bubbling with the new life of freedom that had followed the "liberation." University students were building new dormitories with their own hands. Dr. H. O. Eversole, Director of the American Red Cross, was performing miracles and managing a new child center. The Red Cross had gathered together the pitiful starving bands of war orphans, whose only home was the streets, and settled them in a comfortable building. Eugenia Patterson, the American nurse whom I had met with the Siberian Legionnaires in New York, was holding down an official job in Prague.

During the New York fete for the Czecho-Slovak soldiers, Jeanne had met and become friends with Eugenia Patterson, who had accompanied some of the soldiers across parts of Siberia in the last days of the conflict. Through Ms. Patterson, Jeanne had also met Dr. H. O. Eversole, the director of the American Red Cross in the Czechoslovakian Republic. Now, in Prague, she renewed her acquaintance. Eversole told her about some of the work his staff had done, and although she had promised Jan Masaryk not to

5. The second letter is a brief note: "Sweet Lady—Will come down about 9 P.M. to say 'Hello.' —hope it will not be too late—Faithfully / Jan M." Both letters were written during JRF's trip to Czechoslovakia.

publish anything, her reporter's instinct did not allow her to miss the opportunity to record Eversole's words about Pribram, then a town of about twelve thousand inhabitants. He spoke of the squalor caused by extreme poverty. His description of malnourished children reminded her of those she had met in her beloved Ireland. He told her about mothers who walked more than five miles from other villages so that their babies could receive care. Others arrived on wagons drawn by cows, and reports daily arrived of others who needed medical attention but who were too weak to make the trip. Finally, the Red Cross center acquired enough help to send a Czech physician and an American nurse and social worker to the outer areas: "In one village last week, the Mayor spent the entire day actually running all over the village to tell the mothers that the Americans were there and to hurry the children in. Several places the Mayor found the parents were away at work, and he brought the kiddies in to the doctor himself," Dr. Eversole claimed.[6]

The Red Cross split Czechoslovakia into districts by need and located areas where children were most undernourished. Some of the cases Jeanne observed were youngsters with crooked legs and backs, and with open, festering wounds. Five centers began the program, which was gradually expanded, and the Red Cross, with assistance and participation from the government of the republic, gave aid and instruction in preventive medicine, prenatal and postnatal care, first-aid training, and nutrition. The Czechs, who named the program "To Our Children," were to take over the complete administration within two years. It was imperative that Czechoslovakia not become dependent on outside aid.[7]

Jeanne Foster's arrival in Czechoslovakia came at a particularly difficult time for the Masaryk government. Strikes and riots had spread through the country during the summer, and part of the government resigned on 14 September 1920. A Marxist faction tried to establish itself by forming a rump congress in late September, but by 27 November, near the end of Jeanne's visit, a faction of Social Democrats formed their own rump congress. During all of this turmoil, from September through November,

6. Quoted by JRF (LC).

7. In the essay, Eversole mentioned that the Czechs would assume control by July 1922 (LC).

Czech-German conflicts—conflicts great enough that troops had to intervene—broke out in Tœplitz (Teplitz), Cheb (Eger), and Prague (Praha).
Jeanne was in the middle of just such a conflict on 13 November in Prague:

> The second night after my arrival there was trouble on the streets between
> the Czech soldiers and some of the German residents. Eugenia and I went
> down to the German Casin Hall with some of the Legionnaires [from the
> Siberian expedition]. Although it was two years after the "liberation," the
> Germans were still displaying a life-sized colored lithograph of the old Aus-
> trian Emperor in uniform. One of the Czech soldiers tore the picture down,
> divided it into three parts, and gave one to me with an inscription and his
> name, "Joseph Terneren." The trouble between the Germans and the Czech
> soldiers went on all night. The next morning, President Masaryk drove down
> into the city unaccompanied and "talked to the boys," as he said. There was
> no more trouble.

The general strikes were quelled at least in part by the powerful personality of Tomáš Masaryk. Although some violence occurred in Slovak regions (Vráble, for example), the Czech workers had no desire for long-term
revolutionary action. By mid-December, though, nearly three thousand
had been arrested for strike-related offenses, and Masaryk faced one of his
biggest tests. Some people were unfortunately prosecuted without the benefit of jury trial, but widespread reprisals did not occur, and by June 1921 a
general amnesty was offered to those who applied. Even the left-wing radi-
cals, who refused to ask for it, were included under the general amnesty that
President Masaryk proclaimed in early 1922. He wanted to move his country forward, and to do so he recognized that his government must allow political groups the opportunity to organize openly. For a time, the problems
of 1920 and 1921 actually made Masaryk's republic stronger. Its apparent
dedication to law and order gave the fledgling state respect in the international community (Mamatey and Luza 1973, 102–7).

Jan Masaryk took Jeanne on several sight-seeing trips around the neighboring villages near Prague. She said that the younger Masaryk much admired his dynamic and famous father and wanted to do his own part in the
promotion of the republic. But Jan was temperamental, Jeanne said, and reminded her of an artist who might have great moments of inspiration and

joy, and then just as quickly find himself despairing for his lack of vision. One of Jan Masaryk's friends later said of him: " 'Despite his apparent joviality and good humor, Jan was an unhappy man. His jokes, his splendid esprit, his exuberance, his disarming smile, all that made him such a perfect companion, were a façade hiding an unbalanced and occasionally even desperate man. . . . He was impulsive, often rash and erratic, and always restless. He made a brilliant goodwill ambassador; no one matched him in that respect' " (qtd. in Taborsky 1981, 197–98, 200).

It was Jan who most often escorted Jeanne Foster around Prague, and it was Jan who spoke with her for long hours about politics, philosophy, art, and music. Jeanne recorded one experience with him because, she said, "it showed his passion":

> One of the several trips arranged for me by Jan Masaryk was a trip to the village of Lany to inspect the Red Cross food station. We started at five in the morning. On the way we saw old men and women gathering faggots to keep their fires in the majestic forests of tall pines. As we were passing a farm, Jan stopped the car. (Although we had a chauffeur from the Palace, Jan drove the car.) Down in the field to our left in the misty light of early morning, an old cow and a woman were pulling a plough to turn the furrows. The plough was guided by another woman. (There were no milch cows or oxen left in the country at that time.) Jan Masaryk's face reddened as he got out of the car and hurried down into the field. We saw him talking to the women. When he came back, he said, "I'm sending help to those women. Please God that I never see a sight like that again as long as my father is President of the Republic!"

The appalling conditions of the people in Prague and of the surrounding countryside formed a bizarre contrast with the castle where she stayed. Indeed, she may have lost critical perspective because of the attentions that the president's family paid to her:

> We drove beyond the village into the beautiful park that held the castle that had formerly belonged to Crown Prince Rudolph of Austria. This castle, intact with all its gorgeous furnishings, had been offered to President Masaryk for a summer residence, but he had refused the gift. The castle contained a museum notable for its collection of ancient and modern firearms and for in-

numerable statues of St. George and the dragon. On our return, I was a guest at a dinner for the Masaryks and the diplomatic corps given by Richard Crane, the American Minister to the Czech Republic.

Jeanne enjoyed her evenings and her excursions with the Masaryks and at the time had no idea about the tremendous strain the president was under from the strikes and from the Marxist movement in the government. He showed no trace of the pressure, she said. Later, when she knew more about the circumstances, she said that his decorum, his "public front," impressed her enormously. When she was in Prague, what did catch her notice was Masaryk's careful attention to his presidential expenses. Castle meals were spartan and cost-efficient. He was more concerned with building hospitals and schools, and with trying to build a sense of "nation" between several groups who seemed to get along best when threatened by an outside force. Peace could be an elusive commodity in the republic in 1920:

> The meals at the Castle were very simple. Lunch might be small lamb chops, one vegetable, and for dessert rice pudding. Wine was never served. If the embassies had special luxuries sent in from Paris in hampers, the President would have none of it. The food served on his table was that which could be obtained in the country itself, which was at that time suffering a dearth of nearly everything.
>
> With Alice Masaryk and Eugenia Patterson, I visited the ancient city's historic shrines, the Red Cross headquarters, the Veterans' Hospital, and watched the students of the colleges and universities building new dormitories. While I was in Prague, President Masaryk held an official reception for guests from the three provinces—Bohemia, Moravia, and Slovakia. Many of the young girls attending this reception with their parents wore their colorful national costumes laced with very beautiful heirloom embroideries.

On 6 January 1920, ten months before her great adventure through Germany and Czechoslovakia, Jeanne had attended a reception in New York City at the Hotel Plaza for Jan Masaryk, who was then chargé d'affaires of the republic. The evening consisted of music by Dvořák, Smetana (two of her favorite composers), Novák, Suk, and Nedbal. The printed program contained four poems by Antonin Sova, translated by Ladislav Urban, with

"English Rhythms by Jeanne Robert Foster."[8] In May of the previous year, she had written "The Music of the Czechoslovaks" for the *Review*, which she began, "There is a saying, 'Where there is a Czech—there you hear music.'" She explained the differences between Czech and Slovak music— the former being "of a lively, rhythmical, dance-like character," and the latter being "a more poetic form, a freer rhythm, and a tendency to introduce church modes" (Foster 1919a, 547–48). Jeanne's article briefly examined the qualities of her favorite Czechoslovakian musicians and of singer Emmy Destinn.[9] At the end of the article, she reminded her readers that Czechoslovakia was its own self-determined country and had received political recognition by the Allied nations and the United States (1919a, 548).

The music had not been forgotten. One evening during Jeanne's stay in Prague, Jan Masaryk, an accomplished pianist, sat down at the castle's grand piano and played some of her favorite pieces. That evening was only a precursor to another—one of the most memorable of her life:

> I will never forget the torrent of wild melancholy music that poured out of the grand piano from his fingers, all the sadness and the feverish gaiety that is typical of Slav music. That night, President Masaryk asked me if I would like to hear an opera. "If you do," he said, "Jan will ask the director of the Narodini Divadio (the Prague National Theater) to give a performance of the one you prefer."
>
> I told him that I would like to hear Dvorak's fairy tale opera, "Rusalka." As I recall the date, it was the night of November 21 that the opera was given. I had only one evening dress with me, as I had brought a single suit case. It was black and gold tissue and quite lovely, although it was not an expensive costume. Just before we left to go to the National Theater, Jan Masaryk produced a velvet case containing some lovely jewels. He said he had borrowed them and insisted that I wear those he selected.

8. A copy of the original program is in LC. Antonin Dvořák (1841–1904), Bohemian composer. Bedřich Smetana (1824–84), Czech composer. Viteslav Novák (1870–1949), Czech composer influenced by native folk melody. Joseph Suk (1875–1935), Czech composer and violinist. Oskar Nedbal (1874–1930), Czech violinist, conductor, and composer. Antonin Sova (1864–1928), Czech writer known for lyrical verses.

9. Emmy Destinn (1878–1930), Bohemian operatic soprano.

Today, I can still feel the thrill of that evening almost as much as I did then. We waited in an ante room of the theater until the audience was seated. Then we were ushered into the booth reserved for our party. When President Masaryk entered, the entire audience rose to their feet and cheered their president. I felt like a fairy princess in my black and gold dress with the borrowed jewels glittering in my hair. Whatever happened to me in the future, I would always have this night to remember.

Much has happened since then. The glorious young Republic for which the Czechs fought so bravely has known many changes. Tomás Garrigue Masaryk, the lion heart, and Jan Masaryk, who tried so valiantly to salvage the seeds of Czech freedom, are long gone. The day following the performance of "Rusalka," I obtained an emergency passport at the American Legation for my return to Paris. On December 1, I embarked at Cherbourg for New York. In my heart, in my mind, was locked away the most unforgettable experience in my life.

Letters that reached me later from Major Thomas Russell, now British military observer at Warsaw, carried the information that despite the protests of his government, he had never been able to retrieve his passport, and that the five unlucky passengers on the Orient Express who did *not* escape were held many weeks in Karlsruhe.  ·

Jeanne Foster's work for the new republic continued. Dr. Alice Masaryk wrote to her on 15 January 1921 (NYPL) to ask her to organize a bazaar in New York City—a display of Czechoslovakian art (sculpture, etchings, watercolors). Jeanne also wrote an article, unfortunately never published, about the life of Alice Masaryk, from the time she became one of the first women to attend the University of Prague to her internment in a Vienna prison.[10] It was exactly the story Dr. Masaryk needed to win the sympathies and the attentions of the American public:

Dr. Masaryk . . . was obliged to carry her trunk on her shoulder all through the city and was put at once in a cell together with not only other political prisoners but also prostitutes, thieves, and murderers. The sanitary conditions of the prison were horrible and the people about it painfully rough and

10. Alice Masaryk was held in prison in 1915–16 by the Austrian government. Letters written to her mother, Charlotte Garrigue Masaryk, during this time are at the Manuscripts Department, Lilly Library, Indiana University, Bloomington.

feelingless. A little window in the top part of the wall through which the
prisoners could see a bit of sky and old chimney were the only comfort of the
place. . . . After nine months she was released for want of proof and thanks to
the protest the American women sent to the Austrian government. It took a
year before she recovered her health. (LC)

Jeanne's role in the movement became less active after 1921, but in 1923
she published "The Winter Song" in *Rock Flower* (91). It was her tribute to a
country she had come to love:

> In Strasbourg, the Tricolor streams on the ancient square;
> In Dover, St. George's cross lies crimson upon the wind;
> Beyond the sea, there are stars above the sunrise
> Upon tall ships in Atlantic harbors.
> But I am dreaming of another flag.
> In Praha, in golden Praha,
> There is a new flag of freedom upon the streets,
> As the soldiers march singing the "Winter Song" softly.
> Softly, softly it comes to my ears—
>                                        (lines 1–9)

Americans sometimes have a tendency to view other nations and their
conflicts—or their possibilities—too simplistically. We may turn a blind
eye to centuries of turmoil, and we may hope, as Woodrow Wilson did, that
self-determination will in some measure erase long conflicts between rival
groups. Jeanne was no different from many in her uncritical view of
the Czechoslovakian Republic, in her love affair with the idea of the new
country.

In reality, she knew that Masaryk faced many challenges. His land-
reform policies were sometimes unfair to Hungarians and Germans living
within his borders, and their attitudes did not make other Czech leaders
feel very generous. Graft had to be controlled; some Czechs stood to make
fortunes from the misfortunes of others. The Slovaks never had complete
equality with the Czechs, and many of their leaders viewed their participation in the republic as the lesser of several evils and not necessarily a permanent solution. By 1930, accusations by former ally Karel Pergler of
misuse of funds made life difficult for Masaryk and his eventual successor,

Benes. It disturbed Jeanne to hear such rumors, and she didn't honestly know which of her friends was in the wrong.

Pergler had been appointed the Czech Republic's commissioner in the United States not long after Jeanne met him. Later, in 1918, he was named the republic's first ambassador to the United States, and in 1920 he was given a similar post in Japan. Before he left for the Far East, he visited Jeanne and her sister Cara for several days at the Foster summer cottage at Higgins Beach, Maine.

In one surviving letter between the two—dated 5 June 1919 and written to Jeanne from Washington, D.C.—Pergler enclosed a special edition of a booklet "on the Czechoslovak State with a photograph of President Masaryk . . . because I think you will be interested in the artistic makeup of the book." In another letter, dated 26 December 1919, Pergler wrote to Jeanne that he would be in New York for a dinner on 7 January but that he planned to arrive a few days early and would like to have dinner with her on both 1 and 2 January. He wanted to discuss "several additional ideas" that "have occurred to me." Jeanne was editing some articles by Pergler, which later appeared in *Current Opinion* (May 1919) and in *Annals of the American Academy of Political and Social Science* (July 1919); so, though they were friends, these meetings were largely business dinners. During this period, Jeanne wrote a biographical sketch of Pergler's life up to and including his appointment to Japan.[11]

The last letter from Pergler, dated 3 April 1939, is a response to one from Jeanne. Their concern focused on the recent German invasion and the tragedy of Czechoslovakia. Pergler blamed his old friends Tomáš Masaryk and Edvard Benes for much of the trouble. Masaryk had died in 1937, and Benes was now the leader of a crumbling nation. Pergler was furious at the state of his republic:

Munich and what followed is to a large extent the result of the fatuous policy of Benes, and his utter political incapacity, aside from the question of his methods in domestic politics.

. . . One of the last acts of the Hácha government, by the way, two days before Hitler walked in, was a declaration to the effect, not in so many

11. The letters from Pergler to JRF and JRF's biographical sketch of him are in LC.

JRF with Czechoslovakian politician Karel Pergler at Higgins Beach, Maine, 1920. Londraville private collection.

words, that unseating me from Parliament was an illegal act and one of virtual force.[12] My standing at home is now unquestioned. This satisfaction came too late, however, to do any good.

I hope we may be able to discuss these matters personally in the near future.

Jeanne said that the falling out between Pergler and Masaryk started in late 1920. She had heard rumblings of it during her stay in Prague, when reports arrived about money being embezzled from the Japanese embassy. Pergler was eventually dismissed and disgraced, although it was later discovered that his assistant, a man named Novak, had probably been the thief. In any case, by 1930, Pergler, back in the Czechoslovakian Republic, accused Masaryk and Benes of similar misdeeds. Masaryk acted swiftly, expelling his old ally from the country. Pergler moved to the United States, where he became a respected professor and author. He died in Washington, D.C., in 1954.

No other letters between Karel Pergler and Jeanne Foster survive. She lost contact with him shortly after World War II started in September 1939.

In 1948, Jeanne's good friend Jan Masaryk died. Reports circulated that he had committed suicide, but Jeanne did not believe it. Dr. Hajo Herbell, a pro-Soviet historian, wrote in 1969 that "lies are spread such as the one about the alleged murder of . . . Jan Masaryk who, in actual fact committed

12. Emil Hácha replaced Benes as president and tried to adjust to Hitler's ideas of a "New Order." See Mamatey and Luza 1973, 469.

suicide in 1948, and whose 'murder' was invented by a creature named Veigl" (171). But in their book on Alice Masaryk, Ruth Crawford Mitchell and Linda Vlasak note that "evidence brought to light during the Dubcek 'Spring' of 1968, that brief relaxation of the Soviet grip on Czechoslovakia, supports the belief [that Jan Masaryk] was murdered by Soviet secret-service agents" (1980, 203). This version of his death would have made sense to Jeanne. Her friend, she said, would never leave his country "by choice." [13]

Jeanne's relationship with Czechoslovakia ended by 1940, but her dedication to the republic had made her feel a part of the great experiment. Though the government was flawed, Jeanne Foster never regretted her efforts on behalf of the Masaryks and their noble plan.

13. JRF, interviewed by RL, 9 August 1969.

# 9

# John Quinn, the Man from New York

"Who is John Quinn?" a reporter for a local paper in Schenectady once
asked Jeanne Robert Foster. "Mrs. Foster smiled very patiently. . . . It
was a smile and an expression—conveying—or concealing—fathoms
of intention."

—Coral Crosman, "Who Is John Quinn?"

JOHN QUINN WAS THE IRISH AMERICAN LAWYER to whom
Maud Gonne wrote, "[I] feel wild that you do not belong to Ireland entirely,
for you would have led the people and made history as Parnell did" (Gonne
and Quinn 1999, 124). He was the man about whom journalist Frederick
James Gregg wrote, "John Quinn . . . was probably the most courageous
patron of the arts of his time. It was not his way to wait until men's reputations were made before buying their work" (qtd. in *MFNY*, 637). Quinn's
friend, John Butler Yeats, wrote to his son William Butler Yeats, "John
Quinn is the nearest approach to an angel in my experience" (qtd. in *MFNY*,
3). To Jeanne Foster, he was, quite simply, the love of her long life.

When B. L. Reid's biography of Quinn, *The Man from New York*, was published by Oxford University Press in 1968, Jeanne was thrilled. She wrote
on 19 October 1968: "Dr. Reid has used a full length page picture facing the
JBY painting, of me, and other small pictures. There are forty-four references to me in the index. I had no idea he was using so much; he quotes
Ford[1] and gives JQ's last days under my care, in detail, notes the Italian trip,
in fact memorializes me with JQ, and is careful to show that it was a spiritual debt and differentiate me from others that are mentioned" (JRF to RL,

---

1. Ford Madox Ford (1873–1939), English author, poet, and editor.

in LC). Reid says nothing of this spiritual debt, but does omit the gossip of the time that Jeanne Foster and John Quinn were lovers. Her later notebooks mention Quinn in the same manner she used to write of Albert Shaw—speaking of their deep feeling for each other, but never owning a physical relationship.

Most of those who knew Quinn and Jeanne assumed that they were intimate, but she remained adamant that they were not.[2] She certainly equivocated about the definition of the sexual relationship, arguing that Quinn was impotent from his February 1918 cancer surgery even before she met him later that same year. On 24 December 1968, she wrote: "Quinn was incredibly brave to function at all after 1918. He had to be laced up in an intricate harness before he could adjust his clothing. He could function 'as a man' no longer" (JRF to RL, in LC). Jeanne does, however, write to Quinn about the joy of going to sleep at night and waking up the next morning in his arms. She certainly was smitten with the man, no matter what spin she chose to put on the relationship.

Jeanne never denied that she loved Quinn. In the early 1920s, she had even written to Dorothy Pound about her desire to have a child with him. Others had the same wish for her. Quinn's friend, Henri-Pierre Roché, wrote to Jeanne in 1922:[3] "An outsider can not imagine you not becoming a mother—and him a father. For me you complete each other. —There ought to be nothing against that, even if one has to look for freedom in another continent."[4] Having a child was only a dream for both Quinn and Jeanne. It would have been an unacceptable reality for each: the Irish Catholic Quinn and the very married Jeanne Foster.

It was the emergency of J. B. Yeats's influenza in 1918 that brought John Quinn and Jeanne Foster together, and after that point they were rarely apart. The first time they spoke was on the telephone. "This is John Quinn," he announced. He asked her if she was afraid of the influenza. (Quinn was.) When she answered no, he asked her to look after old Yeats, "and send the bills to me." After John Butler Yeats was well, Quinn invited Jeanne to dinner

2. JRF, interviewed by RL, 15 August 1969.

3. Henri-Pierre Roché (1879–1959), French author and art agent.

4. Roché to JRF, dated only 1922 (NYPL). Unless otherwise noted, Roché's letters to JRF are located in the Foster-Murphy Collection, NYPL.

at his apartment. When he answered the door, he said, "My God, I thought you were an old lady" (letter, JRF to Murphy, 27 March 1968, MC).

JBY had tried for several years to get the two together, telling Jeanne that "Quinn needs a good woman to rest his head" (*MFNY,* 313), although his own judgment was that "it was futile to seek 'everlasting' happiness in love. Love is not happiness; it is torture. Love kills by satiation; it destroys itself like the Phoenix" (*PF,* 422).

Jeanne had first caught a glimpse of Quinn at the Armory Show of 1913, when she watched him escort his friends, Theodore Roosevelt among them, around the exhibition. But she was not eager to make his acquaintance, for she had been warned that Quinn was a notorious womanizer. Over the years, she learned of his affairs with Annie Foster, daughter of the former governor of Ohio;[5] with Ada Smith, daughter of his landlady;[6] with Alice Thursby, journalist Arthur Brisbane's sister; and with May Morris, daughter of poet and designer William Morris. Jeanne also knew of Quinn's brief affair in early 1912 with Lady Augusta Gregory, one of the founders of the Irish literary movement of the early twentieth century, when Lady Gregory was fifty-nine and Quinn was forty-one. Gregory wrote to him after she returned to Ireland: "Oh my darling, am I now lonely after you? Do I not awake looking for you—and long to be alone sometimes that I may think only of you? Why do I love you so much? . . . I think I love you better every day" (D. Murphy 1987, 129).

John Quinn had listened to J. B. Yeats's praise of Jeanne Foster for several years, but he was certain that any lady friend of the old man would likely be

5. JRF wrote to Aline Saarinen on 1 January 1958: "In regard to Annie Foster, she was a dim memory when I met [JQ]. His happiest recollection of her was as she appeared in white satin at a New Year's ball. One of her letters which I do not have was written from Atlantic City. It may have been 1910. She had visited him in New York at that time but the love-affair had not been renewed. She died suddenly—sinus trouble— . . . and J. Q. laid her memory away although he sometimes called me 'Annie' " (NYPL).

6. JRF wrote to Aline Saarinen on 1 January 1958 that JQ had rented a cottage at Manhattan Beach one summer for his sister [Julia] and little niece, Mary. Ada Smith cared for Mary, who was about five at the time. "John spent as much time as he could with them. During all the years I knew John, he never saw [Ada] at his home. I know she and her mother ran a restaurant in Westchester. . . . She did not persecute him as Dorothy Coates did . . . but when she was mentioned, John looked at me silently as if for pity" (NYPL).

similarly old and wrinkled, even though JBY had written a letter to Quinn that not only described Jeanne but included a pen-and-ink likeness. It had intrigued him, Quinn later told Jeanne, but he had a suspicion that JBY had made her more beautiful than she was. In fact, the opposite was true, he confessed to her after opening the door to his apartment that night in the fall of 1918. Even John Butler Yeats could not completely capture her loveliness (*PF*, 395, 503).

When Jeanne Foster arrived in John Quinn's life, he was involved in a decade-long relationship with a former schoolteacher, Dorothy Coates. He had difficulty untangling himself from Coates, whom Jeanne called "the dragon." Using the same technique he had used on May Morris—"do nothing and she will go away"—he simply ignored Coates. But Coates was not to be cast aside easily and often showed up unexpectedly and at embarrassing moments for Quinn. His secretaries, and even Jeanne herself, often had to run interference for him.

Later, when B. L. Reid was writing *The Man from New York*, it was important to Jeanne that Quinn's "womanizer" title be erased. She wrote on 24 December 1968: "I persuaded Reid to do Quinn justice in certain ways by giving him my intimate handwritten diary of his last days. After reading that, Reid changed his mind and knew Quinn was not 'a conqueror or a crusher' of women" (JRF to RL, in LC).

Perhaps. Quinn had a long list of conquests, each of whom was shocked and dismayed when she learned that he was finished with her. Many women were certainly drawn to such an attractive, vibrant, unmarried man. One cannot be surprised that over the years he would have liaisons with several who caught his eye. Jeanne's attempt to minimize these adventures is difficult to understand, especially because she dealt with the evidence of correspondence from many of them and was discreet enough to return the steamier letters to May Morris and Lady Gregory after Quinn's death. She evidently considered herself to be the end of his lifelong search for true love and was thus able to dismiss his earlier adventures as youthful experimentation.

John Quinn was often around beautiful and intelligent women who understood art and literature. What made Jeanne Foster so necessary to him? Of course, that inexplicable essence, "chemistry," no doubt had something to do with it. But there was more. Her belief that genius resided only in men made her feel that her own considerable talents as writer and editor were better utilized in the service of some superior man, and this attitude appealed to Quinn. Her philosophy carried over to her views about art and artists as well. In 1920, she wrote in her diary: "When I no longer care to see, art alone remains to me with moments of conscious delusion—and art cannot spring from me save through the masculine vision" (LC). Jeanne felt that her choice of husband had stifled her development: "Life mis-cast me. If I had been married to a man who needed my type of brain, I would have done nothing but promote his glory and felt no lack. Genius is male" (letter to Murphy, 3 June 1970, MC).

Coral Crosman interviewed Jeanne for the *Schenectady Union Star* on 7 November 1968. Their discussion centered around the newly published *The Man from New York* and hinted at Jeanne's theory:

> Gazing out into the autumn sunlight from her quiet parlor, Mrs. Foster, a gentle, grey-haired lady with the grace of an opulence of aesthetic aristocracy and the clear, lucid mind of a much younger spirit, speaks affectionately of Quinn, with a respect for his neglected achievements:
>
> "This should be his story, not mine. I want you to write about [*The Man from New York*] and not about me and my part in it."
>
> It is typical of this modest, unassuming woman, whose life is a biography in itself, that she not want to sound as if she were climbing on the bandwagon with someone else. She made available to Reid materials, drawn from correspondence, for his book. And she also had shared with him her own memories of this gifted man. (24)

John Quinn had for some time been looking for an associate to assist in his literary and artistic business. He was quickly becoming one of the foremost collectors of modern art in the world, and he needed someone of sensitivity to help him keep an eye on his varied interests. He employed competent people to handle affairs in his law office (although he often fired assistants who he felt were not keeping pace with the work), but there was no one to arrange the other half of his life. He needed, more than anything, someone who was knowledgeable but whose ego would not compete with his own. Quinn was also used to dictating to his secretaries, but when the topic was other than law, he needed someone who could take notes and understand the subject, someone who would be able to advise him as he composed and to adjust to his quick rush of ideas. Jeanne was perfect for the job. Although she was not a professional stenographer, her experience as a reporter and editor had forced her to develop her own method of rapid notation.

Shortly after they met, Jeanne began to supply the kind of editing that Quinn needed and wanted. She became the companion that he leaned on for the rest of his life, trusting her to be the recorder for his interviews with famous figures and his intermediary with people such as Gwen John and Henri-Pierre Roché. In the meantime, she kept writing, sometimes combining her art interests with her journalism, as in the case of her articles on Constantin Brancusi, and always working on her poetry.[7]

Of course, Jeanne Foster still had a husband in her life. In 1918, Matlack Foster was sixty-four and ill. Jeanne visited him frequently in Schenectady, and on rare occasions, health permitting, Matlack would travel to New York City to see his wife and his brother Gardiner.[8] After Quinn met Jeanne and fell in love, he became jealous of her time, especially with her husband. On one occasion, she reassured Quinn that her relationship with Matlack needed to be respected but was not intimate, calling her husband a "lobster" and no threat. Fearful of losing her, Quinn wrote a letter expressing his concern, echoing cadences in *Hamlet*.[9]

I could not dodge the issue presented Wednesday. It was useless to blind myself so. I saw it like a flash—first impulse to try to stay you—but second thought said, No use: she wants to go or she would not go. If she is willing or wants to go, if not tonight it will be tomorrow. The willingness was the blow. . . . I had and have money and it was for you. But—what's the use. You know and you know I know you did not "simply have to see the man from home." There is no man from your home you have to see if you did not want to see him. "A lobster"—yes but you spent the night with him. . . . If not that night—the next or the next so why speak . . . the willingness was the thing.

7. Constantin Brancusi (1876–1957), Rumanian artist.

8. JRF had by now taken an apartment at 300 West Forty-ninth Street in New York City.

9. JQ's letter to JRF is dated only 20 July. Someone penciled in 1918, but JQ and JRF did not meet until later that year (NYPL).

I would have no right to be angry. Even at night writhing like a man in hell at
the picture of your dressing to hurry to the arms of the fellow.

Quinn certainly had "no right" to the feelings he described. He need not
have worried, however. Jeanne could not have been more enthralled. Only
a vestigial sense of propriety and the fact that her husband lived with her
parents kept that marriage intact. Quinn was the superior male that Jeanne
had always longed to serve. Whenever she spoke of him, even decades
later, it was obvious that she was still captivated by his power.

When they were able to arrange time together away from Matlack,
Jeanne sometimes read Quinn's law briefs to him while he was shaving in
the morning, and from that time on he needed no notes; his memory was
exceptional. He also had a great sense of the moment, especially when it
came to the celebrities he knew, and he wanted Jeanne to share in this experience. Thus, he orchestrated informal moments with people such as
Brancusi, Matisse, and Picasso. In one instance, when W. B. Yeats and his
wife, George (1892–1968), were visiting New York City in 1920, Jeanne
helped prepare their quarters at Quinn's apartment. When the Yeatses were
about to appear, Quinn, without explanation, pushed Jeanne into a closet in
their room. That night she rather uncomfortably eavesdropped on their
private conversation. When they left, Quinn explained that he had wanted
her to experience genius unguarded.[10]

During that same visit, when WBY was preparing to set out on his cross-
country lecture tour, Quinn took the opportunity to interview him at the
Algonquin Hotel. He brought Jeanne along in order to record the occasion.[11] Jeanne by this time already knew the Yeats family, so her presence as
a note-taker didn't inhibit either man. Pleased with the success of the Yeats
meeting, Quinn thought that he would collect several such documents and
amass his own literary history of the early twentieth century. And so it was

10. B. L. Reid wrote that JQ pushed JRF into a room across the hall (*MFNY,* 419), but she
told RL it was a closet in the Yeatses' room, which seems to make more sense. She wouldn't
have been able to hear the conversation from a room across the hallway. See also *PF,* 642,
note 17, and Maddox 1999, 162.

11. The result of the interview was edited and published in 1988 as "John Quinn's 'An
Evening in New York with W. B. Yeats' " (Quinn 1988).

that Jeanne sat in on conversations between Quinn and a number of writers, including Pound, Ford, Eliot, and Joyce.

It was through John Quinn that Jeanne Foster amassed most of the important items in her art and manuscript collection, either directly or indirectly. Although he disposed of the bulk of his library (including manuscripts) in several sales, he did retain special items, as well as his own correspondence, and he would occasionally give some of them to Jeanne, especially if the writer interested her. This is how she came to possess many of the letters between Quinn and English painter-writer Wyndham Lewis, and between Quinn and Irish politician Frank Hugh O'Donnell. He gave her art, as well. Jeanne loaned one of those treasures, a painting by Georges Braque, to Georgette Passedoit, Quinn's secretary, for an exhibition. During the stressful times of the late 1920s, Jeanne forgot about the painting, and, sadly, it was never returned to her. Its current location remains unknown today.[12]

In June 1921, Jeanne accompanied Quinn on a trip to Europe. It was particularly important to her that he have a peaceful and happy time. He was ill, and she hoped the trip would extend his life. She wanted to take him away from the pressures of his law practice, at which he still worked excessively long hours, and to give him some respite from his worries about John Butler Yeats, who was failing more and more as the weeks went by. The trip would take them both away from Dorothy Coates, who probably thought that she could outlast Jeanne as she had outlasted some of Quinn's other paramours. To avoid confrontation, his travel plans were kept a secret, even from most of his friends, so that Coates would not interfere. For the sake of propriety, Jeanne left separately, and she and Quinn met again on the other side of the Atlantic (PF, 527).

12. The correspondence between Wyndham Lewis (1882–1957) and John Quinn is published in Lewis and Quinn 1990a and 1990b; the Frank Hugh O'Donnell (1848–1916) correspondence is in Londraville and Londraville 1991. JRF described the painting by Georges Braque (1882–1963, French artist) to RL only by saying that it had a lemon or lemons in the center. There was an exhibition of Braque's works in 1926–27, which might well have been the exhibition JRF mentioned. It was held at the Brooklyn Museum from 19 November 1926 through 1 January 1927; at the Anderson Galleries (where JRF knew several people) in January and February; at the Buffalo Albright Art Gallery in March; and at the Art Gallery of Toronto in April.

Respectability was an issue for both John Quinn and Jeanne Foster. She was, after all, a married woman, and he was a bachelor who had a professional reputation to protect. They had the false impression, not unusual for people in their position, that only their closest friends knew of their affair and that it would thus not do for either one of them to be found in a compromising position. This impression may be why Quinn wrote rather peevishly to W. B. Yeats on 9 November 1923, when John Butler Yeats's partial autobiography was posthumously published. In his preface, WBY mentioned that Jeanne and Quinn were with John Butler Yeats on one occasion in the middle of the night. Quinn took offense: "The . . . mistake . . . consists in your statement that your father was 'taken ill in the night' and woke up and found his friends Mrs. Foster and John Quinn sitting at his bedside" (Quinn 1983, 290).[13] He felt that this description might give the impression to some that he and Jeanne were alone in the middle of the night, from which rumors might start.

Quinn returned from Europe in the summer of 1921, but Jeanne stayed on to look after his interests and to do some work of her own. She missed him enormously and was worried about the heap of concerns, his own and others, that always bedeviled him. Soon after his arrival in New York City, she wrote on two occasions:

> John, you are not trapped by life: you are free—and you are my lover and friend only as long as I give you joy—no longer. I love you, not things, or a status. . . . You are wonderful. There is no one like you. If I do anything it will be because of you, and for you, John. I miss you—your arms, your "goodnight"—your "good morning." (16 August 1921, NYPL)

> John, you are to me the sun, the blue sky, the sea, the blue marsh-flowers, the wind in the firs, the tall firs themselves; and all lovely natural things. Love me or love me not, it makes no difference. To have found you is enough for me. You are, that suffices.[14]

13. The JBY autobiography is *Early Memories: Some Chapters of Autobiography* (1923).

14. The second letter is not dated, but was certainly written on the same 1921 trip (NYPL).

Although the letters were for Quinn's eyes only, they seem at the very least reckless. They could have been intercepted by any of a number of people in his office. Could it be that at this juncture Jeanne was half wishing to be discovered?

In 1923, Quinn and Jeanne traveled again to Europe. He had never been to Rome, and she wanted him to see the "seat of culture" before he died. But first, duty called. Clients in Paris and Berlin demanded too much time, and Quinn's health, already compromised, faltered. By the time he and Jeanne set off for his "spiritual bath" in Italy, as he called it, he was "exhausted, irritable, preoccupied, bored, contemptuous," and he had a growing awareness of his own mortality (*MFNY*, 594). More than forty years after his death, Jeanne still found it painful to speak about Quinn's battle against the inevitable. In a 10 December 1968 letter, she described his brave attempts to continue an active life: "John had to be encased in a kind of harness to get about after his first operation. Where John wanted to get[,] Pierre [Roché] and I took him. Finally JQ wanted a trip to Italy. That was the last year before his death. It took Pierre and I, together, using all our strength, to make this trip possible. I have told you about teaching Italian chefs to make 'compote de pruneau' every night as that was one of the things John had to have at 7 in the morning" (JRF to RL, in LC).

When they returned to Paris, Quinn still wanted to search out art treasures. When he was too tired or ill to examine the paintings and sculpture for himself, he gave Jeanne the authority "to buy and search out art" for him. She had acted as his assistant on previous trips, and he trusted her opinions.[15]

For Quinn, surrounding himself with art was his way of denying his impending death. But when he sailed back to the United States, alone on 27 October, he had that drawn, emaciated look that is characteristic of the final stages of cancer. Jeanne again remained behind to attend to some of his affairs, to visit with Gwen John, and to do some writing for the *Review*.

On 18 December 1923, she returned to New York to find Quinn much

15. JRF to RL, 24 December 1968, LC. One painting JRF convinced JQ to purchase was *Portrait of Cézanne's Father*, painted in 1875 and acquired from Georges Bernheim in Paris, October 1923 ($5,300). It is now at the National Gallery, London.

JRF and John Quinn on their last trip abroad, 1923. William M. Murphy private collection.

worse than when he had sailed for home in October. On the first day of 1924, Roché wrote to him from Paris that he had just seen a second finished portrait of Mrs. Foster by André Derain and that "it is more like the 'atmosphere' of Mrs. F. than herself." The first, painted in 1923, Quinn thought "too sensual" (*MFNY*, 593). Derain commented, "I know Quinn's trouble. He doesn't want a portrait; he wants 'a Derain'" (*MFNY*, 593). The second portrayed Jeanne as a romantic beauty, and Quinn was pleased. The piece was titled *Girl Reading a Book of Magic*.[16]

Quinn grew weaker as the days and weeks wore on, but still his love of art, of possessing art, drove him. In 1958, Jeanne wrote to Aline Saarinen about his last purchase, Rousseau's *The Sleeping Gypsy:* "The last painting he bought was Rousseau's gypsy woman in the desert with the lion. Roché had sent over photographs. J. Q. asked me to walk down town with him. . . . We stood under the elevated below Trinity in New York—it was raining— and he asked me to decide as he knew he was not a well man. I said, 'Buy it.'

16. The painting was called *Portrait of Jeanne Robert Foster* in the 1978 Hirshhorn retrospective of JQ's collection. JRF bequeathed it to B. L. Reid. *Girl Reading a Book of Magic* was JRF's own title for the piece. Current location unknown.

He was very happy and cabled Roché at once. The price then was $12,000" (NYPL).[17]

In May 1924, Jeanne was called to Maine for ten days to nurse an ailing sister, and when she returned, Quinn looked near death. She remained by his side for most of his last two months. On 21 July 1924, she wrote in her diary: "John is still alive. His head is a skull with yellow skin drawn over it— his face a mask of pain—his eyes faded to a light blue—but filled with light and unearthly. His arms are flails of bone—his poor body a skin swelled with water" (*MFNY*, 630). She made certain that his room was filled with roses and larkspur. He spoke to her of his love, treasured words she never forgot: "Hold me, hold me," he told her. "I must have been mad to have ever had you out of my sight. I must not leave you; you must not leave me for an hour, ever, ever." She said that sometimes "he dreamed we were on a long voyage together, dreamed until the mental cloud numbed his mind."[18] At Quinn's request, she sent for the Paulist fathers, and he made his peace with the Roman Catholic Church, which he knew would please his sisters. A year or so earlier, Jeanne had changed her own faith for him. "I became a Catholic for his peace of mind," she wrote to Aline Saarinen in 1962 (n.d., NYPL).

Two days before Quinn's death, Roché wrote a letter to Jeanne filled with concern for the woman who would be left behind; he did not know what she might do. The letter did not arrive until after Quinn had died:

I am happy John lives a dream-paradise, and that you are the maker of it.
. . . Do not die, Jeanne. God is big. —I understand and respect your re-
gret that you have not had fully what some other women may have had.
Though I know that you have had, and given, much more than any other.
What they have had would have been one more crown in your head because
Love was in you—but for them it has gone, left nothing, because that dies at
once, is ashes, when Love is not there. (26 July 1924)

17. JRF to Aline Saarinen, 1 January 1958 (NYPL). Zilczer lists the purchase price at $7,772 (1978, 182). *The Sleeping Gypsy* is now owned by the Museum of Modern Art, a gift from Mrs. Simon Guggenheim. Henri Rousseau: Henri-Julien-Félix, known also as Le Douanier (1844–1910), French artist.

18. JRF to Aline Saarinen, 1 February 1962, NYPL.

John Quinn finally died on 28 July 1924, at 6:30 in the morning. His last words to Jeanne Foster were, "Where have you been so long?" and "Goodbye, dearest" (*MFNY*, 630). "I felt I must die at that moment," she once wrote about Quinn's death (letter to Murphy, 28 July 1969, NYPL).

In the days and weeks that followed, letters and telegrams from world leaders, artists, and writers arrived at Quinn's office and at Jeanne's apartment. One of the first was from Gwen John: "I am dreadfully unhappy and you must be more unhappy. Will you come over and we can talk of him and you will see how I love you always" (NYPL). Another was from artist André Dunoyer de Segonzac, whose letter Jeanne always kept:[19]

> Since learning the sad news of Mr. Quinn's death I have intended to write so as to say how deeply I share your pain.
>
> I had a very hard time accepting the thought of this great misfortune, I who had seen Mr. Quinn in such good health and so very active at the moment of his last trip to Paris. Alas—we must come to terms with fate. . . .
>
> I hold an unforgettable recollection of him—: even though I only had the pleasure of seeing him twice—: one sensed so strongly that he was a man of exceptional intelligence and superior character.
>
> This impression came across immediately: there was such loyalty and lucidity in his eyes, along with the passion he had for the Beautiful, the Good and the Just—
>
> As for me, he showed me such kindness and generosity that I feel I've lost a true friend—, and his memory will stay with me for the rest of my life—
>
> Please accept my most respectful and sad condolences.

The great patron was gone, and many had lost not only his financial support but his friendship. "He was a generous and a noble soul, free from guile," wrote sculptor Constantin Brancusi. Lady Gregory wrote in her diary on 30 July, "A great blow yesterday— a cable from N. Y. 'John Quinn died this morning'. . . . America will seem very distant now." James Joyce cabled that he was "deeply shocked": "Please accept my sympathy in grateful remembrance of his friendship and kindness" (*MFNY*, 634).[20]

19. André Dunoyer de Segonzac (1884–1974), French painter and engraver. The letter was translated from the French by Dr. John Cross, SUNY-Potsdam (MC).

20. See also JRF [1925b], 14.

But the tribute that meant the most to Jeanne was the one written by her friend W. B. Yeats: "I have known no other so full of over-flowing energy and benevolence, and this always arising out of his nature like a fountain and having the quality of his nature. I mean his benevolence expressed him as a work of art expresses the artist" (Foster [1925b], 14).

Yeats's sister Lollie wrote, "This is terrible news": "I will always think of him as the impersonation of splendid energy and infectious buoyancy—he was a great man" (letter to JRF, 31 July 1924, NYPL). Her sister, Lily, also paid Quinn tribute: "I remember Uncle George Pollexfen—who never allowed himself to be carried away by feeling of any sort, and was the most unimpressionable man I ever knew, said after meeting John Quinn once—that he felt there was something noble about him" (letter to JRF, 11 September 1924, NYPL).

Jeanne Foster and John Quinn had brought each other love and friendship; they had been personal and professional soul mates. But Quinn was gone, and Jeanne had other difficulties to overcome.

One was Dorothy Coates, who sued the Quinn estate, saying that for twenty-five years she had been Quinn's "legal wife in the eyes of man and God." She reported to the court and to the *New York Times* that Quinn had asked her to keep silent about the marriage because he was "a prominent Catholic" and she a Protestant. She could not provide the court with any evidence of a marriage, though, and she ultimately withdrew her case. The unpleasantness lasted for two years, and it made the mourning period obviously more difficult for Jeanne (*MFNY*, 644–45). Quinn had asked her and his staff during the last months of his life not to allow Dorothy Coates in to see him under any circumstances. "That would kill me," he told Jeanne. The situation took its toll on her as well.[21] Lily Yeats, concerned for her friend's troubles, wrote on 20 July 1926:

I never met her [Coates], but Papa constantly wrote to me of her, always as that D—— Miss Coates, she behaved most treacherously toward him, by

21. JRF told Murphy that she thought Ms. Coates had moved to Delaware, where she lived with her mother. She also mentioned that Coates had an affair with Dr. Shaw about the same time that JRF had a liaison with him. Shaw, too, gave orders never to allow Coates beyond his reception desk. JRF, interviewed by Murphy (Murphy notes, not dated, MC).

getting him to discuss J. Q.'s character and actions with her and you know
how Papa could hurl himself into any discussion on character [and] she went
and repeated and altered and isolated remarks of Papa's to J. Q. . . .

She surely knows that without marriage certificates and marriage wit-
nesses—merely saying you are married is not enough. (NYPL)

Jeanne had promised Quinn to look after his interests as best she could
after he was gone, and with the Coates case gathering some publicity she
was glad to have extra work to occupy her mind and her time. She tried to
convince Thomas Curtin, Quinn's executor, that the sale of the enormous
art collection would so depress prices that there would be a "slaughter"
from which the art market would not recover:

Who will . . . buy twenty Picassos in this country? Why the dealers . . .
hardly know the "pink" and "blue" periods and the value placed upon these
early works by Paris and the continent. Who will buy fifteen Matisses? And
does any one think that the very large collection of Derains can be sold here
. . . for a fifth of what Mr. Quinn paid for them?

. . . Since we do not love art sufficiently in this country to preserve
the collection intact as a memorial to him, let us not go down in art history
as eternally disgraced by our method of its disposal. It will be a hundred
years or more (or perhaps never) until we see a man of Mr. Quinn's nature
again. (letter, JRF to Curtin, 18 October 1924; given in Zilczer 1978, 58–
59, 60)

Quinn had stated in his will that he wanted his paintings to be put on the
market after his death, but, according to Jeanne, had changed his mind
about the dispersal of his collection shortly before he died. She lobbied for
a home for Quinn's treasure in the United States or, failing that, for a more
reasonable dispersal.

Curtin's hands were tied by Quinn's will and other trustees of the estate.
In addition, Curtin himself was seriously ill from tuberculosis. He died suddenly on 2 March 1925. Jeanne had to face grief again. On 5 March, she attended his funeral: "I cut two locks of Mr. Curtin's silky blue black hair for
his sister and Mrs. Curtin. He smiled in death—he was beautiful. I could
not bear to think of placing his body in the ground." When Jeanne returned

to Quinn's office to work, she noted it was "like a tomb."[22] Her forty-sixth birthday on 10 March was filled only with sadness.

Through this period of grief, Jeanne continued to write. On 26 April, she gave a reading of her poetry at the Shoreham Hotel for the Poetry Society, as well as several other readings in the months that followed. Later that year, she and Roché visited the Albert Barnes Foundation. Barnes had once refused her request to see his collection because she was a friend of Quinn, and there had been deep-seated jealousy between the two collectors. Barnes, however, finally relented. When he met Jeanne and Roché, he explained that he had made arrangements to leave the artwork he owned to the University of Pennsylvania.[23] It broke Jeanne's heart to think of the Quinn collection: "Roché and I were very sad. Why, we asked ourselves, must the John Quinn Collection be sold? I felt I must go once more to the executors and plead to have it given to the city and housed with dignity" (Foster 1925a).[24]

But after Thomas Curtin's death, she had no allies, and all her pleas fell on deaf ears. The great art collection went to auction in several sales in the United States and France, and there was, as Jeanne predicted, a slaughter.[25] Lily Yeats wrote to her on 12 May 1925: "I often think of the fine man that went in July—and who ought to have had so many more keen years in the saddle. . . . I suppose all his pictures are scattered and all his footprints lost in the crowd who never knew him" (NYPL). She wrote again in April 1927 that she was at least "glad" to know that Jeanne had acquired two John Butler Yeats paintings, a self-portrait and one of his son, William Butler Yeats.[26]

Henri-Pierre Roché and Jeanne Foster had shared a long friendship, and

22. JRF, diary 1925 (not paginated, MC). JRF wrote at the top of the first page, "While Reading John Quinn Letters Beginning January 8, 1925 [and] Ending May 5, 1925."

23. Dr. Albert Coombs Barnes (1872–1951). Barnes decided to create the Barnes Foundation instead of leaving his collection to the University of Pennsylvania, as he had told JRF. His will stipulated that the paintings were not to be moved after his death. A 1991 court ruling has allowed parts of the collection to travel. See Hughes 1993.

24. In 1959, Roché wrote a tribute to the Quinn collection, "Adieu, Brave Petite Collection!"

25. For details about the Quinn art sale, see Zilczer 1979, 1982, and 1985.

26. This letter is paraphrased in RL's unpublished catalog of JRF's collection (LC).

they became even closer after Quinn's death, as they shared their grief. Inevitably, Roché's interest in Jeanne became more than platonic. In the same month that they visited the Barnes collection together, Roché wrote to her: "I still love the same your love for John and your suffering for his being far. At the same time I always want more to hold you in my arms, and there is no opposition in me between those two feelings."

In another letter dated 23 December 1937, Roché wrote to Jeanne about long ago wishes: "I often think of the son we could have had together, Jeanne, if you had been willing to, if I had . . . earlier been pushed to the 'determination' of having one by nearing age, and if we both had felt that John was approving and protecting us. —Too many 'ifs.'" Certainly a strange suggestion in a letter about their mutual love for Quinn. The correspondence between Foster and Roché is always affectionate, and perhaps he thought his proposition might be cheering.[27] He was no stranger to unusual liaisons, as his own *Jules et Jim* testifies.

In the same letter, on a more practical note, he told her that Quinn should have made better arrangements for her in his will: "I am sometimes most angry against myself not to have written or cabled to John after his last letter (where he was feeling better) on the necessity to marry Jeanne, or to leave her the property, or at least guard and responsibility, and paid management of his Collection." Roché had expressed similar wishes on 1 August 1924, only a few days after Quinn died: "Since he is there no more I am more sorry you are not his wife. His family may be fine and everything, but who knew John's tastes and intentions and mind as well as you? . . . What happens of you, Jeanne? . . . We shall never find another John. Le trou en nous ne se remplira pas [The void in us will never be filled]."

Quinn left her little, she said, because she did not want anything from him, and it would not be judged in the best light by society if he gave art treasures to a married woman. This nod to convention was in the main ineffectual because most who knew them assumed that they were intimate. Matlack Foster would have been dismayed if a bachelor with Quinn's repu-

27. In their biography of Roché, Reliquet and Reliquet quote from Roché's diary, in which he wrote of the women he remembered "nostalgically": Beatrice Wood, Cligneur-Lou (Arensberg), JRF, and others (1999, 165). Roché never claimed to have had a sexual affair with JRF.

tation left money to his wife without explanation, but certainly some bequest disguised as gratitude and payment for her editorial services would
have been appropriate.

John Quinn trusted Jeanne Foster's judgment to such an extent that he
directed that she be the person to make a selection from his thousands of
letters and decide which should be given to the New York Public Library,
and so, even as the fight raged to keep Quinn's collection together, she
worked tirelessly to create what she considered her own memorial to him,
the collection of his letters; it is largely because of her work that we have
the John Quinn Memorial Collection in its proper place in the New York
Public Library today. For more than a year she worked with Florence
Thompson, one of Quinn's favorite secretaries, to bring some order to the
voluminous correspondence he left behind.

In *The Proud Possessors*, Aline Saarinen applauds Jeanne's work: "She fulfilled her task intelligently, devotedly, and discreetly" (1958, 234). Jeanne
understood early the contribution Quinn's letters would make to later
scholarship. In her unpublished preface to his letter collection, she wrote:

> Mr. Quinn found time during his short life and strenuous business career to
> correspond with hundreds of persons. That these persons were in the main
> the greatest political and literary figures of their time, that they freely poured
> out the treasures of their minds and the intimacies of their hearts in their let-
> ters to him, will establish him in the minds of those who read these letters in
> time to come as—what he was to those who knew and esteemed him in
> life—an authority on aesthetics and the foremost art collector and connois-
> seur of his time. (Foster [1925b], 1)

During the decades that followed Quinn's death, Jeanne looked forward
to the next life they would share. She wrote to Aline Saarinen in late 1961
that she would be with Quinn someday again: "It has seemed to me that at
times the guidance of John's mind has been with me over the long-long
years. I believe that he will reincarnate when he is needed and I pray that
since I came back with his group, I will come again with him" (NYPL).[28]

In March 1969, she spoke of Quinn in relation to W. B. Yeats's theory of
the "Dreaming Back," which suggests that we become attached to an inci-

28. The letter is not dated but was probably written in the autumn of 1961 (NYPL).

dent—good or bad—in our life and thus have difficulty in moving forward
in our lives (W. B. Yeats 1938, 223–24). Although Jeanne had moved on
with her life, she still missed Quinn enormously. A dream in 1969 seemed
to reassure her that her efforts on Quinn's behalf had not been in vain:

> I've had my first dream or vision of John Quinn, the first since he left us in
> 1924. It was some kind of reality. He was a young man, and his mother was in
> the dream, approving. Part of the vision—reality—or dream—was finally ar-
> riving at a house where his mother and I prepared food for him. There I was
> taken to another room lined with bookcases and below the cases were large
> drawers for manuscripts, etc. John opened one near the archway. "Here," he
> said, "are all these papers and manuscripts concerning me that you kept so
> long. I have them all here."
>
> In my dream or vision, I wondered how they could be there. He opened
> the adjacent drawer. "These are your papers," he said. Now the strangeness
> of this vision was that I awakened and came here to this room at night, but
> when I fell asleep again I moved once more into the same detail.
>
> I hope, I pray, that he visits again.[29]

29. JRF to RL, 5 March 1969 (LC).

# 10

# Artists and Actors

IN THE HEADY ATMOSPHERE OF PARIS, Jeanne Robert Foster felt a special vitality. Long before she met John Quinn, when she was traveling with her husband but in the midst of her love affair with Albert Shaw, Paris—the city of art and artists—gave her some measure of comfort: "I ab-sorb—feel—re-create within myself the beauty of the art—the life of Paris. Alas—there are no high passions sought so long and vainly of late. If love bringing a kind of high passion destroys the more ethereal passion (art) then love, adieu" (diary, 24 August 1911).[1]

In her diary, Jeanne at times expressed remorse for extramarital physical love and attempted to sublimate it in what she deemed the more acceptable love for art. The diary was her vehicle for confessing her lack of desire for Matt: "M. F. is good, kind, wise, a genial companion—an excellent friend, yet not one word of his tongue or deed of his doing can stir within me one thrill of quickened life" (25 August 1911). She understood why she could not love him: "He invited one to explore his mind, but once set out on the journey and you found—a great cave—a grotto fetid with Lilliputians" (13 September 1911).

Jeanne turned to art not only as an escape but as a way to shape her phys-ical body. Her belief that she could give up anything but her own beauty—as if she herself were an art object—was a revealing comment on her life. On a larger scale, it represented the limited options available to unhappy women:

> I shall conquer—only please God *give me art*, give me high achievement. I
> look at my hands, short milled type fingers and wonder what they can do,

1. Unless otherwise noted, all JRF diary entries in this chapter are from diaries in LC.

what the mind they symbolize may accomplish. I summon the powers that be, Goethe's demon. . . . I will sacrifice all save beauty, that must still be mine, such poor beauty as I possess but *which is mine* because I made it from ugliness. I have molded my face, my form— . . . the essence within me. (diary, 24 August 1911)

Jeanne realized the importance of a woman's beauty in a man's world and, further, knew that such beauty was an abstraction, a concept she had supported in order to give herself power.

Nine years later, in the summer of 1920, Jeanne returned to Paris. John Quinn asked her to accompany to France a "wealthy and flighty" young woman who had made a bad marriage and whom Quinn represented in the divorce proceedings. He wanted her supervised to avoid "trouble." Jeanne sailed on 28 June 1920 (*MFNY*, 464). She wrote to Quinn about her charge: "The girl is terribly over-sexed. She is hysterical and has absolutely no control over herself at times. . . . as I was a teacher before I was anything else— I commenced her re-education" (14 September 1920, NYPL)). The young woman was Dorothy Lindsey, the daughter of William Lindsey (1858–1922), the writer and businessman for whom Jeanne had worked in Boston a decade earlier. After her attempts to reeducate Ms. Lindsay on the voyage, Jeanne disembarked and went in search of artist Gwen John, whom Quinn had asked her to visit.

When she and Gwen John met, they became friends at once. They went to galleries together, lunched with Henri-Pierre Roché, and stopped at the convent in Meudon, where Jeanne first saw the portrait *Mère Marie Poussepin*, a John painting Quinn very much wanted and one about which Jeanne would later hear a most fascinating story. The friendship was suddenly put on hold, though, when Jeanne received an invitation from the president of the new Czechoslovakian Republic to visit Prague.

When she returned to France the following summer, she easily renewed her acquaintance with Gwen John, who, although a recluse, felt comfortable with Jeanne. It was a happy time because Quinn was with Jeanne, and she was looking forward to introducing him to one of his favorite painters for the first time. Gwen John was uneasy about meeting him, at least in part because of his reputation as a man who could sometimes be brusque with people. But Jeanne served as an effective buffer between the quiet painter and the domineering lawyer.

Quinn had first known John through letters, after receiving an introduction from her brother Augustus in 1910, and they remained epistolary friends after Jeanne introduced them in 1921. Cecily Langdale, Gwen John's biographer, writes: "During those years he [JQ] purchased almost every picture that she sold, ultimately acquiring about a dozen paintings and scores of drawings. That this was the period of her greatest artistic productivity is attributable in good part to Quinn's enthusiastic encouragement" (1987, 47). It was in 1921 that Quinn commissioned Gwen John to paint the portrait of Jeanne, and at that time the painter introduced him to the mother superior of the Meudon convent, from whom he purchased *Mère Marie Poussepin*.[2]

Jeanne and Quinn were busy visiting other artists as well. One photo shows them with Roché and Olga Picasso at a luncheon provided by Pablo for the American art buyer and his lovely companion. Jeanne's diaries reflect the flurry of activity. Entries are sometimes disjointed. Dashes and fragments abound. One entry, for instance, records events on an art-buying trip with Quinn:

> Early Derains from 6–12 thousand. Best landscape village . . . small heads unimportant. Small bust $3/_4$ high—boy—hat—rich tones—much admired: —JQ bought Matisse interior 1300 frs. —Can spot a Derain on sight. Large # Modigliani—*caricatures in paint*—black blobs for eyes, or one eye punched out . . . puckered mouth . . . Best Modigliani—portrait of his wife—least of a caricature . . . —Roché: "When sober Modigliani very silent—when drunk eloquent, brilliant, quarrelsome and even dangerous—had no studio of his own—painted in friends' studios wherever he happened to be. Unappreciated, unrecognized, unbought, hard time to live—paintings sold for few frs. . . . Died of tuberculosis—wife pregnant—on hearing news she jumped out of window, committed suicide with unborn child. Shortly after death— fame." Not great artist. Might have developed—for all features distorted . . .

2. Zilczer dates the painting 1915–21, taking into account the various versions that JRF described (1978, 167).

JRF in France, 1921. *From left to right:* Henri-Pierre Roché, JRF, Olga Picasso, John Quinn. William M. Murphy private collection.

long necks . . . eyes black flat or discolored smashed—small puckered mouths—color good. (diary, 26 July 1921)[3]

John Quinn later used Jeanne Foster's notes when he considered and reconsidered paintings they had seen. Even though Henri-Pierre Roché recommended Modigliani, Jeanne's opinion finally helped to persuade him that there were other painters whose work was better. Cézanne, for instance, was frequently mentioned positively in her diary. On 27 July 1921, she wrote about one Cézanne paintings that she particularly liked: "roughly painted . . . dark blue and green clouds—rough landscape. Whole effect—gathering storm—majestic, strong beautiful." At the time of his death, Quinn owned five Cézannes.

On one occasion (27 July 1921), Jeanne and Quinn visited the studio of French art dealer Ambroise Vollard (1867–1939), who told Jeanne a story

3. Henri Matisse (1869–1954), French painter. Amedeo Modigliani (1884–1920), Italian painter and sculptor.

about Cézanne's temper: "Cézanne a man of violent feeling,—temper, when aroused destroyed things or slashed paintings, that 1 time painting he cut with a knife because he was enraged because his son stayed out too late at night. When Vollard told story of Cézanne slashing his paintings JQ said, 'Better for artist to cut up painting than to cut off ear Van Gogh.' " Vollard told them that the "legend of trouble between Gauguin and Van Gogh was not true, that Van Gogh had gone to a whorehouse that he liked and admired Gauguin very much and that in a fit of remorse over his staying at the whorehouse—token expiation—he sent Gauguin his ear."[4]

On the same day, they visited Serge Férat's studio and saw several paintings by Rousseau, which Quinn especially liked.[5] At a third stop, they examined some Vlamincks, Rouaults, and Braques. Quinn selected some to buy and continued to yet another gallery. A notation in Jeanne's diary for 2 August 1921, for instance, says simply, "bought the two Picassos." Quinn liked them so much that Jeanne's note for 3 August reads, "bought another Picasso, dress, and sweater."

Although Jeanne still had work to do in Paris for both Quinn and the *Review of Reviews*, Quinn himself had to leave in late August. Shortly before his departure, he introduced Jeanne to Constantin Brancusi. The sculptor admired her beauty, her charm, and her appreciation of his vision. She was able to understand the lyricism in his abstractions. One photograph illustrates their special relationship better than any description. Jeanne is standing in a model's pose with one foot pointed at the camera, and Brancusi is two paces away, looking not at the camera but at her, a smile of apprecia-

4. In *Van Gogh's Progress*, Carol Zemel writes that the facts around Van Gogh's ear amputation remain unclear, but that "psychoanalytical scholars have interpreted [the act] variously as an introjected displacement of rage toward Gauguin—as father-figure, a reenactment of unexpressed guilt over his father's sudden death, a symbolic castration in the face of repressed homosexual desire for Gauguin" (1997, 267). *Le Forum Républicain*, a contemporary newspaper, reported at the time that "Last Sunday night at half past eleven a painter named Vincent Vangogh . . . appeared at the maison de tolérance No. 1, asked for a girl called Rachel, and handed her . . . his ear with these words: 'Keep this object like a treasure' " (qtd. in Hulsker 1977, 381).

5. Serge Férat (also Jastrebzoff, 1881–1935), Russian-born artist who worked and died in Paris. Maurice De Vlaminck (1876–1958), French painter. Georges Rouault (1871–1958), French expressionist painter.

JRF with Constantin Brancusi in France, 1921. Londraville private collection.

tion and approval on his face, the artist appraising his model. Although they were not able to spend much time together in 1921, Jeanne and Brancusi would renew their friendship in 1923.

In Paris, without Quinn, Jeanne stayed with Gwen John most of the time. They gossiped about friends and acquaintances, and Gwen John gradually became more comfortable. She said little at first, but Jeanne had a talent for making a person feel at ease in her presence: "We talked of Rhoda Symons—of their gossip about Augustus John, of Rhoda's studio, and of the Symons marriage.[6] Gwen had not liked the Rothensteins, although she said they were most affectionate with her. Rothenstein had kissed her on her neck. She did not like it" (diary, 4 September 1921).[7]

Other, more serious talks centered around the very private life of Gwen John herself. One night she told her new friend a secret story. It is recorded nowhere else but in the 1921 diary of Jeanne Foster:

6. Arthur Symons (1865–1945), English writer, had a breakdown in Italy in 1909, and after that event his wife and sometimes actress, Rhoda, continually predicted his demise and asked friends for financial help. She told JQ that she and Symons "must" live apart and asked JQ to help her find a way to keep her flat in London and to provide her with a motor car (MFNY, 197). See Gonne and Quinn 1999, 224, for JQ's letter to Pound about Rhoda Symons.

7. Sir William Rothenstein (1872–1945), English artist noted for his portraits.

Gwen John came in at eleven: she looked very ill. I asked her about herself and she said she had had a great grief. Little by little she told me her story. After her first experience with her first lover—Rodin no doubt—she had been comforted by the love of a priest who had been at Meudon many years but who had been sent by his Bishop to Versailles.[8] This priest had always loved her: but their relationship had been platonic on account of Rodin—or the "other man" as she said. He had made her an artist—not Rodin. When she came to Paris she met the priest: he became attached to her and asked her to paint Mother Poussepin of the Presentation convent. In a burst of enthusiasm she accepted and even agreed to paint several Mère Poussepins for the various branches of the order. She did not have technique: she had not painted figures. She didn't know her craft. In terror she started to study, starved herself to hire models, and painted, painted, painted. The convent refused to loan her a nun's costume. She bought the cloth and had one made. Twice it was ripped apart and remade before it was right. Then—she pretended to work very slowly. She painted and repainted seven Mère Poussepins, hiding or destroying all of them. Seven years of agony passed. She never had a portrait she dared show the priest. Finally he lost patience and said: "Are you or are you not going to paint Mère Poussepin?" Then, desperate, she began this painting and the miracle happened, the technique—borne of seven years trouble had been perfected.[9]

She says she never would have been an artist if it had not been for this priest. His encouragement and her desire to please him gave her the art she has achieved.

Then he was ordered to Versailles. She saw him infrequently: She did not need him now as much as he needed her. She neglected him without knowing it. She had one long perfect day with him before she went to England. She did not write. Shortly after her return, she heard he had died. She was overcome with grief. She went to Versailles to make her drawing of him for his sisters, the nuns. She heard from them that he had died of grief over the death of an elder sister who had brought him up and who had died some months earlier. She noticed that his shroud was drawn up high around his neck. She saw a violet bruise on one side and thought it strange. Next day

8. Auguste Rodin (1840–1917), French sculptor.

9. JRF told RL that she posed for the body of the *Mère Marie Poussepin* painting that JQ bought. It was exhibited at the Hirshhorn Museum's retrospective of JQ's collection in 1978 and is currently owned by Thomas Conroy Jr., JQ's grandnephew.

she read in the Journal that the rector had committed suicide by hanging, or strangling himself with the window cord. She asked the sisters. They did not affirm it and he was hastily buried in holy ground while the Bishop of his diocese was away. She blames herself for the tragedy. If she had given him more, he might not have killed himself, she argues.

. . . Gwen said later, "I have become corrupted and depraved. I am eating food now and thinking it is good. I am lying—that is, I lie sometimes. I no longer desire to live a religious life. Had I gone to Versailles with my friend as I intended, I might not have been able to endure the long hours in church. He was intensely religious: he really had faith." (4 September 1921)

Jeanne told her some of her own private stories about her experiences with Aleister Crowley—about how the magician had put a curse on her mother. Gwen John had a willing and sympathetic listener as she shared her own beliefs in the otherworld:

She asked much about what I thought of the condition of souls after death: of the possibility of reunion with our loved friends. Also of elementals. Malicious animal magnetism. She complained of being annoyed by evil forces. One interesting fact came out during the conversation. She knew the mysterious country of flowers—which I have visited in dreams since childhood. She described the same luxuriousness, the masses of blooms, the strange forms, the size of the blossoms, the white star flowers. I told her of the flower-fields described in the apocrypha—the flowers of the field of Ardoth. I firmly believe that this field exists, that mystics and the pure-minded and the very young may go there at night. . . . Tears came into her eyes now and then: She said she wanted to die but did not want to commit suicide. (diary, 4 September 1921)

Jeanne tried her best to reassure John that she had a valuable life. She understood the artistic torment and pain her friend was feeling and tried to get her to take care of practical matters. She took John to a bank to cash a check for one thousand francs from John Quinn: "I showed her how to make out a deposit slip and check," she wrote in her diary (6 September 1921).

Jeanne helped the reluctant artist as much as she could. John's mood improved, and as time went on, she began sharing happier stories with Jeanne.

One was of a great adventure with her brother Augustus's wife, Dorelia, as they traipsed through Europe with no money. They slept out-of-doors, escaped thieves, and stayed with a band of gypsies.[10]

Two days after Gwen John told Jeanne Foster her story about her adventures with Dorelia, the artist decided to dress her up for a painting for Quinn. She realized very quickly that the bright and fashionable trappings appropriate for most models did not suit Jeanne, who seemed from another time and place. The clothes she suggested Jeanne wear were not unlike the simple clothes of an Adirondack woman:

> Gwen brought out an old faded raspberry colored corduroy jacket—and put it on me (Dorelia had made it, she said.), and a wide skirt of a kind of plaid generally colored raspberry. Then she tied a ribband around my waist of a deeper raspberry and made her drawings. She said, "Mr. Quinn will not like it perhaps if I make you look like a simple little girl. You look curiously smaller in this dress. You do not make enough of yourself with your clothes. But perhaps you would not like the clothes artists like. Dorelia always dresses very beautifully. She wears dresses like these paints. I think you should wear period dresses— . . . Never fashionable clothes. They do not suit you."
> (diary, 20 September 1921)

The intended portrait would, characteristically, never be finished, but Jeanne didn't mind. Her friendship with the "lost little artist," as she often called Gwen John, was more important. In the final days of her visit, she helped John by sorting through drawings and helping to frame pictures. "Gwen John is feverishly ambitious," Jeanne wrote in her diary, "[and she] only cares for things connected with her art" (23 September 1921). She observed John's dedication to her art, her singleness of purpose, and she understood that it was John's center, "the air she breathed," as Jeanne put it. She knew why it was so difficult for this painter to part with her work. It would be like giving a piece of oneself to the world. John felt vulnerable every time she sold a painting.

This trip was a busy time for Jeanne, who also visited other artists and

---

10. In her diary (18 September 1921), JRF recounts the entire escapade as told to her by Gwen John.

writers, in part out of curiosity, in part on business for Quinn. On 9 September, she met Juan Gris at his studio:

> He is a dark stocky Spaniard with very beautiful dark eyes and gentle appealing manners. . . . He had been ill and did not look well. His easel stood in one corner of the room. He showed me portrait drawings—very pure in line—old work—pleasant, academic—and some new water colors. These last were most pleasing. His other work was—he said all at Leonce Rosenberg.[11] He said Rosenberg was a dishonest man—that he put his [Gris's] work in the cellar and did not try to sell it—and still he—Gris—had to keep to his contract and could not sell any from the studio or to other dealers. (diary, 8 September 1921)[12]

Jeanne became friendly with Gris and his wife, "a young blonde French woman—slim—with dark blue eyes, black lashes and black eyebrows," and saw them on several more occasions during her final days in Paris in 1921.

On 11 September, she wrote in her diary, "went to Phil Sawyer's. He made line drawings and I sat for details of his mural paintings." Again on 30 September, she modeled for Sawyer. They shared dinner at a café, a "charming little old place with jazz music. We talked of art" (diary).[13] She admired his work, and they corresponded occasionally for a number of years.

On 30 September, Jeanne wrote, "Gwen John. Bought sweaters, wraps." It is the last entry that mentions the painter. On 1 and 2 October, Jeanne again posed for Philip Sawyer. These notations are the last in this diary. Several days later, she sailed for America.

Jeanne's connections to the journalistic world made her a powerful ally, which—as she well understood—also made her more attractive. In 1922, back in New York City, she did not hesitate to publicize some of the artists she had met and admired in Paris. She tried to promote Philip Sawyer, who

11. Léonce Rosenberg (1877–1947), French art dealer and collector.

12. Juan Gris (also José Victoriano González, 1887–1927), Spanish painter who moved to Paris in 1906.

13. Philip Ayer Sawyer (1877–1949), American artist who studied at Ecole des Beaux-Arts with L. Bonnât. JRF owned Sawyer's *Portrait of Jeanne Robert Foster*, a 1921 oil (flesh tones and blues), but its current location is unknown.

wrote to her on 13 April to ask if his portrait of her had been "favorably received." (She told him it had.) He told her of his hardships—a year "of trial, and struggle and disappointment"—and wrote that she was a person "always thinking of the good and comfort of others."[14]

In May 1922, she published an article in *Vanity Fair,* "New Sculptures by Constantin Brancusi: A Note on the Man and the Formal Perfection of His Carvings," in which she gave a short biography of the artist and then examined the art:

> Like Picasso, who can in a very small painting of great figures give a sense of immensity, Brancusi can in his birds of marble and bronze give the sense of space or of flight in the air. One would like to see his last bird [*Yellow Bird*] in its perfected form crown a tall column. He has made many birds in bronze and marble. An essay could be written on the development and evolution of Brancusi's birds. In their last forms they [*Yellow Bird* and *Golden Bird*] are sheer perfection. (Foster 1922, 68)[15]

Jeanne knew that most of her readers still did not understand abstract art, and she tried to introduce the artist as well as the art, hoping that the audience would be more responsive:

> His work is the expression of an original mind, with a great sense of beauty and an endless search for perfection of form. His genius is a lyric genius. One feels that he might design a beautiful edifice even if he lacked the patience or the time to work out the minute details. . . . Not all of his work is abstract. Brancusi's early sculpture was representational, but for a long time it has grown more and more abstract. Some of his latest work might be called Euclid plus Leonardo. . . . The artist in the end always desires to express by his work his own personality. That is one of the sources of Cézanne's genius. Brancusi, like Cézanne, wishes to give the world his own images, his own vision of beauty. (124)[16]

14. JRF, interviewed by RL, 17 July 1968. There is no record of any correspondence between JRF and Philip Sawyer after 1922.

15. In 1969, Athena Tacha Spear wrote the work JRF envisioned, *Brancusi's Birds.*

16. For a recent evaluation of JRF's analysis of Brancusi and modernism, see Masteller 1997.

In 1923, she renewed her acquaintance with Brancusi, Gwen John, and several others artists after she and Quinn arrived in Paris on their last great adventure together. On this trip, Brancusi and Jeanne became closer. From a special combination—friendship with the artist and familiarity with his art—was born Jeanne's poem "Constantin Brancusi: Roumanian Sculptor." It contains eighty-two lines and five sections titled respectively "L' Ouvier" (The Cave), "L' Homme" (The Man), "L' Arbre" (The Tree), "Le Portrait," and "Diner Avec Brancusi" (Dinner with Brancusi). Brancusi must have been charmed when it appeared in *Rock Flower* (59–62) later that year:

> Pan thewed with sinews of ilex trees;
> A faun's head, black curls,
> (One suspects onyx horns).
> A beard touched with white;
> Darkness between two white fingers;
> The throat—a column;
> Quick hands, gestures
> Faultless of intention,
> Flinging aside knowledge,
> Reaching for perfection
> As a child reaches for a flower;
> Dissolving wisdom
> Tragically for the wise.
> ("L' Homme," lines 16–28)

Although the poem is yet another instance of the difficulty Jeanne had in establishing a critical distance from subjects who were her friends, she had a better grasp of Brancusi's work than did many art critics of the time. One may speculate that Quinn aided her understanding, but as early as 1913, before she met Quinn, she herself saw that some modern works, such as Duchamp's *Nude Descending a Staircase*, No. 2, would infuse vitality into the world of art. Jeanne recognized that artists no longer felt any allegiance to realistic depiction, but had instead discovered a new sense of freedom in their use of color and form.

Visits during Quinn and Jeanne's stay in Paris in 1923 included stops at the private residences of André de Segonzac, Georges Braque, Walter Pach, Georges Rouault, Raoul Dufy, André Derain, and Pablo Picasso. Pictures taken at the time show Jeanne with Roché, with Brancusi, and with art collector Alphonse Kahn.[17] B. L. Reid tells the story of one night's adventures as this last trip was coming to a close. Quinn, Jeanne, and Roché visited Brancusi: "From there they trooped to Derain's studio, up 7 flights of stairs, he lighting the way with a match from above. After champagne with Derain they . . . crossed the courtyard to Segonzac's studio . . . before finally departing for their hotels at two-thirty in the morning" (*MFNY*, 593).

There was some discussion that evening of the portrait Quinn had commissioned Derain to do of Jeanne. In a 24 December 1968 letter, she wrote about her final sitting: "I wore the black dress and ivory beads. Took down my hair. Derain came over and pushed it around to the left side. He kissed my hands—'for the last time,' and said he was 'désolé' " (JRF to RL, in LC).

In the autumn, when Quinn returned to New York, Jeanne once again stayed on in Paris to look after his interests. She enjoyed spending time with Gwen John, selected some of her pictures for Quinn, and visited art studios with her during a period of several weeks. They made plans to produce a small book. Jeanne would write nursery rhymes, and Gwen John would supply illustrations.[18]

André Derain finished Jeanne's portrait sometime after she returned to New York in December. It didn't arrive in the United States until shortly before Quinn died. He gave it to Jeanne as a last gift.

In the late 1920s, Jeanne continued to advertise her favorite artists. In the 21 February 1926 issue of the *New York Herald Tribune*, she wrote again about Brancusi and gave her audience a picture of the artist himself in his ordinary daily activities:

For diversions he takes photographs and develops and prints them himself. Also he likes to cook and serve a dinner for his friends over a fireplace that he has built for his atelier. There will be a round white cement table—it may be freshly trowled for the occasion, flowers of deep brilliant color on the table

17. Walter Pach (1883–1958), American critic, art historian, and painter. Raoul Dufy (1877–1953), French painter. Alphonse Kahn (1865–1926), art collector.

18. The nursery rhyme book was never published. JRF lost her copy, and after JQ died, her thoughts turned to other projects. See JRF's letters to Gwen John in the Gwen John Papers at the National Library of Wales, Department of Manuscripts and Records, Aberystwyth.

JRF in France, 1923. *From left to right:* Henri-Pierre Roché, Alphonse Kahn's secretary, JRF, and Alphonse Kahn. Londraville private collection.

and against the white walls, perhaps capucines with scarlet velvety petals. There will be a pullet or a fat capon roasting on the spit, while Brancusi whips a salad delicately against a wooden salad bowl. And wines—for he is a connoisseur of wines—and a Rumanian liqueur after delicious fruit with coffee, which Brancusi will grind in a Turkish brass coffee mill.

. . . At one of the last dinners I attended in Paris chez Brancusi, Derain and Braque and Satie were there. After dinner Derain mounted one of Brancusi's white pedestals and gave imitations of the poses of classic statuary. Shortly after this dinner I saw Brancusi playing golf at Saint Germain (he had just learned the game), with Erik Satie as an onlooker. He demonstrated the play of the other members of the party by his wit and his furious vigor with his unaccustomed clubs. (Foster 1926b, 4)

In the *Vanity Fair* article, Jeanne wrote that Brancusi always set before her—with a gallant gesture—"the handsomest plate in his cupboard, and arrange[d] a bowl of flowers that drip[ped] the colours of Matisse and Redon into the cool twilight" (Foster 1922, 124).[19] Four years later, she de-

19. Odilon Redon (1840–1916), French artist.

scribed his studio in detail, calling it an "Olympian cave, a workshop of the gods, filled with massive blocks of marble and stone and time-stained beams of ancient wood," and she explained his approach to his art:

> Brancusi has no elaborate art theory; he might resent talk of symbols; nevertheless he has said of one of his abstract heads: "With this form I could move the universe." He gives us forms of a mathematical exactitude of proportion upon whose smooth surfaces we may shape our dreams and give them at least momentary reality. Through a certain withdrawal of the particularized, one learns how the infinite may blend with the finite to stand visible and, as it were, attainable. (Foster 1926a, 4)

There is no better explanation of the modern artist's movement toward the abstract. Where there is an attempt to be realistic, there is always the possibility of the viewer confusing the art with the subject. It is difficult, for example, to look at Whistler's *Arrangement in Black and Gray: The Artist's Mother* without seeing a realistic portrait of an old woman, but the first part of the title directs us to the artist's concept.[20] As he moves away from representation, he can concentrate on the essence of his vision.

Jeanne had the opportunity to study Brancusi's work closely. Quinn purchased *Mlle. Pogany* at the 1913 Armory Show and, later, a number of other Brancusi works, including *The Golden Bird*. Jeanne dubbed the Pogany piece—her favorite—the "egg head" sculpture, first in her April 1913 Armory Show article for the *Review*, saying the portrait "resembles an egg, an ovoid head with exaggerated eyes and two tentacle like arms twining about the neck" (1913a, 446;) and next in her 1926 *New York Herald Tribune* article on Brancusi, designating it "the so-called egg head" (1926a, 4).

Jeanne's interest in American arts also led her to form a friendship with Hollywood producer and director Stuart Armstrong Walker (1880–1941), who founded the avant-garde mobile Pormanteau Theatre in 1915. Jeanne had first become interested in experimental theater when she researched an article on Edward Gordon Craig ("The Drama and the Music") in 1912 for the *Review*.[21] Her own artistic progression toward the abstract in literature

20. James Abbott McNeill Whistler (1834–1903), American artist.

21. Edward Gordon Craig (1872–1966), English actor, designer, and producer; he was the son of actress Ellen Terry.

and art was reflected in her analysis of the theater: "What is the art of the theatre? . . . It is a thing of action, words, line, color, rhythm, all equally important. There may be more art in the graceful performance of a rope dancer than in the careful miming of our actors reciting from memory and depending upon the prompter" (Foster 1912d, 379).

If the spoken word is taken away, Jeanne concluded, a play should remain "unharmed by the loss." Such ideas attracted her to the *Noh* plays of W. B. Yeats, and when she heard about Stuart Walker's Pormanteau Theatre, she was naturally intrigued.

Several times over the years, Jeanne put Walker in touch with actors whom she felt showed promise. She recommended a Mrs. Hagan in 1923 and a Mr. Altman in 1932, and Walker promised he would help them. Jeanne liked Walker's wife, Jane, who called her "my own dearest friend" in a 1932 letter.[22] She lost touch with the Walkers after 1933, the year she closed her New York City apartment, the same year she buried both her father and her husband.

One artist with whom Jeanne did keep in touch, albeit sporadically, was the eccentric and multitalented Paul Spencer Swan (1883–1972). Jeanne first met him in New York sometime before the summer of 1918 and visited him again in 1923 in Paris, where he lived for most of the time between the two world wars. Jeanne was pleased when Swan asked her to be a model, for he was quickly becoming one of the foremost portrait sculptors of his generation. The bust he did is unfortunately lost, although two photographs remain. Jeanne wrote to Swan that she still owned it in 1961, but there is no record after that date.

When exactly Jeanne met Swan is unclear, but they were good friends by 8 July 1918, the date on the earliest surviving letter in his correspondence to her. Swan wrote from his studio on 128 West Thirty-fourth Street, letting Jeanne know how pleased he was with his work: "The bust impresses me very pleasantly," he wrote. He warned her, however, against taking "J. K." under her wing. Swan was referring to J. M. Kerrigan, the Irish actor who was visiting New York at the time.[23] Because of her position on the *Re-*

22. Two of Jane Walker's letters to JRF are dated 21 February 1923 and (quoted portion) 13 April 1932 (NYPL).

23. The letters from Paul Swan to JRF are in the Foster-Murphy Collection, NYPL. J. M. Kerrigan (1885–1964), Irish actor.

*view,* Jeanne was often asked to be—and often served as—a publicity agent for visiting notables; Kerrigan, whom Swan distrusted, was one of many.

At the time Swan sculpted Jeanne Foster, he was thirty-five years old, and she was thirty-nine. A few years later, he appeared for the first time in a major film, Cecil B. DeMille's 1923 production *The Ten Commandments,* and toured the country with the Ben Greet Shakespeare Company. Subsequently, he sculpted the busts of Maurice Ravel, Willa Cather, and John Fitzgerald Kennedy. He was especially honored to be the subject of a 1965 film by his friend Andy Warhol, titled *Paul Swan.* In the late 1960s, he executed a commission by the Vatican to paint the portrait of Pope Paul VI.[24]

Jeanne lost contact with Swan after she moved to Schenectady and so was surprised when he wrote to her in 1960. In a letter dated 14 October, he described his depression over being "expelled" from his longtime art studio at Carnegie Hall: "I need every encomium and praise possible to keep me from suicide . . . and it is only rational to disappear from this transient scene! . . . 20 years of art efforts—and then to [pack] all alone no one of the pseudo admirers to lend a hand." His new apartment "is elegant," he wrote, "but I need money for Nov. rent!" He tried to disguise the hint with a compliment, but couldn't seem to escape his self-absorption:

> I loved your photo on the folder of your book—what a really beautiful person *you* are.[25] I'm just a "Fine old Ruin," and the anguish I've just been tormented with, made me an "old man." I could so easily give up at my age, but I'm doing a lot of praying that I will soon see a meaning to this change. . . . I was made for artistic expression with myself as the medium—21,089 persons came to see me dance. So I hope some new opportunity shows up before it is too late!

Swan mentioned as well that he was glad Jeanne still had the bust he had sculpted. A month later, on 28 November 1960, he wrote, "It was a lovely head of a lovely lady. That I do remember. I remember the Greek figurines around the base!" Some time later she must have given the sculpture to a friend, as she so characteristically did with many of her treasures.

---

24. Swan's obituary appeared in the *New York Times* on 2 February 1972.
25. JRF had sent Swan a copy of *Rock Flower* as a gift.

Bust of JRF sculpted by American artist Paul Swan, 1918. One of two remaining photographs of the bust. Londraville private collection. Location of bust unknown.

In the same November letter, Swan asked Jeanne a question that, she said, completely stunned her. Would she write his biography?

My Très Chère Amie: You have awakened urges in my mind which seem to open up vast vistas of expressive activities. Your letters are so fine and eloquent of a being completely aloof and evolved! I wonder why all this interim of time and silence—except in such a relationship as ours—still unclassifiable, it yet seems, I am turning over my own chronicle of my life—saying "Here, you write the book. Here is the data for you to do a masterpiece of biography." In my case you may understand why it is wiser, from the standpoint of the public that a woman write it and that some one who has been near me for many years. There are too many extraordinary episodes there. . . . I think this phase of things is what has kept 17 publishers from putting it out. . . . Now if you will undertake the biography—from my effort, I have sent to you . . . I'll give you half the money earned from it. . . .

Well, my book should be cut down and just the events used which contribute to the revelation of the person I am—which clarify the strangeness—which show the normalcy and universality of my personality—the soul that looks for beauty in all people and things— . . . I do hope you'll be free to un-

dertake this great work, and I do believe now that there will be a most lucrative return—

At first, Jeanne was tempted: she was eighty-one years old and was
being given a chance at "the old life" again. But she finally declined. She
had thought of doing a biography of John Butler Yeats—or at least an edition of his correspondence—but she realized that it would consume too
much of the life she had left. She had by now become good friends with
William M. Murphy and had chosen him for that project. She was also in
the middle of working on a book of Adirondack poetry and teaching poetry
classes. It would not be easy to muster the additional strength to do Swan's
biography.

Jeanne also understood how difficult Swan might be. His autobiography
was what he really wanted published, but under her name because, as he
told her, "the physical beauty of the subject should not be referred to by the
subject himself" (letter, Swan to JRF, 28 November 1960). She let a reply to
his letter linger for a time and then wrote, gently declining.

In response to her refusal, Swan did not mention his book again but
wrote that he was relieved that Jeanne hadn't "dropped" him, that he "was
really so glad to have your letter yesterday." He hinted that he needed
twenty-five dollars to spend on fixing up his studio for dance recitals and
hoped that Jeanne would write soon: "I feel now we two have sailed out
upon a calm sea. You are an angel you know, Love Paul."[26]

Swan's final appearance in a film role was in Andy Warhol's 1965 movie
*Camp*. Jeanne wrote to him only infrequently during her last years. Her
health was beginning to fail, and she was withdrawing more and more from
public life, saving most of her energy for her poetry and for visits from her
closest friends.

Paul Swan died sixteen months after Jeanne Foster, on 1 February 1972.
His autobiography is as yet unpublished.

26. The letter from Paul Swan to JRF is not dated.

# 11

# Ford Madox Ford
## and the *transatlantic review*

WHEN JOHN QUINN INTRODUCED Jeanne Robert Foster to the novelist and editor Ford Madox Ford in France in 1923, the writer was first struck by her appearance, as so many others before him had been, but he also recognized her astuteness. In his autobiography, *It Was the Nightingale*, he wrote: "Mrs. Foster was the ravishingly beautiful lady who bought Mr. Quinn's pictures for him. She was an admirable business woman and, as far as they were susceptible of management, she managed the American side of the *transatlantic review* to perfection" (1933, 298).

When Ford, Quinn, and Ezra Pound founded the *transatlantic review* in 1923, Jeanne, by then a combination secretary, art buyer, and literary liaison for Quinn, was chosen to be the American editor. Many assumed that she was included in the group as a way to appease Quinn and loosen his purse strings, but her appointment as American editor was anything but an honorary position. In a letter to Bernard Poli dated 26 February 1964, she explained her duties: "Ford placed me in charge of the editorial end in New York. I had an office with the Thomas Seltzer Co. for two years. I carried on for Ford until the magazine could no longer be published, receiving mss. and mail, answer[ing] letters, interviewing would-be contributors, reading all manuscripts submitted, etc. The manuscripts—all except those that were hopeless, were immediately mailed to Ford with commentary, biographical material, etc" (NYPL). A letter from Ford to Jeanne dated 22 January 1924 verifies this claim:

> Of course *you* are the Associate Editor and no one else: yr. functions being to
> give a first reading to mss. and forward a selection to myself and to settle any

editorial questions for the decision of wh. there wo. not be time to refer to me—such as refusing advertisements and the like. (I wd. not for instance take the advts of nude photos that the *Dial* rejoices in.)

As for taking share subscriptions:

You are fully authorised to take these and on receipt of cheque from you to the S. A. *des Editions de la transatlantic review,* I will forward you (the unit of shares being five hundred francs paper) share certificates to the amounts in francs as per the exchange on the day of receipt of cheque. (Londraville and Londraville 1990, 186)[1]

As the correspondence between Ford and Jeanne shows, she was the editor who winnowed out the wheat from the chaff on this side of the Atlantic. Ford wrote to Jeanne about how he handled the publication of some of his novels—to his disadvantage—in order to promote periodicals with which he was connected, such as the *English Review* and the *transatlantic review.* He wrote about his work habits and about how he was driven to "eyestrains and headaches and depressions" (194) because of his occupation. He complained of his chronic financial difficulties. Although the letters to Jeanne generally corroborate established views of Ford, they show more clearly than some of his previously published letters the problems and the fortunes that directly affected his work, its subject matter, its production, and its publicity.

Ford, though often affectionate in his letters to Jeanne, apparently had no intimate relationship with her beyond that of a close friend and confidant. He often mentioned Stella Bowen to Jeanne, who once gave Ms. Bowen a pair of earrings for a gift. When Ford switched liaisons from Ms. Bowen to Renee Wright, he included Ms. Wright in greetings to Jeanne. The letters suggest that Jeanne was more an extended family member than an amorous possibility for Ford. She never felt it necessary to defend the relationship as anything but platonic.

The affection Ford felt for Jeanne Foster, documented in his letters, appears to have been well deserved. She used her position in the New York literary world to advance his fortunes and, encouraged by the example

1. Unless otherwise noted, all quotations from the letters between Ford and JRF are from Londraville and Londraville 1990.

Quinn had shown by arranging and promoting W. B. Yeats's lecture tours, tried to do the same for her friend. She said that Ford's penchant for changing women kept him chronically in need of funds, and she was happy to ease his financial burdens.

Jeanne told many stories of her experiences with artists and writers over the years, but the Ford-Foster correspondence is noteworthy because it establishes her importance in the publishing world of the 1920s. The first letter between them, dated 18 November 1923, is handwritten and addressed to Jeanne from 10 rue Ponthieu, Paris, with the heading, "Three Mountains Press." Jeanne wrote to Ford about contributing her own brand of criticism to the *transatlantic review*, much as she had done for Albert Shaw's journal. Ford encouraged her to do so (18 November 1923), but jokingly warned her that their good friend Ezra Pound might not always like what she had to say: "Of course you are a wicked woman to butt into the art criticism of the T.R.: but, you being a weak and clinging woman Ezra may not break your neck: and anyhow, he is responsible in having brought us together" (185).

At this time Jeanne also composed a biographical sketch of Ford for publication and distribution to anyone who might be interested in his work or in the *transatlantic review*. Even though Ford had by now changed his last name from Hueffer to Ford, much of his work still carried the name Hueffer, and Jeanne wanted to use what was most recognizable. In her essay, she praised his "intuition and sensitivity":

Ford Madox Hueffer, born 1873, son of Dr. Francis Hueffer and Lucy Madox Brown, daughter of Ford Madox Brown, most distinguished novelist, poet and critic, immense knowledge of art, several books on the Pre-Raphaelites and their work, also book on Hans Holbein the Younger . . . knows more perhaps than any man living the ins and outs of intellectual Anglo-Saxondom and of the intimacies and inner lives of the Pre-Raphaelites. No one has written so touchingly or so eloquently of Christina Rossetti. Hueffer rates her poems above those of Dante G. R. He thinks she is the greatest artist in the use of English words in poetry of any writer of the nineteenth century.[2]

2. Ford Madox Brown (1821–1893), English artist. Hans Holbein the Younger (1497?–1543), German artist. Christina Rossetti (1830–94), English poet. Dante Grabriel Rossetti (1828–82), English writer and artist.

... Hueffer has been criticized again and again on his facts, but never on the accuracy of his impressions. As an artist, he has the most uncanny intuition and extraordinary sensitivity. He is not appreciated now. Sometime some one will "discover" Hueffer. Read his early books and find out how very good he is, his great range.[3]

The *transatlantic review* began to run into difficulties in 1923, a year before Quinn died. Understandably, he did not have the energy to spend on promoting the journal or on proofreading text, as he enjoyed doing when his health was better. In an unusual display of temper, Ford wrote to Jeanne from Paris on 22 February 1924 about problems with the magazine. He was irritated at Jeanne for getting copy to him late.

I should be glad of notes on last season's books for No iv which will contain a sort of Literary Supplement—but please keep them in tone with the spirit of the Review—which is that there *is* a great deal of good work being done in America. . . . I suppose your present notes have been long on the way. You must remember that we begin to print seven weeks before the Review reaches you—so copy to be in time should be posted at least two months before the number for which it is intended. (186)

Apparently, he felt remorse a month later and wrote on 14 March 1924, "I just scramble off this note to say that I don't attach any blame to you at all in the matter of the illustrations—far from it!" (188).

The *transatlantic review* would be out of business by late 1924, and until the end Jeanne worked hard to save it. In May, she received a letter from Stella Bowen, who told her that Ford was sailing for New York on the *Paris* to "look after the affairs of the Review, and to see publishers." She hoped that Jeanne might arrange a social gathering, "to 'boost' the Review, but in any case perhaps you will see Ford and look after him a little! I should be so grateful!" (Londraville and Londraville 1990, 204).

But the die had been cast. Bernard Poli writes that Ford placed the blame for the financial failure of the *transatlantic review* on John Quinn and on Thomas Seltzer (the journal's agent in New York) "for the inadequate busi-

3. JRF gave RL a copy of her biographical sketch of Ford. Another typescript is in the Foster-Murphy Collection, NYPL.

ness arrangements they made, on the United States at large for reading the magazine without paying for it, on England for its apathy, on his staff for not being more helpful, on the French for not being more reliable" (1967, 163).

Another problem arose between Ford and Seltzer at this time. Something was wrong with the copyright of Ford's *Some Do Not* (1924), and Seltzer published it without paying Ford any royalties. Seltzer was, as Poli writes, "an idealistic publisher who liked good books but did not have enough money or readers to make his firm a going concern" (1967, 93).[4] Ford wrote to Jeanne from Paris on 8 April:

> The continual lateness of delivery from here and the delay in New York seem to make it impossible to publish in New York before the 10th of each month. So I think it would be better if Seltzer published the 5th number on or about the 15th May and called it the May-June number, then he would publish the 6th number on the 15th or so of June and call it the July number. He would have to send a circular letter to subscribers explaining that they will not be cheated of a number but that their subscriptions will include the number for January 1925 which will be published on the 15th December.
>
> If you think this is a good plan *decide it for yourself* and tell Seltzer to do it. He may as well in that case print the cover himself, so I shall not send over covers with this number. . . .
>
> A small syndicate here is negotiating taking over the *review* and putting more money into it. As to this I am writing to Mr. Quinn. If they do, the organizer of the syndicate—a rich man who wants occupation—will take over the New York management and I hope you will get on with him. He is quite pleasant. (188, 189)

Krebs Friend, an acquaintance of Ernest Hemingway, agreed to back the *transatlantic review* in mid-1924. Frank MacShane explains, "Unfortunately this new arrangement only lasted another six months because the division of authority between Ford and Friend was never made clear, and a certain amount of ill feeling therefore arose between them. In December of 1924, Friend withdrew his support and the *review* ceased publication" (1965, 155).

---

4. See also the letter from Ford to Monroe Wheeler dated 24 November 1924 (Ford 1965, 163–64). Londraville and Londraville 1990, 205.

By the time Ford wrote to Jeanne on 26 March 1925, the *transatlantic review* was completely defunct. Ford was trying to tidy up its affairs and was still calling on Jeanne Foster for some assistance. They had now developed a lasting friendship that would strengthen over the next several years:

> I was very glad to get your letter of the 26th the last half year, but not getting any answer was afraid you were ill. I am glad to see that you seem in better spirits. . . .
>
> Yes, it was a pity that I had to suspend the T.R., but Mrs. Ford and I had spent frs. 120,000 on it—and are indeed still paying its bills, and as my principal source of income comes from my writing and it left me no time to write I had no other course open to me. . . .
>
> When are you coming over here? A number of your friends have asked up that question and we could only answer that we expected you last autumn. There is a certain amount of news here, but I have been so buried in my book that I have missed most of it. My young American friends say that it—the book—is one of the world's masterpieces, to be compared only with the Divine Comedy of Dante.[5] They probably exaggerate. As soon as I have finished an immense amount of belated correspondence I am going to resume turning my *Good Soldier* into French, a job that ought to have been finished by now. (189, 190)

Jeanne did all she could to promote Ford's novel *Some Do Not.* In her review of the book, she tried to intrigue readers with comments such as *"Some Do Not* is for the exceptional reader," and "the theme is . . . difficult and there is still too much barnyard ethics in average human nature."[6] She directed a not so subtle challenge to women readers, telling them about the critic who claimed women would not like the book because they wanted their novels "to have happy endings." She appealed to both the working-class reader and the literati when she explained that Ford had extracted "the heroism out of the lives of failures." She wrote of the main characters:

> Christopher Tietjens and Valentine Wannop have very little choice in the matter of destiny. They are handicapped, the one by a certain perverse hon-

---

5. Ford is referring to either *No More Parades* or *A Man Could Stand Up*, published in 1926.
6. The typescript of the review is in LC. It is not known if JRF ever published it.

esty, the other by circumstances. They haven't a fighting chance of winning out in their particular game. And against their lives foreordained to failure, the novelist has placed contrasting lives that because of birth or fortunate circumstance, or fortuitous accident, are destined to win more or less personal happiness and a full measure of the material lavishness of the gods.

Jeanne helped Ford with his lecture tour, which he was attempting through Lee Keedick's agency. By 1927, still not able to enter the American market, Ford would rely on Jeanne to smooth the way, but in 1925 and 1926 he was more concerned about her health and let rest his requests to her for assistance in settling *transatlantic review* matters:[7]

Why is it impossible to have a letter from you? I have written to you again and again—and now Mrs Dransfield says she has had a very sad letter from you, which dreadfully upsets me.[8] You say you are too hard up to come to Europe—but you know we wanted you to stay with us, so that it might have been ever so inexpensive—and I am sure that if you had spent a quiet month with us in Avignon it would have done you ever so much good.

. . . I leave Liverpool next Thursday week for Montreal which I expect to reach on the 24th, so I may anticipate striking New York on about the 26th or next day. I have been having a really terrible time of anxiety with publishers and shall have no end of trouble to put things straight when I get to N.Y.—but I will tell you all about it when we meet. Do wire me to the boat when and where I may expect to find you.

. . . Do, do, do let me have news of you. And may God bless you! (summer 1925, 190–91)

When he wrote to Jeanne from Paris a year later, he was concerned:[9]

What in the world has become of you! It must be over a year now since we have heard anything at all and that is not nice of you—for I have written to you several times. Do let us hear!

7. JRF told RL that this letter, undated, was written sometime during the summer of 1925.

8. Jane Dransfield (Mrs. C. D. Stone, 1875–1957), poet, playwright, critic.

9. Ford had temporarily left Lee Keedick's agency and was working with James Pond, another lecture agent.

. . . Are you never coming to Europe? Or must we come to the United States to see you? In any case I am coming at the beginning of November, for three months to lecture under the auspices of Mr. Pond, so we will meet then if I have to go to Seattle to find you.

But before then do let us hear. We often talk of you—and you would be astonished to hear how many people ask us after you. (192, 193)

Ford wrote to Jeanne again on 22 September 1926 in reply to a letter from her. If he came to New York, she promised, she would do her best for him:

Anyhow it is very jolly to hear from you again and you are very kind to offer to play fairy godmother and more in Gotham!

Well then: of course I'd love to lecture to anyone you are interested in: I am in the hands of Pond so I suppose you shd write to him: and presumably soon, as I believe my dates are filling up. I fancy the Pond Lecture Agency N.Y. wd. find him.

And equally of course I'd love you to give me a dinner. I shd. naturally prefer a tete a tete one: but if it has to be ten . . . well they say there is safety in numbers. Anyhow perhaps we cd. manage better! (192)[10]

MacShane writes that James Pond "asked [Ford] to go to the United States under his auspices" for a ten-week tour (1965, 196). Ford sailed for New York in October 1926. He lectured in the Midwest and on the East Coast, including stops in St. Louis, Chicago, Boston, and Cambridge. During the early days of his visit to New York City, he enjoyed a special dinner Jeanne gave in his honor. They saw the sights together and often dined out, having several dinners with Ford's good friend Carl Van Doren, editor of the *Nation*, and his wife, Irita.[11]

Jeanne was doing whatever she could to make Ford's trip a success. Her 29 November 1926 letter to William Aspinwall Bradley, the literary agent, detailed her plans. Mr. Ferris Greenslet (publisher and literary figure from Boston, and an editor of the *Atlantic Monthly*) "will see that [Ford] is enter-

10. Ford was unaware that JRF was in Paris and London in September 1926.
11. Carl Van Doren (1885–1950), American editor, critic, and biographer. Irita Bradford Van Doren (1891–1966) was editor of the *Sunday Literary Supplement* of the *New York Herald Tribune*.

tained at the clubs [in Boston] with a view to publicity" and will introduce him to others who might promote him. Mrs. William Z. Ripley, head of the Lecture Bureau of the Women's City Club, will "pay the usual fee" when Ford speaks to her group in January. Leighton Rollins, a publicity agent for authors, "may arrange a lecture." "I have also planned a large tea for publicity purposes—whenever Mr. Ford comes to Boston," and "Mr. Frank Cheney Hersey is canvassing the chances at Harvard." Mrs. Oakes Ames "will entertain Mr. Ford at luncheon or dinner" and later arrange "something larger" in Boston:

> I shall need . . . some regular publicity photographs, the conventional smiling head, or face, smooth prints done by one of the commercial photographers. . . . I shall also need a "galley" of provocative piquant quotations from Mr. Ford's book and a complete list of his books together with a short vivid biographical sketch written in a way that will stimulate curiosity.
>
> Will it be possible for you to go to Boni & Boni and ask them to arrange with the Boston Herald and the Boston Transcript to have Mr. Ford interviewed as soon as he comes to Boston? Also, please ask them to arrange ahead for interviews in the leading newspapers in every town Mr. Ford expects to visit. (LC)[12]

Jeanne told Bradley about the problems—some quite humorous—that she had encountered in her promotion of Ford:

> There is no trouble about putting Mr. Ford over. He puts himself over wherever he is known. The trouble is that he is not known. I hear these comments from more or less prominent people with whom I have talked about Mr. Ford's lecture tour:
>     1. "We don't know anything about his work."
>     2. "Why has he never been put forward by his American publishers?"
>     3. "Is he really nice? We thought his newspaper photographs so unattractive?"
>     4. "Has he written very much?"
>     5. "Isn't he the man who writes like James Joyce?"
>     6. "Isn't he a German?"

---

12. Albert Boni (1892–1981), American publisher, was the head of Boni & Boni.

7. "Hasn't he three wives like Augustus John?"

8. "Did he write anything previous to the war?"

9. "Is he a relative of Henry Ford?"

You see the ignorance about Mr. Ford is abysmal. Oh, I forgot one other question. "Will Mr. Ford speak on the League of Nations?"

A month after Jeanne wrote to Bradley, Ford presented her with a gift. When Joseph Conrad died in 1924, Mrs. Conrad returned several of Ford's autographed books to him, a gesture that could be interpreted as thoughtfulness or spite, but Jeanne said that Ford thought it to be the latter. He decided to show Jeanne his appreciation of what she had done for him by giving her one of these books, *The Soul of London* (1905), which he had originally inscribed "Joseph Conrad from Ford Madox Hueffer 5th May, 1905." On 15 December 1926, twenty-one years after he had written this inscription, he presented this book to Jeanne and reinscribed it, "Jeanne Foster from Ford Madox Ford 15th Dec, 1926 *Habant sua fata libelli*" (Books have their own lives).[13]

Whenever Ford was in New York City, he and Jeanne enjoyed going to church together. Even though Jeanne was not particularly interested in organized religion, she came to enjoy her outings with Ford. He had converted to Catholicism some years before his 1926 New York trip (when he was staying in Paris with his uncle Leopold) because he felt that Protestantism was gloomy and illogical. The ritual, the Latin liturgy, and the stained glass of Catholicism attracted him more than its doctrines (Macshane 1965, 14), as one letter to Jeanne shows:

Xtmas Day in the morning [1926]

My Dear:

I have just come in from Mass. N.Y. is very lonely without you: I wish we'd have gone to Mass together. I had quite—oh quite dreadfully!—a touch of nostalgia when they sang the adeste . . . not really for England or Paris—but I believe it was truly to live amongst Papists. I think they are, really, the only people one understands. *au fond*. They are one's real family as you and I are

13. This book is now in the collection of Edward O'Donnell, Johnson and O'Donnell Rare Books, Syracuse, New York.

more kin than if we were related by blood. Perhaps what I really need is to be reconciled to the Church. I was looking at a plaster of paris statue of the Virgin and she said: "This is the last Xtmas Mass you will ever attend." . . . just like that . . .

I meant to stop in bed all day—but I thought I had better get up and go to Mass: Naturally I am taking the Germans to lunch at the N.A.C. opening, to the Bullitt's for their Xtmas tree and supper.[14] And afterwards to the Van Dorens!

Tomorrow however I won't go out. I won't. I won't. I won't.

I hope you are not being too worried by your blood kin! It is a shame and it infuriates me that you cannot have a life of yr. own. . . . But I suppose you never could. You immolate what you have of an outside life, as it is, on the altar of my imbecile worries.

God bless you my dear: I think of you very much and write with true affection! And I prayed for you—like Hell—just now. (193)

In January, Jeanne was back in New York City. There she served as a literary agent for Ford and tried to smooth over the troubles caused by a rift between Ford and Jessie Conrad, Joseph Conrad's widow, over Ford's book on Conrad's life. Jeanne felt that he had not gotten a fair hearing years before in the controversy surrounding the question of his collaboration with Joseph Conrad, and it was her contention that disagreement between the writers was largely an invention of Mrs. Conrad, whose antipathy toward Ford was well known.[15] Jeanne maintained that the personal and professional relationship between the two men was always amicable and that Ford was disappointed that Mrs. Conrad described it otherwise.[16]

Jeanne wrote to some of her powerful acquaintances—including Heywood Broun (10 January 1927), the journalist who wrote for the *Morning Telegraph, New York Tribune, World, Nation*—and to others, hoping that they might be able to help Ford:

14. William Christian Bullitt (1891–1967), American diplomat, author.

15. Joseph Conrad (1857–1924), British novelist, Ukranian born of Polish parents.

16. JRF, interviewed by RL, 12 March 1967. Information not otherwise noted in this chapter is taken from a series of interviews between JRF and RL, dated 22 December 1966, 12 March 1967, 11 July 1967, and 14 July 1967.

I do not know whether I made myself clear when I talked with you at Elinor Wylie's party.[17] We find that a general misunderstanding exists throughout the country in regard to the friendship of Joseph Conrad and Ford Madox Ford. This misunderstanding seems to be due to the widespread attention given to Mrs. Conrad's letter published in the New York Times which followed the publication of Ford's life of Conrad, or *Reminiscences of Conrad* [sic].

The result of this misunderstanding is evidenced by the refusal of certain librarians to buy Ford's books, by the refusal of various committees in certain cities to consider a lecture engagement. Now Mr. Ford is in this country on a lecture tour. I want that lecture tour to be a successful one. I thought if a writer of such widespread popularity as yourself, Mr. Broun, could undertake to discuss the imaginary differences, that is, imaginary in the minds of various individuals throughout the United States, we could straighten out this Conrad matter once for all.

Mr. Ford has Conrad's letters to him and other material in contradiction of Mrs. Conrad's claim that no close friendship existed between the two men in recent years. There is also a good deal of material in contradiction of Violet Hunt's book "My Flurried Years."[18] Perhaps if it could be managed by way of a discussion or a review of Miss Hunt's book, it might be the most effective and least obvious way to get the truth before the public.[19]

History has shown that Jeanne Foster's opinion about the Ford-Conrad matter was correct. It is now accepted that Ford and Conrad produced two novels jointly (*The Inheritors*, 1901, and *Romance*, 1903), and that Ford wrote some sections of *Lord Jim, Heart of Darkness, Nostromo,* and *The Secret Agent* when Conrad became too ill to meet particular deadlines (McCarthy 1999). H. G. Wells wrote, "Conrad owed a very great deal to their early association; Hueffer [Ford] helped greatly to 'English' him and his idiom" (1934, 531).[20]

17. Elinor Morton Hoyt Wylie (1885–1928), American author and an editor of *Vanity Fair.*

18. Violet Hunt (1866–1942), Ford's former companion, wrote in *I Have This To Say,* "[Jessie Conrad says that] 'After 1919 Conrad never sought a meeting.' Why, surely, to call at our house which he frequently did implied rather more effort for Conrad than to receive us at Ham Street" (1926, 273).

19. The letter to Broun is reproduced in Londraville and Londraville 1990, 199–200.

20. Herbert George Wells (1866–1946), English writer, sociologist, and historian.

On 7 January 1927, Jeanne sent a letter to Ezra Pound, telling him about some of Ford's troubles. Ford was not a good speaker, so she showed him how to project better. A recent lecture by Ford had been most successful, and she was pleased with her work.

When Ford next wrote to her (24 March 1927), he was back in Toulon and was disheartened that because of his departure from New York, he would not be able to see Jeanne any longer:

> I have meant to write every day but I have been writing hard at *New York Is Not America* and, having naturally mislaid my spectacles have been suffering from all sorts of eyestrains and headaches and depressions.[21] So that if I had started to write to you at the end of a day I might have cried.
>
> However, now I have had some new glasses made and can more courageously confront the world.
>
> . . . As you see, I am using your machine all the time. It is an admirable instrument—but I am a pretty dull performer. Still I continue, faint yet pursuing. But I am a rotten letter writer at all times. I have a hundred things to say which I shall think of when I am in bed or on the sea.
>
> . . . I do hope to see you here in July; do just make a bolt of it and come. I would much rather you did that than that you went West and made engagements for me—for I do not in the least want to go to West; but of course engagements for Ezra are another matter. In any case do keep in touch with me. I expect—indeed I am sworn to Boni's—to be in New York about the 20th September; we shall probably go to Paris in May and then to Avignon with us and swim in the Rhone. That would be great fun. But Stella is writing about that.
>
> God bless you, my dear; keep very well and very cheerful and sometimes pray for the being who inscribes himself
>
> Yours very affectionately<br>FMF (194–95)

21. Mizener says that Ford wrote *New York Is Not America* during his New York trip in the autumn of 1926 (1971, 352, 584), but, according to the Foster letter, it would seem the book was not finished until at least the following March. On 28 March 1927, Ford wrote to Pound from Toulon, four days after he had written to JRF, mentioning that he was "finishing a book now" and that he spoke to "Lee Keedick with empressement of your lecturing in the U. S. A" (Ford 1965, 173). This comment matches the information in the Foster letter, and so the date of the letter must be 1927.

The "machine" Ford mentioned was a typewriter. When Ford was still in New York, Jeanne gave it to him when she noticed that his own was in poor working order. He was grateful and used it when he wrote *New York Is Not America*. By December 1927, Ford was back in New York and presented Jeanne with an early Christmas gift, an autographed copy of *New York Is Not America*. The book's published dedication reads:

My Dear Jeanne:

    Here I am back after all, just in time to dedicate this New York edition to the kindest of New Yorkers.

Yours gratefully and with affection,<br>F.M.F. (182)

Ford was in New York City the following year, but it is unclear how often he and Jeanne saw each other. When he wrote to her on 27 July 1928, on his way back to Europe, he did so from his shipboard desk. He regretted not seeing her again before he left, but had been unable to reach her. By this time, Stella Bowen had been replaced in his affections by an American woman, Renee Wright.

What in the world has become of you? I rang and rang and rang you up but never could find you home—and now here I am on the way to Europe again. I really have worried about you for such a prolonged silence can only mean that you are ill or nervously troubled. Pray, pray, pray let us have some news of you that will calm these apprehensions.

    All the while I was in New York I just wrote and wrote hardly going out at all. I think I must have written at least 90,000 words in sixty days and I finished my book exactly a fortnight ago.

    . . . God bless you, my dear: I will put up a candle for your happiness in the church of Batalha in Portugal where there is a very famous Virgin M. She might help you.

    Renee sends her love. She is very much recovered by now—and do believe that I never forget you. (195)

On the same evening that Ford wrote this letter to Jeanne, he wrote the dedication of *A Little Lesser Than Gods* to Renee Wright, but when he returned to France, his relationship with her dissolved. She wanted Ford to marry her, but his first wife, Elsie Martindale, refused to give him a divorce. Ms. Wright did not want to be known as Ford's mistress, and his American "sentimental attachment" ended. He moved from Toulon to Carqueiranne.[22]

Ford was in New York again by April 1929 "to secure advances for his new novel and to renew acquaintances in American literary circles." At this time, Ford's personal and literary reputation was beginning to suffer for a number of reasons, his vanity among them. He didn't like publishers and reviewers, and he was not shy about telling them so (Macshane 1965, 204).

When he tried to locate Jeanne and was unable to because of her extended stays in Schenectady, he contacted her brother-in-law, Gardiner Foster, in New York City, but Dr. Foster, too, had trouble keeping track of his busy sister-in-law. Ford wrote to Jeanne on 14 April 1929:

> I do wish you would let me know how to get in touch with you, for I can't even get in touch with Mr. Foster now, but the last thing he said was that you were going to be in Schenectady some time this week. Jane, on the other hand, says she heard from you that you were stopping in Boston, so I just don't know what to make of things.[23] I do hope you are ever so much better. It seemed perfect madness for you to be going to Boston when you did, but I suppose you had to. Do drop me a note. (196)

This 1929 letter is the last of the letters in the Ford-Foster correspondence. There were no others in her collection, but more were certainly written. Jeanne said that she corresponded with Ford until his death in 1939, and she made the same claim in two letters to Ezra Pound, dated 26 July 1939 and 4 November 1956 (NYPL). One can only speculate that she may not have preserved the later letters or that she gave them to friends as gifts.

Ford had a rather inconsistent career, particularly near the end of his life. Jeff McCarthy writes that during the years between 1928 and 1939 Ford was "either the pleasant figure of the great man reflecting from his comfortable success or the slightly pathetic figure of the writer who continue[d] to produce even though he [was], apparently, beyond his best work." The

22. Although Ms. Wright went to Paris that fall "to buy clothes" and had Ford return with her to New York at the end of 1928, Ford knew, as Mizener puts it, that "Mrs. Wright would not have him on the only terms he could offer her" (1971, 385–86).

23. Jane Dransfield. There is no evidence that JRF was in Boston at this time.

books Ford produced in his later years, explains McCarthy, are "less the penetrating and energetic proselytizing of the pre-war Ford . . . and more the misty memoirs of an old man in need of an editor. . . . Still, these last works repay the reader's effort with entertaining vignettes about modern artists and provoking assertions about civilization" (1999). H. G. Wells wrote in 1934, "What [Ford] is really or if he is really, nobody knows now and he least of all; he has become a great system of assumed *personas* and dramatized selves" (1934, 526). But three decades later, in 1967, Bernard Poli would write: "Today Ford is credited with being one of the key figures in the renaissance of post-World War I English literature, and in particular for his sponsorship of American writers who had fled—primarily to Paris— at the end of the war" (163–65).

Jeanne never mentioned Ford or his work in anything but the most positive terms. What counted most to her was that he stood by her while some other friends and acquaintances drifted away after Quinn's death, that he was always concerned for her happiness and welfare, and that he never wavered from his offers to assist her in whatever way he could. She did the same for him.

In 1939, she lost two people she loved and admired. W. B. Yeats passed away in France in January, and on 26 June, while on a trip to Provence, Ford Madox Ford died suddenly. Twelve days later (8 July 1939) Jeanne received a sad letter from Yeats's sister, Lily, sharing her pain over the death of her brother.[24] Jeanne said that Ford's death, coming so soon after Yeats's, gave her a "great heaviness of spirit for many months."[25]

In many ways, Jeanne Foster's relationship with Ford Madox Ford was a model for her association with other famous men of the time. There is the initial reaction to her beauty, followed by a deepening awareness of her intelligence and goodwill, and then a friendship that recognizes a kindred spirit. As we read their letters, we see glimpses not only of the woman who captivated the likes of John Butler Yeats, Ezra Pound, and John Quinn, but of the person who could offer these men that rarest of gifts, complete and unequivocal affection. For those who knew her even when only a vestige of her famous beauty remained, that gift was rare indeed.

24. The letter is summarized in RL's catalog of JRF's collection. Location of letter unknown.

25. JRF, interviewed by RL, 5 February 1967.

# 12

# The Modernists, Part One
## Pound, Joyce, and Eliot

AS SHE HAD EARLIER with John Butler Yeats, Jeanne Robert Foster found a good friend and an excellent reader of her work in Ezra Pound. He recommended, as Yeats had, that she curtail her attempts in what he considered outdated "Victorian" forms and return to her Adirondack roots.

Although the exact date of their meeting is not clear, it is most likely that Jeanne met Pound in the early summer of 1921, when she and Quinn were in Europe together. Quinn asked Pound for an introduction to James Joyce, and he obliged. Jeanne understood almost immediately that Ezra Pound could open doors otherwise firmly shut against outsiders.

The meeting with Joyce took place on 14 July 1921. On one occasion in the previous year (22 February 1920), Quinn had invited Jeanne to accompany him to the Algonquin Hotel in New York City for an interview with W. B. Yeats, where she served as Quinn's amanuensis.[1] Now he wanted her to do the same when he spoke with Joyce.

Jeanne's typescript of that meeting and her diary account describe Joyce's dark salon, a "tasteful gray and yellow room" with a Marie Laurencin watercolor of Joyce hanging on the wall.[2] When Joyce entered, she noticed that "in the gloom his face was very white and drawn—He protected his right eye even behind the glasses by squinting his face."

Jeanne said that Joyce's eye problems (iritis) forced him to write parts of *Ulysses* on butcher paper in red ink with words large enough for him to see.

---

1. JRF was JQ's secretary for the meeting with Yeats. See Quinn 1988.
2. NYPL owns both JRF's diary account and the more formal typescript of the interview.

Quinn thought that the eye disease was caused by Joyce's infected gums and gave him money to see a good dentist.[3]

The three spoke about writing, and Joyce said, "writing should always be conditioned by the subject. It would be impossible for example to put Bloom's thoughts and words into the language of Ruskin."[4] He spoke of *Ulysses*, which particularly interested them, and said that he had had a "great boyhood interest in the story": "There was a prize offered in school on 'My Favorite Hero.' Other boys wrote on Wolfe Tone and Robert Emmet and Daniel O'Connell. My subject was Ulysses. I didn't get the prize."[5]

The conversation turned to other writers—Austin Clarke, George Russell, Francis Ledwidge.[6] Then, when Quinn suggested that Joyce publish a key for *Ulysses*, the Irishman laughed: "My notes would make one or two volumes, each bigger than the book itself. I shan't even give the divisions their names as you have them—The book falls into three parts—the parts will simply be numbered . . . —But it does not matter if I go around this table around each leg—and climb up on the mantle to get to my chair; how I get there is my affair—"

He excused himself to put more drops in his eyes, and when he returned, he resumed the conversation, "sweetly making an effort to be amusing." The interview ended a short time later, and Jeanne recorded her final thoughts: "I wanted to give him something to do, something to drive the pain out of his face. We left—he promised to lunch or dine with us. A very great man." Quinn later told Jeanne that Joyce looked like "a man who has been through hell. Dante must have looked that way. His face is full of pain."

For the remainder of Jeanne's stay in France, most of her literary stimulus came from discussions with Ezra Pound. On 10 August, she recorded an early visit with him: "Ezra Pound for dinner. Pound spoke of the Cantos

3. See also *MFNY*, 492.

4. John Ruskin (1819–1900), English art critic and writer.

5. Theobald Wolfe Tone (1763–98), Robert Emmet (1778–1803), Daniel O'Connell (1775–1847), all Irish nationalists.

6. Austin Clarke (1896–1974), Irish poet and playwright. Francis Ledwidge (1891–1917), Irish working-class poet killed in action in Belgium during World War I.

published in the August ('21) Dial. Said he wrote numerous notes to first draft and then condensed them into the poem. Said the Cantos followed the general plan of the Divine Comedia. Said one needed notes with the Comedia. It was 'hard (Pater's hard) reading.' "[7]

Quinn left for New York on 15 August 1921, but Jeanne stayed behind to visit friends and oversee some of Quinn's art concerns. On 20 August, she had dinner with Pound and later wrote in her diary:

> Dinner with Pound . . . read Pound's hand, discovered he had studied magic and approached it at a different angle from W. B. Y. Regarded W. B. Y.'s early practices as questionable. "You have no right to force a symbol like a steel triangle through another person's images." Found Pound very learned in all things of the psychical mind. We talked of J. Q., about stories told by Joyce and J. Q. Celtic triumphant social animal etc. . . . We talked pictures. He seemed to know a great deal about them.
>
> . . . I read Pound's hands a little in the light of the Élysées Gardens. Right and left differ enormously. One (the left) Pound calls "the hand of a modern mood man" . . . [and] his hand is Renaissance.
>
> The right harder, practical, shrewd—colder—Pound is nervous, sanguine—tremulous, happy, childlike—yet practical.

Jeanne did not see Pound every day, but because she did not make daily entries, it is difficult to know how often they met. She received friendly letters from him during her stay, and one she kept (dated 27 August 1921) announced the birth of W. B. Yeats's son, Michael, on 22 August.

About the same time, an incident involving Pound made Jeanne feel uncomfortable, at least for an evening. He had not remained faithful to his wife, Dorothy, whom he had married in 1914, and was infamous for his roving eye. It was part of Jeanne's special tact that allowed her to remain friends with him even after he had embarrassed and compromised himself in front of her. Early in their friendship, probably late August 1921, when Quinn was not with her (Would Pound have been so bold with John Quinn nearby?), Jeanne faced her most difficult moment with her passionate friend. William M. Murphy recorded the story in his personal notes on 29

7. Unless otherwise noted, quotations from JRF's diaries are from diaries in LC. Walter Horatio Pater (1839–94), English essayist and critic.

June 1966, immediately upon his return home after a visit with Jeanne. She told him that when she was in Paris, she attended a dinner with Georgette Christ, a very beautiful Georgian Russian—who in Jeanne's opinion was a nymphomaniac:

> After dinner one night JRF in all innocence returned to [Christ's] apartment with her. Georgette ripped JRF's gown off and kissed her passionately on the shoulder. JRF told her off, said she must have a cloak to put over her dress to go home. Georgette told her to go into a certain room and fix herself up. When JRF opened the door there stood Ezra Pound stark naked, looking like a Greek god, lithe, muscular, handsome. ("With my Pagan soul, I'm glad I saw him that way. I've always loved beautiful things.") She said, "Ezra, what are you doing here?" He replied, "She brought me up here to make love." "To whom?" "To you," he said. "I thought you knew all about it." Georgette had apparently planned a triple play, though [in 1966] JRF "still doesn't know what exactly she had in mind for the three of [them] to do. It's not in the handbooks." Georgette had told Ezra that JRF was in love with him and wanted to meet him in GC's apartment. JRF told Ezra to get dressed and then took a taxi home. She told him she wasn't in love with him "that way" at all, never had been and never would be. She told him she would forget about the incident and never mention it again. And she never did until now.
>     . . . JRF knew Dorothy Shakespeare Pound, thinks her a fine woman . . . and can't understand why Ezra would leave her for Olga Rudge [who gave birth to Pound's daughter, Mary, in 1925], whom she doesn't know. But she first suspected Ezra and Dorothy didn't get along at the time of the Christ incident.

Jeanne Foster never mentioned the incident to Dorothy Pound, nor did she let it intrude on her friendship with the couple. She continued to have pleasant times with Ezra and Dorothy in Paris.

On 7 September 1921, she and the Pounds went to dinner at Café Voltaire. She later recorded the event in her diary:

> We had a merry dinner. Talked about the attack on modern art and about various persons we knew.
>     Pound said he was reading a manuscript written by a well-known American writer who wrote regularly for The Saturday Evening Post and Mc-

Clures. He wished to take an article he had already sold to the McClures for
$600 and have it published in the Dial for $40. Pound said that so far he
could see "no reason why it should go in the Dial." He said he did not think
the man would write any more after he finished his criticism of his work. Several had not.

I: Yes, that is why I haven't brought my poems. I feel that after you looked
at them I should not be able to hold a pen.

Pound: Nevertheless just bring them over.

The Pounds have taken a studio for six months from October 15 and
Pound has bought an enormous bassoon.

He wore the bright blue shirt with the wing collar . . . and looked remarkably well. He is happy with Natalie because she loves him devotedly
and quite simply.[8]

Two days later, on 9 September 1921, Jeanne drove to 59 rue des Saints-
Pères to see Pound, who served her a cordial. "God knows what it was," she
wrote. "It tasted like fire."

Jeanne, with Pound's urging, finally became brave enough to show him
her work, and she recorded their conversation. The typescript (located in
MC) is dated 17 September:

We came back to the Villa Calypso and Pound suggested that I bring down
the MS of my book of verse. I carried it down to him and left him in the salon
to look it over. Mrs. Pound and I went upstairs and laid down on my bed to
rest. After a half hour I went down to Rue Terre Neuve with Mrs. Pound to
get Gwen John. We came back alone as Gwen was not ready. I sat down beside Pound and we began. Pound was sitting at the table in the salon impa-
tiently. He said:

"I can't do anything for you as long as you keep on imitating Browning
and Tennyson and Morris and Swinburne. Here's a poem that is a frank imitation of Morris," naming a poem. I said, "Well, Mr. Pound, I may be imitating Browning and Swinburne, but as a matter of fact I have never read that
poem of William Morris's. Do you mean that you feel that my verse is frankly
imitative?"

8. Natalie Clifford Barney had a home in the Faubourg St. Germain and was famous for
her Friday *salon* (Norman 1960, 269).

Pound: "No, I only mean that you use the old forms. There's nowhere any direct imitation, only echoes of the Victorians. I can't do anything with that kind of verse. *(Then, hastily:)* Here in these verses for Japanese prints I have marked several things. I don't like archaicness in modern poetry—'shapen' *(indicating an end word in the first)*, and here I can't see that the inversion helps much; I don't like inversion, and *(turning the sheet)* I think *(indicating another)* there are too many figures."[9]

He turned to a poem where I had written of my metamorphosis into a faun—"onyx horns" on forehead without any means of my knowing that they were onyx. "Here," he said, "if you want them onyx, you must have the horns seen in the pool. Otherwise they might be smooth, cool if you touched them, but you could hardly know that they were onyx. And here you begin, 'I am a faun . . . or Apollo.' Don't confuse your readers. Have it a *faun* or come out and make it *Apollo.* You have to set your scene as it were, make a composition like a painter, no matter how lovely your sounds may be."[10]

He picked up a section of songs and light lyrics called 'The Singing Mask." "I find the best things in the collection here. There is more genuine passion in them. Take this ["Margot's Song," *RF,* 12], it has emotion."

"Yes, but such poems are rare—they come only with certain moods."

"The great genius like Swinburne can make any number of technical errors. His passion covers them. In poetry it is really a matter of how much of that power you have. The influence of Swinburne and the *Rubáíyát* broke the back of Victorian poetry. I think you will find your best chance following the lead of the verses."[11]

I: "I am sorry, Mr. Pound, that I have not a copy of my Adirondack verse with me [*NOY,* 1916]. In that volume you would find ballads written to shanty tunes and the simplicity you like in these lyrics."

9. When Murphy reproduced this conversation in his article "Jeanne Robert Foster," he noted that JRF and Pound were talking about poems from *Rock Flower:* "Shapen still stands at the end of the first line in 'A Pair of Lovers: Moronobo,' contained in the section, 'Verses for Japanese Prints,' [*RF,* 41]" (1971, 9).

10. JRF took Pound's advice. On page 17 of *Rock Flower,* 'The Escape" contains the opening lines: "Let us bend over a pool / And slip off the familiar flesh. / Look! / I am Apollo." Murphy writes that JRF used the metaphor of the faun with onyx horns in "L' Homme," a section of the poem "Constantin Brancusi: Roumanian Sculptor," p. 59: "Pan thewed with sinews of ilex trees; / A faun's head, black curls, / (One suspects onyx horns)" (1971, 9).

11. Omar Khayyam (c. 1048-c.1122), Persian poet who wrote *The Rubáíyát.*

Pound: "I would go on with that work. You have a kind of background there. W. B. Yeats was very fortunate in having the background of Irish folklore. And you must work for the *mot juste*. You should know how Dante manages technique, and Arnaut Daniel."[12]

I: "Would you burn all this and start afresh?"

Pound: "No, you have a book there. Publish it and keep on working. Your work is in transition. You'll find your métier after a while."

"I know—I understand. Those moods or moments are the only ones that do produce poetry."

"By the way, there are some in the section marked 'doubtful' that I suggested putting back. This one [*turning the leaves*], 'The Winter Song,' and these lyrics."

On 20 September 1921, she and the Pounds had dinner again and made plans to see each other "on Thursday," and "Pound advised me not to pose any longer." Why, she didn't say, but she ignored his advice. On 30 September and 1 October, at least, she sat for Philip Sawyer. This particular diary ends a few pages later, with no more mention of Pound. Her thoughts had turned to her return to America and to John Quinn.

Six months later, Pound was still encouraging her when he wrote to her in New York on 21 February 1922: "J. Q. has sent me your poem on the late JBY; the best thing I have seen of yours, I think further reflections [by others about JBY] useless."[13] As thanks for his help and for his friendship, Jeanne included in *Rock Flower* (94) her tribute "Ezra Pound":

> You,—who have given me strange music,
> Leave me dumb because of the voices
> Crying beyond you.
> I perish of silence—
> Die in the depths of a terrible stillness,
> Hearing no more, lovers in springtime

12. See Salvato 1996. Arnaut Daniel (c. 1150-c. 1200), Provençal poet, member of the court of Richard Cœur de Lion.

13. Unless otherwise noted, Pound's letters to JRF are located in the Houghton Library at Harvard University, Cambridge, Mass.

Singing songs of love in the valleys,
Singing of hands and lips meeting together.

Jeanne approved of Pound's unselfish desire to promote talented artists and writers. It is what she too wished to do when she reviewed the works of Vachel Lindsay, W. B. Yeats, and George Moore. Though she was not as well known as Pound, whose proprietorship extended to "a half-dozen careers aside from his own" (MFNY, 248), and though she did not have the influence or money of a John Quinn, Jeanne certainly did her part. This facet of her personality helped to deepen her friendship with Pound. He saw her as a kindred soul, someone who did not get lost in her own career; and he saw her as a fellow poet, one whom he might be able to help. He had, after all, advised some of the greatest writers of the time, including T. S. Eliot.

Jeanne Foster first became involved in Eliot's career some years before she met Pound, but only peripherally. Quinn and Pound had proposed to Alfred Knopf that a brochure be published about Pound in order to introduce him to a wider American audience and to advertise the forthcoming Pound-Fenollosa book, Noh, or Accomplishment.[14] Pound had resolved for Eliot to write the piece but insisted that it remain anonymous. "I want to boom Eliot," he wrote, "and one can't have too obvious a ping-pong match at that sort of thing" (MFNY, 280). The essay Eliot wrote (with three changes made by Pound) was "Ezra Pound: His Metric and Poetry."

The essay appeared before Jeanne Foster met John Quinn, but he later told her a strange tale—that there was a secret about the "brochure": Eliot hadn't written it at all. Pound had done more than make a few "deletions." He had written the essay himself and eventually let it be known that Eliot had written it in order to promote him. On 17 November 1969, Jeanne wrote to William M. Murphy: "Quinn believed that Pound really wrote the supposed Eliot MS. for it was interlined and corrected heavily in Ezra Pound's handwriting. The Pound letters that I gave [to the Houghton at Harvard] with it had comments . . . about Eliot as I was doing publicity for Pound at that time, and he was loyally promoting Eliot. Even

14. Ezra Pound and Ernest Fenollosa, Noh, or Accomplishment (New York: Alfred Knopf, 1917). Alfred A. Knopf (1892–1984), American publisher.

the Houghton Library did not—at first—recognize it as genuine Eliot!!" (MC).

In any case, the brochure appeared just before Quinn's 5 February 1918 operation. Even though overworked and ill, Quinn proofread the copy and paid Knopf four-fifths of the publishing costs ($117.92). Pound wrote on 7 April 1918 that he was delighted with the professional-looking results: "You certainly have done me proud, and it is very crafty to present me in gold and old rose madder, as if I had just that graceful and saddened tonality that the American 'patron of the perfumed shelf' has so long desired and been accustomed to. . . . Certainly if America finally decides to pay my rent, it will be your doing" (MFNY, 342).

In 1919, Quinn asked Jeanne to shop around a collection of Eliot's poetry. He and Pound had decided to push Knopf to publish it, but Knopf wanted more poems, which were not forthcoming. Pound added some of Eliot's essays to the volume, and Knopf rejected it in late 1918 because he wanted to publish only poems. Quinn got the manuscript back in February 1919 and sent it to Horace Liveright (1886–1933). When that publisher didn't work out, Quinn (who was angry because he thought that Liveright was waiting for him to offer to pay part of the costs) turned the manuscript over to Jeanne. She immediately sent it to John Lane's American office, hoping that Eliot's American-European duality would appeal. Quinn told Eliot that he would be willing to give Lane a $150 subsidy, but he may not have told Lane, and the book was rejected.[15] Jeanne suggested to Quinn that Knopf might be their best offer after all. On 9 July, Eliot wrote to Quinn and agreed to Knopf: "I leave it in your hands in all confidence, but with the always stronger feeling that you ought not to accept or have forced upon you so much disinterested labour. My only justification is that I do not know anyone else with either the influence, the intelligence, or the generosity necessary to undertake it. It is quite obvious that, without you, I should never get anything published in America at all" (MFNY, 405).

On 29 September, Eliot sent Quinn an addition for the book, a new poem Quinn particularly liked entitled "Gerontion." Knopf published the collection "essayless," as he had wanted to do from the first. Eliot approved the contract on 5 November 1919, writing Quinn: "I earnestly hope that

15. MFNY, 404, and JRF, interviewed by RL, 15 October 1966.

my affairs will not take any more of your time and thought; if you took no further interest in them whatever you would still have earned my lifelong gratitude which, I assure you, you shall have" (*MFNY*, 405).

The book, *Poems by T. S. Eliot*, appeared on 18 February 1920. Quinn bought thirty-five copies and gave a number away as gifts to special friends. Jeanne read the poems aloud to him, and, as with his court briefs, it wasn't long before he had most of the volume memorized. He wrote of his delight to Pound: "They are great. . . . some of Eliot's things are like fugues, and others awfully witty. The Hippopotamus and Sweeney—hell, *all* of them, are great" (*MFNY*, 434).

But life was difficult for Eliot. When Pound wrote to Jeanne in February 1922, he told her there were pressing concerns to discuss with her: Eliot needed money. His wife was ill, and bills were overdue: "The case of Eliot has got beyond a joke. Nothing is any use but a permanent guarantee, for 'life' or for as long as he needs it. And the minimum, all things, health, wife, etc. considered is 1500 dollars or £300" (NYPL).

Pound's plan (detailed in the February 1922 letter) was to give Eliot an annuity by selling shares of "support" for the poet, not with any hope of future monetary return but simply as a way to keep Eliot going. He and Richard Aldington had purchased one share each at ten pounds, due each year, and he assumed that "the ever resolute J. Q." would purchase two shares.[16] Eliot was as much American as European, and Pound felt that America ought to do her part "as least as much as Paris or London. Certainly bankrupt Europe oughtn't to do it all." World War I killed not only artists and writers but civilization, and its rise from the ashes depended on new artists and new writers: "Civilization has got to be restarted. Preferably by honest people. After all the thirty people who want literature to exist ought to be willing to pay & cant expect boobs and blackguards to do so." Pound asked Jeanne for help in drumming up additional "stockholders." He specifically mentioned Irene Lewisohn, who sponsored one of Pound's Japanese plays in her theater:[17] "Say simply that Eliot is the one tragic poet de nos

16. Richard Aldington (originally Edward Godfree, 1892–1962), British writer.

17. Irene Lewisohn (1892–1944), American theatrical artist who combined poetry and music in her productions. See, for instance, *A Pagan Poem, Symphonic Poem by Charles M. Loeffler, after Virgil, Stage Version by Irene Lewisohn* (1929–30).

jours; and that I think him the best of my contemporaries; and that it is simply a case of the work NOT getting done; the patron in a case of this sort really performs part of the creation." Some help was immediately forthcoming. John Quinn offered Eliot three hundred dollars a year for five years.

A few months after Jeanne had received Pound's February 1922 request to be an advocate for Eliot, Quinn mentioned to her that he had received another letter from Eliot about a new poem. "I . . . have a long poem in mind and partly on paper which I am wishful to finish," the poet told his patron (*MFNY*, 489]. Jeanne looked forward to reading it. She had previously presented a copy of Eliot's essay book *The Sacred Wood* to John Butler Yeats, and the three—she, Quinn, and old Yeats—had enjoyed discussing its ideas about poetic theory. Her favorite essay in the book, "Tradition and the Individual Talent," intrigued her, and decades later she still liked to discuss its ideas. She was especially interested in Eliot's concept that each genuine new piece of art restructured the whole literary universe and subtly altered every other work in the canon.[18]

Knowing Jeanne's enthusiasm about Eliot's poetry, Quinn promised her a copy of the new poem as soon as he received one. It was to be called *The Waste Land*. Eliot wrote to Quinn on 19 July 1922: "As it is now so late I am enclosing the typescript to hand to [Liveright] when the contract is complete. . . . I had wished to type it out fair, but I did not wish to delay it any longer. This will do for him to get on with, and I shall rush forward the notes to go at the end. I only hope the printers are not allowed to bitch the punctuation and the spacing, as that is very important for the sense" (*MFNY*, 535).

A copy of that typescript, protected for years in Jeanne's files, is now at the Houghton Library at Harvard University, a gift from her in 1961. The catalog gives the history: "Made in the office of John Quinn from typescript sent to him by Eliot; mailed by Quinn to Jeanne Robert Foster 31 July 1922. Varies at several places from published versions, and includes one additional line." (For an account of what happened to the original typescript, see chapter 14.)

Jeanne would not meet Eliot until 1923 in Europe and then only briefly,

---

18. JRF, interviewed by RL, 15 October 1966.

but she continued to be intrigued by his work. Toward the end of Quinn's life, she watched his concern for Eliot intensify. She would be able to do little for the poet when Quinn was gone, and she knew that the Quinn estate would not continue to support the entourage of artists and writers he had so carefully cultivated. Eliot was one of Quinn's favorites. The poet seemed driven ("I have not even time to go to a dentist . . . I am worn out. I cannot go on" [*MFNY*, 582]), a problem Quinn understood all too well. He tried, somewhat successfully, to drum up more money for Eliot and sent additional subsidies himself. But Quinn was sick, and the money he had promised through 1927 stopped on 29 July 1924, when he died.

Decades later, after B. L. Reid interviewed Eliot for *The Man from New York* in 1964, he wrote to Jeanne to tell her that the poet "remembered little about Quinn." [19] It saddened her that Quinn had been so easily forgotten.

19. On 20 September 1964, JRF wrote to Murphy about Reid's visit (NYPL).

# 13

## The Modernists, Part Two
### Pound, Yeats, and Other Friends

ON 5 APRIL 1922, two years after Ezra Pound had first written to Jeanne Robert Foster about T. S. Eliot, Pound wrote a newsy letter to her about his experiences cultivating the publisher Horace Liveright, who had recently been in Europe. Pound introduced him to Joyce, Eliot, Wyndham Lewis, and Constantin Brancusi, and his scheme to court Liveright as a publisher worked. Liveright "is going toward the light, not from it," he wrote to Jeanne. "Much more of a man than publishers usually are."[1]

Around this time, Jeanne signed a contract with Liveright to have *Rock Flower,* her third book of verse, published. He also offered her the position of editor in chief held by Toby Seltzer, but she declined. Jeanne would have felt uncomfortable (she said Liveright expressed more than a professional interest in her), and she was simply too busy with her other undertakings (Dardis 1995, 68).

Letters were exchanged rapidly between Pound and Jeanne that spring of 1922. Pound wrote on 12 April, 23 April, and 6 May 1922. "I am dead," Pound began his letter of 12 April. He was writing, he said, from the World of Spirits, and it was not a happy world. He was frustrated about almost everything. Why wouldn't America support its struggling, talented artists? "Every American village supports 6 or 7 parsons," he informed Jeanne. "Why shouldn't they support a writer or artist instead of the 4th or 5th parson—parsons wholly unproductive." Why couldn't he get paid for his arti-

---

1. Unless otherwise noted, Pound's letters to JRF are located in the Houghton Library at Harvard University, Cambridge, Mass.

cles? Francis Crowninshield of *New Age Magazine* had ordered a piece from him, "a perfect definite," but it had never appeared in print, and the promised money had never arrived.[2] Pound told Jeanne that if she was "more than metaphorically hard up," if she could get his article published, she could take the proceeds for herself.

Eleven days later (23 April) he wrote again of further frustrations, reminding her, "Remember I'm officially dead." It is an important letter because for the first time he wrote to Jeanne about his interest in Japanese art, a subject about which they shared many long conversations. Pound was promoting Tami Koume, "the first Jap really to absorb the new occidental art." He enclosed some photos of Koume's work and hinted that he had "some other work on the horizon, however this is for yr. private ears." He didn't mention what the work was.

His letter of 6 May 1922 contained a list of chores for Jeanne, duties that focused primarily on promoting T. S. Eliot to various people and asking her to find out how much *Vanity Fair* might pay to have *The Waste Land*. Again, he asked her not to contradict "news of my demise." She was not to resurrect him for at least several months.

Neither Hugh Kenner (in *The Pound Era*, 1971) nor Charles Norman (in *Ezra Pound*, 1960) nor other Pound biographers mention this self-imposed death that Pound asked Jeanne to concoct with him. She did not know the reasons behind it and never asked. She assumed that Pound, being such a great promoter, was only trying to re-create interest in his work with a kind of joke. The work of a recently dead writer is often more sought after. "A beautiful publicity stunt," Jeanne suggested, and she was only too happy to help him in his efforts to dupe the publishers of the world.[3]

The two other 1922 letters from Pound are dated 5 September and 30 September. Both, again, are filled with requests for assistance: convince Quinn to give Eliot more money; find some patronage for William Carlos Williams; help Pound solve various problems with the *Dial*; tell publisher Seldes that "any mss. from [Franklin Pierce] Adams will probably be worth

2. Francis Welch Crowninshield (pseudonym of Arthur Loring Bruce, 1872–1947), American editor, publisher, and art collector.

3. JRF, interviewed by RL, 15 October 1966.

considering" (30 September).[4] He reminded her, "You can be more use as an interpreter than as a subscriber (to support writers). I am not writing this to squeeze your angelic pocket." Pound ended his letter with one of his aphorisms, "Nothing matters but innocence."

In a 1923 postcard from Venice (postmarked 6 April), Pound wrote to Jeanne that, as always, he was on the hunt for money, this time for himself: "I see that Mr. Juillard (A.D.) has left $10,000,000 to 'music.'[5] Wot about my opera?? Who runs the 'Juillard'?? Ever. Ezra."[6]

Only one other note survives from 1923, dated 3 December and concerned with the business of the *transatlantic review,* in particular with selections for the art section of that journal. Pound needed some help and knew that Jeanne Foster had her finger on the pulse of the contemporary art world: "Will you send me Braq-s [Braque's] address and will you write to him and Picasso to send on photos of anything they'd like reproduced." She was glad to oblige.

The 1924 correspondence between Pound and Jeanne reflect all the events of that important year in her life. Although she received a thank you note from Dorothy Pound in April for her introduction of the Pounds to composer Charles Martin Loeffler, the letters from Pound and his wife after July that year express concern for Jeanne because of John Quinn's death.[7] His loss was a blow to Pound as well. "I can't tell, from here, whether you are now overwhelmed with work [of settling the estate]," he wrote on 4 August. "There is no use trying to count things up. But this much seems certain: I should not have had any books published in America since 1912 but

---

4. William Carlos Williams (1883–1963), American author. George Seldes (1890–1995), American publisher and journalist. Franklin Pierce Adams (1881–1960), American author and humorist.

5. Augustus D. Juillard (1840–1919), American merchant and patron of music, whose bequest established the Juillard Music Foundation and the Juillard School of Music.

6. The opera was *The Testament of Francois Villon, A Melodrama by Ezra Pound, Words by Francois Villon, Music by Ezra Pound.* See Norman 1960, 253–54, 260, 269, 280–83, 309. The postcard from Pound to JRF is in LC.

7. Charles Martin Loeffler (1861–1935), who was born in Alsace and lived in Kiev as a child, spent much of his adult life in Massachusetts and was connected with the Boston Symphony.

for him. That's one item. Also the two vols, of the L. R. [*Little Review*] and the printing of Ulysses seem to come under that head."

Jeanne wrote to let him know that the week before Quinn died, he spoke of Pound. She sent him Quinn's words: "Tell Ezra that when I get well, you and I will come over in early winter or late autumn and we will all . . . go on a trip somewhere. I want Pound to make me really see Italy. . . . And tell him I want to know about his health, about the appendicitis and what he is writing. I don't think he ought to stay in Paris. He is too kind-hearted. Vagrant Americans impose on his kindness" (23 August 1924, in Pound 1991, 175).

Pound's attention soon turned to concerns over Quinn's art collection. What would happen to it? Would Jeanne like him to contact Albert Barnes, who might be the only living person able to purchase the entire collection? If *Red Duet* by Wyndham Lewis didn't run too high at auction, would she secure it for him? Would she please come to Europe to stay with him and Dorothy? (31 December 1924).

Pound remembered Quinn with great affection, but Quinn was "pushed aside by the living," Jeanne later said. "Have you a little spare time?" Pound wrote in the same 31 December letter. "If not . . . oh well, there is (and that may not sound like a compliment) NO one else to act for me in them bhloody stites."

He had read "The Four Winds," a manuscript by R. C. Dunning, and had asked Jeanne if she could convince Horace Liveright to publish it, even though he had already refused it once:[8] "The style is the style of Swinburne and the Rubáíyát. A few years ago NOTHING could be printed that was in any other. Now they are all daft on the new gongorism and can see nothing that hasn't got an anti—straddled over six fences."

Jeanne did as Pound asked and promoted the manuscript, with some success. Under a different title, *Windfalls*, the book was published by Edward W. Titus in 1929, at least in part through her efforts.[9] In return, Jeanne asked Pound to do what he could for Gwen John, who had with Quinn's death lost her best patron. As much as Jeanne loved Quinn, she knew

8. Ralph Cheever Dunning (1878–1930), American author.

9. Edward William Titus (1870–1952), American bookseller and publisher.

Pound was correct: attention must be paid to the living. She worked tirelessly in a futile effort to keep the Quinn collection together, as much to
protect artists still living (and their prices) as to memorialize Quinn. "Don't
see anything to be done re/sale," Pound wrote to her on 31 December 1924.
He understood her fears: "Bad for artists to have it dumped on market." A
year later (4 September 1925), he lamented to her: "It's amazin'; its like the
dissolution of a renaissance condottier'd state."

Pound repeated his invitation to her to visit (31 December 1924), fearing that he couldn't know her state of mind and state of health without seeing her: "You had better come over—as soon as you get things in order." He
wouldn't be going to America, he told her, because it was "too late . . . past
the time when it wd amuse me to poke up the animals. Suffer the lil children
to come unto me."

Pound's 1925 letters begin on 7 January with concerns about the *transatlantic review*. In a late attempt to resurrect the failed magazine, Jeanne went
to great efforts to find American dollars for it. At one point, it appeared that
if the magazine continued, much of the responsibility would fall on her
shoulders. Ford Madox Ford, the driving force behind the original journal,
could not take any more time away from his novel writing. Pound, ensconced in Rapallo for the most part, would not be able to promote the
journal from afar. "I shall not be in Paris," he told her. "I can only promote
this matter by letters—& will not have even a typewriter with me for several
months." He asked her if she would be able to run a review, promote it,
manage it, and find money for it. He warned, "Do you understand that NO
one connected with the review, except myself has the faintest idea of economics?" Although Pound told her that it was not too late for a resurrection,
he did her a great favor in pointing out the pitfalls. It was the death knell for
the *transatlantic review*.

But Jeanne Foster was not finished. Her connections with editors led her
to Ernest Walsh and Ethel Moorhead, and she encouraged them to con-
struct another, slightly different magazine.[10] She knew many of the best
writers, and she was certain that they would contribute. Pound finally met
Walsh in Bologna in late May and was pleased with the plans for *This Quar-*

---

10. Ernest Walsh (1895–1926) and Ethel Moorhead (no dates available), American
writers.

*ter:* "[The editor] seems prepared to go the whole hog," he wrote to Jeanne on 7 June 1925, "wants most funds to go to writers, in fact, a commendable enterprise." Jeanne was once again quietly in the center of things, arranging subscriptions, promoting, doing what she could to ensure the success of the new magazine. Pound was happy: "An the review itself considerable improvement on the transat. None of the ole mush about 'extreme right' 'left' etc. . . . It is not loony like the Lit. Rev.; or wuzzy in the head like the transat in its weaker moments."

The first issue (1925) of *This Quarter* was dedicated to Pound. After four large issues and a move from Paris to Monaco, the journal passed to the editorship of Edward W. Titus. The last issue was published in September 1932. Friends of Jeanne and of Pound all contributed—Brancusi, Djuna Barnes, William Carlos Williams, H. D., Ernest Hemingway, and Pound himself.[11] However brief the existence of *This Quarter*, its quality was unsurpassed.

Pound was also angry when he wrote to Jeanne on 7 June 1925—not with her but with those handling the Quinn estate. He had not been told if Quinn estate trustees would allow him to buy Wyndham Lewis's *Red Duet.* Other Lewis paintings could "damn well . . . be [advertised] by a special number of the T. Quarterly," but "will the goddam estate supply me wif photos?" They did not send Pound photos and did not seem particularly concerned with dispersing the art slowly so that it might bring the highest prices.

Pound's anger and frustration did not abate by 4 September 1925, when he wrote to Jeanne again: "Someone will probably thank you fer savin the Q, correspondence about 2147 a,d, HELL." He was not happy with Quinn's heirs, who he felt knew nothing about art and literature: "You may be faintly cheered to see John's honest sailor in the capital of CANTO XII back side to the audience. . . . You can threaten the family that if it don't behave I will print it J. Q. instead of lightly veiling the narrator. On the whole you'd better not, as they wd. Get the hole book put on the HINDEX and stopped in customs."

When John Quinn and Jeanne Foster had visited Europe in 1923, Quinn

11. Djuna Barnes (1892–1982), American poet and painter. Hilda Doolittle (H. D., 1886–1961), American poet whose early imagistic work was published by Ezra Pound.

had told Pound the sailor story.[12] Pound decided not to identify Quinn by name:

> 24 E. 47th, when I met him,
> Doing job printing, i.e. agent,
>     Going to his old acquaintances,
>     His office in Nassau St., distributing jobs to the printers.
>                                                         (Pound 1986, 53)

Pound was also concerned about Jeanne's own family and the attention they demanded when she could have been doing great things for artists and writers:

> Damn your family. I mean, I fully sympathize. Or might if I knew anything interesting about 'em. I really have no sympathy or interest in anything that don't fit into my particular scheme for restarting civilization, or at least pre-servin the fadin traces of same. . . .
>     You better allow your family 75 a month, and live in yourup on the other 75. Better than the great suburb.

The new year of 1926 would see the complete dispersal of the Quinn collection in several auctions in New York and Paris, and the end of Jeanne's relationship with the Quinn estate.[13] There was nothing left for her to do for the man she had loved so dearly. Acting as an agent for others who knew of her expertise, she went to Europe to visit the Pounds, to look at art for some American clients, and to escape, for however briefly, her family in Schenectady.

When exactly Jeanne left on her trip is unclear, but she was still in New York on 14 April 1926 when Pound wrote to her from Rapallo about want-

---

12. In 1923, Quinn told Pound a story, "The Tale of the Honest Sailor," and Pound used it in Canto XII. Kenner explains that the sailor rises "to the ownership of 'a whole line of steamers,' all the time supposing the boy he was bringing up had sprung from his belly, begotten by 'a rich merchant in Stambouli' " (1971, 425).

13. The 1926 catalog of "the memorial exhibition of a portion of the collection of paintings and sculpture belonging to the late John Quinn" (Brummer and Weyhe 1926) gives a partial listing of some of the artwork sold in the New York sales.

ing to purchase some of Lewis's drawings. He had not heard from her for some time and was concerned. Jeanne probably left New York shortly after receiving a letter on 5 July 1926 from Lollie Yeats, letting her know that a new book by William Butler Yeats would soon be out and that the family looked forward to seeing her again soon.

Jeanne was in Paris near her good friend, Dorothy Pound, when Omar Pound made his entrance into the world on 10 September 1926. It was a difficult birth for both mother and child, and there were some fears for the baby. On 20 September, Mrs. Pound sent a note to Jeanne to thank her for two separate gifts of flowers and to reassure her that her baby son was a survivor ("Omar improving rapidly") and that "A little later I hope he'll be in Italy to learn to speak Italian! more easily than his lazy mama." Mrs. Pound invited Jeanne to visit again and to "ring up Ezra at Foyot." She ended with a touching response to what Jeanne had told her was her own private dream: "I can but wish and hope that you may have the son you desire" (NYPL). But Jeanne was forty-seven years old in 1926. Quinn was gone, and although she and Albert Shaw saw each other occasionally, she had an invalid husband still living. There would be no son. She never knew Omar Pound as he grew up, but she felt a connection because of these early moments of his life—even though she never actually got to see him—and thought of him always as a kind of spiritual child.[14]

Besides spending time visiting galleries and friends, Jeanne also paid a visit to James Joyce. He was happy to see her, which surprised her, she said. Years earlier, he and Quinn had a disagreement about the payment for the manuscript of *Ulysses*, and Jeanne thought that Joyce might think her "guilty by association." (Joyce always suspected that he was getting short-changed. It isn't clear if Quinn actually knew of the "falling out.") But Joyce was kind, and she was able to talk openly about Quinn:

I told him of Quinn's illness making excuses for the unfortunate sale of the MS of Ulysses, which Quinn never intended to be sold. Joyce told me of the

14. JRF, interviewed by RL, 15 August 1968. By September 1926, JRF was making plans to return to New York. On 22 September 1926, Ford Madox Ford wrote to her about her invitation to "play fairy godmother" when he arrived in New York. He mentioned that he planned to sail on 20 October.

American pirated edition, also of a volume of forgeries purporting to the correspondence between Joyce and a Swiss inn-keeper over lost luggage. Joyce
said:

"I never had such an argument."

. . . Story of library, more talk of Quinn, the burning of his book Dublin-
ers long ago. He remembered telling Brancusi that he, Brancusi[,] looked like
Carlyle. He cannot believe that his play Exiles will be produced until he sees
the curtain rise. He said Valery Larbaud would translate certain parts of
Ulysses into French, that he, Joyce objects to the publication of fragments of
Ulysses and thinks German translation might be better than the French.[15]
He thinks the Teutonic and the Latin language better suited to Ulysses than
French. (Foster 1926b)

Jeanne Foster was delighted when Joyce agreed to her visit because she
wanted to ask him about his writing process. Like Quinn, she was always interested in inspiration. But after a short conversation, Joyce turned the subject to cooking. She said that even though she was quite frustrated, she
came away with some very good recipes for artichokes.[16]

After leaving France, Jeanne stopped in London for a few days before her
ship sailed for America. While she was there, during the third week of September, she met with D. H. Lawrence for an afternoon and discussed doing
some work as a literary agent for him in the States. She said that Lawrence
was "broodingly handsome" and pleasant to speak with, but she decided
that she already had too much to do.[17]

By the time Ezra Pound wrote to Jeanne on 18 November 1926, she was
back in New York doing some editorial work and occasionally escorting
Ford Madox Ford around town. In a subsequent note on 7 December,
Pound asked "what my stock (pussnl. Licherary stock) is now quoted at in
N. Y." His friend Ford was there and, largely through Jeanne's efforts, was
finding that the lecture circuit paid his bills. Pound continued:

15. Valery Larbaud (1881–1957), French poet and critic, and close friend of James Joyce.

16. JRF, interviewed by RL, 15 August 1968.

17. D. H. Lawrence (1885–1930), English writer. JRF, interviewed by RL, 15 August
1968.

I feel up to a lecture tour; but not without a guarantee. I suppose there is no one in America who is in the least trustworthy. I mean for sums above 40 dollars; and that no guarantee is worth a damn unless a certain amount of it is actually on deposit in the Equitable???

. . . 2 or at the outside 3 months with fat guarantee. . . . but prob. My ideas are exaggerated. Who makes 10,000 bucks on a lecture tour? And what sum less than that wd. Pay one for the trouble and waste of time and effort?

On 7 January, Jeanne wrote back:[18]

The times are right for your appearance here. I want you to come. Your literary stock is high where you are known and I believe you would have an amusing tour and make some cash. Pond, the agent, has done little for Ford. He really doesn't like Ford. . . .

So I would advise you not to have Pond. I do recommend Lee Keedick. Ford is with him at this moment (I have just had a telephone message booming your stock and probably trying to arrange a western tour for himself).[19]

Ford has told me that he would take an apartment and ask you to live with him if you cared to do so, if you would come over next year. Ford intends coming over as he has now such a large personal following in New York among amusing people of all kinds that he finds life vastly entertaining. He is called don Juan at present and any number of women are mad about him. Truly—truly!

. . . Ford has just called me up to say that if I am writing to you to "say all the nice things he wants to say." Well, he is happy and spoiled and neglects no opportunity to tell the great Amurrican public that Ezra Pound is the greatest living poet.

. . . I have been doing a little work and a little publicity for Ford. Let me know as soon as you decide to come over for I want to arrange some social things. You'll have to play that game a little. And I can do quite a lot that will sell your books. . . .

My family register about the same amount of invalidism but I am used to captivity.

How is the young O. Pound? I swear to you that I think of him every day

18. The letter in its entirety is published in Londraville and Londraville 1990, 197.

19. James Pond and Lee Keedick managed lecture agencies.

of my life—a baby I've never seen. I know you don't like to write about him but sacrifice yourself when you write again.

On 23 January 1927, Pound wrote again about a lecture series, mentioning lecture agent Lee Keedick:[20]

As to Kekeedik, not *some* money but a *LOT. A LOT.* I assure you the amusement side wd. Not come off. When it is a LOT and ABSOLUTELY assured, the question of duty (jewty as W. B. Y. wd. Call it) might arise.
. . . Tell Kekedikky, if you see him, that I have been known to stop the traffick in Piccadilly Circus simply by raising my voice. You understand, I seldom do raise it; but the vocal cords, evidently resemble those of the enraged gorilla.

Pound ultimately decided against the trip to America.

In the spring of 1927, Jeanne Foster took a final trip to England and France, primarily on art business for private clients. Although she was disappointed at being unable to see the Pounds, it was on this trip that Jeanne visited William Butler Yeats as she was passing through London:

When Yeats invited me, when I was in London in 1927, to dine with him and his sister Lily, of whom I was exceedingly fond, in a restaurant of their selection, he, curiously, left Lily at the restaurant and drove over . . . to fetch me . . . I had a remarkable psychic experience.
WB had a hansom waiting; . . . I felt he was thinking of Maud Gonne and almost oblivious of me so I asked him, as I have told you, what she was like.
I have told you what he said, without looking at me, that "Maud Gonne" was "like apple blossoms with the dew on them in May."
He did not go on talking after he had answered my question but bent a little forward over his cane, and seemed to be lost in thought.
I began to be aware of a psychic cloud, or atmosphere, a penetration from his mind, sensed my mind flowing, for all time as I have found, into that magnificence so far above and beyond me. I was aware of all his poetry and plays, compounded.

20. The letter is in the Foster-Murphy Collection (NYPL).

... I have never lost the interpenetration of my mind and spirit that to him of course was an unconscious gift. (JRF to RL, 14 July 1968, LC)

During her 1927 visit, Jeanne told Yeats she knew his family was a "last remnant of an ancient noble race with comprehension not known to men today, a disappearing race except for the few, who having perhaps lived in ancient times, remember dimly and record their memories." Yeats "remembered a part of the old heroic days in Ireland when he was an ancient bard." She was grateful that she had seen him in London, for she never had the opportunity again.[21]

Jeanne returned to New York to find her mother gravely ill. Lucia Oliver died on 25 June 1927. It was a period of intense mourning. Jeanne had lost her best friend, and the financial care of the family invalids now rested completely on her shoulders. On 2 September, she received a letter from Pound, suggesting "If . . . you are reprehensibly working fer a livink; or MORE reprhnsbly working for someone else's; you might both turn an honest (or dis-) double eagle from time to time acting as agent for several expotriotts." Pound, who was concerned about Jeanne's financial state, would assist her with acquiring these clients: "Not opening an office with overhead; but drawing comission on less' say Hemingway, McAlmon, and even me. If I have at last reached the stage of receiving royalties."[22] As usual, Pound filled the rest of the letter with various requests about publishers and about other possible sources of money.

On 8 October and 20 October 1927, Homer Pound, Ezra's father, wrote to Jeanne from his home in Philadelphia. He was confused, as she no doubt sometimes was herself, by various requests from his son. He had been working diligently to get Pound's prose published, as his son had asked, but now

My son has just informed me that you have agreed to act as his agent in the US. Therefore you and I will have to get together and understand just what

21. JRF reminisced to RL in letters dated 13 April 1970 and October 1967 (LC).

22. Robert Menzies McAlmon (1896–1956), American author and publisher. With his Contact Publishing Company, McAlmon was for a time the leading expatriate publisher in Paris.

he wants done. Not having been aware that he had made any arrangement with any one but his Dad, I have already started . . . getting his prose works *published*. . . .

Ezra tells me I am to let you know what I have done. Please write me, what steps you have taken about it. (8 October, NYPL)

Jeanne said that Mr. Pound was upset. Her friend Ezra sometimes asked several people to do the same thing for him. But she had nothing but praise for Pound's father, who had shown her special kindness shortly after John Quinn's death, when she stayed with Homer and Mrs. Pound for a few days in Pennsylvania. He was sometimes frustrated with his son, but so was everyone who dealt with Ezra Pound.

On 31 July 1928, Pound sent Jeanne a list of ten questions and asked if she might "haff . . . any adwice or any adwices about any of the following matters, or are you bored stiff with all the lot or part of the lot of said subjects." They ranged from inquiries about Ford Madox Ford to "nooz of dear Horace [Liveright]" to a request for information about publisher Pascal Covici, inquiring if Jeanne thought it might be wise to court Covici for Pound's purposes.

She had already had some dealings with Covici because of her brief association with musician George Antheil.[23] A year earlier, she had investigated the publisher at Pound's request and had found him to be reputable. Pound had then arranged for Antheil to meet Jeanne, telling her that he was a "remarkable new violin." Antheil himself had written to Jeanne on 16 February 1927, scheduling a meeting with her, giving her his New York address, and expressing his great hope to see her as soon as he arrived from Europe (LC). They did meet, and she introduced him to several of her literary contacts. Although she never mentioned that she was specifically involved in Covici's 1927 edition of Pound's *Antheil and the Treatise on Harmony, with Supplementary Notes* it is likely that she was once again a facilitator.[24]

In the same 31 July 1928 letter, Pound also asked Jeanne for some advice regarding his new literary journal *Exile*: "IF I put Bill Wms' and Zukofsky in

23. Pascal Covici (1885–1964), American publisher and editor. George Antheil (1900–1959), American operatic composer.

24. JRF, interviewed by RL, 11 April 1967.

charge of N.Y. editing end. wd. there be any necessity of six or ten intelligent people in N.Y. meeting every month or so, and discussing the USE of next issue to promote general vivacity or bearability of vie licheraire etc. in the neighborhood."[25]

There is no way to know if Jeanne Foster answered Pound, and this is the last letter extant from him to her until 1956. By then, the years had changed them. Yeats and Ford, such close friends to both, were dead, and World War II had torn apart the world again. Pound, charged with "giving . . . aid and comfort" to enemies of the United States during World War II, had lived for more than ten years in St. Elizabeths Hospital in Washington, D.C., judged by psychiatrists to be "mentally unfit to advise properly with counsel."[26] Jeanne was by 1956 seventy-seven years old. She considered her time on this earth limited and began to plan a few projects—some important work yet to be finished from the old days: John Butler Yeats's biography, her Adirondack poetry collection, something more about John Quinn.

With a synchronicity that Jeanne attributed to an "awakening of spirits," Aline Saarinen contacted her to say that she was doing a book, *The Proud Possessors*, about famous American art collectors. She wanted to talk to Jeanne about John Quinn. Knowing that Saarinen would need to meet Ezra Pound, Jeanne sat down at her desk on 4 October 1956 in Schenectady and wrote to her old friend at St. Elizabeths: "Dear Ezra, This is the long lost and forgotten Jeanne Foster writing. Immured as a social worker to support the various members of my family (now all deceased except one), I was vowed to silence. To bring back even to mind the friends and happiness of former years gave me such pain that I wrote to no one" (McDowell 1984, I-12).

She told him of her plans, of Saarinen's book, and asked for his help. He replied on 6 and 7 October and 8 November: "FERgotten !! me foot !!! Having made various efforts to trace yu, etcettyroar. but never able to do so. An yu aint vurry visible in the pale print. I spose my letters to J.Q. are legally MINE so far as printing 'em is concerned, and that I could free them for publication whatever stuffiness J.Q.'s bloody biGoted sister might have wished or does wish" (6 October).

25. Louis Zukofsky (1904–78), American author.
26. The Grand Jury and the psychiatrists are quoted in Norman 1960, 405, 411.

Characteristically, after filling her in on news of friends and family, he asked her a favor: "Can yu make the local lieBURY scribe to 'Edge' . . . Of course IF there were ADULT acquaintances of J.Q. left . . they cd / be useful." And about Saarinen's proposal: "phrase 'great art collectors.' Most of 'em mere accumulators stuffed-shirts with money. Quinn was a reality." Pound wanted to help her, especially with the John Quinn material:

> Grampaw's mind moves slowly/ butt IF yo aint got no pension a twist of the wrist might mobilize a bit of frozen asset/ Paige [*sic:* Dr. Denys Page] did fine job with my letters/ published cause there was a frog in the firm and didn't know that the filth of kikery which J.Q. so admired, wouldn't want 'em printed.
>
> BUTT . . . there is no reason why Jeanne with a twist of the writst shdn't put out a nize li'l vol of Letters from Poet to Bank Lawyer.[27]
>
> There must be enuf for a vol/ esp with the N. Age art / 1 that opened the correspondence / and J.Q's first, which if his BLOODY Schwester wont release/ could be summarized / i.e. I wd/ write my recollection of what it contained. i. e. saying he suspected I had him in mind when I sd/ buggar the bastids that buy dead men's woikz from dealers/
>
> And J.Q. sayin he wuz gittin off it, and buying from the living.
>
> . . . You might propose the idea to New Directions, 333 Sixth Av. N.Y. 14.
>
> . . . Any how tell No Directions bout the Quinn being held up/ and that we need noise to spring grampaw (after eleven years, and Admiral Donetz etc.) Naturally dumb buzzards who don't know the score are innocuous, etc.
>
> J.Q. wd/ have had me out of here ten years ago. etc. Thatzz one trouble, knowing no adults in this defiled country.
>
> . . . All yu shd/ write to New Directions is statement that the letters are of interest/ that they have been too lonng buried/ that they are not in Paige's collection, cause E.P. files date only from Rapallo.
>
> And that you "believe" a satisfactory HHHarrangement can be made with E.P.

Jeanne wrote back, telling Pound that hearing from him "was like living again." "Dear Ezra, I am old," she wrote. "You are not so much 'grandpaw' as

---

27. The letters were finally published as *Selected Letters of Ezra Pound to John Quinn, 1915–1924* (Pound 1991).

I am 'grandmaw.' I haven't much gray hair but the years have slowed me down" (McDowell 1984, I-12). Pound was intrigued by the Saarinen book and thought of ways the famous journalist might be able to help contemporary artists that he knew: "All right, let Mrs Saarinen get a good fellowship for Sheri Martinelli one of thse piffling and stincgking Foundations which always give support to the unfit, and boycott EVERYTHING of any value" (8 November).[28]

The letters written between 15 January 1957 and 4 December 1957 are disjointed and touch on many subjects, in no particular order. Pound wrote about *Edge*, about an old manuscript of his that Jeanne had kept safe for him, about a planned publication of Gaudier-Brzeska papers,[29] about senators "cowering in terror," and about getting rights for his letters to Quinn to help Jeanne with a publication. On 18 May, he told her about a visit from Saarinen: "La Saarinen arriv/ you didn't tell me her husband is one of the FEW architects. She was to have come back, but hasn't showed. I wonder, can it be yet AGAIN/ al that chaRRm . . . and merely the journalist technique . . got data re/ J.Q. as they do, just what they can use for their own job/ ." And then, sadly, he added, "yu think you have made a friend for life and then they Evaporate."

On 4 December 1957, Pound responded to a letter from Jeanne in which she had expressed concern about the future of art. From the time of her early work on the *Review of Reviews*, she felt that the worth of a nation could be measured, at least in part, by the support it gave to its living artists. Pound felt the same and was always angry at the neglect: "Yes these bastardly Foundations will raise monuments but they will do NOTHING for living artists who aren't working for hire / they wdn't give Gaudier 3 cents if he were alive to day. they do nothing to get me out of quod after gornoze how long . . . country governed in terrorem of a few punks like Javits, Eug Meyer and Winchell."[30]

---

28. Sheri Martinelli (1918–96), American poet, painter, and model.

29. Ezra Pound, *Gaudier-Brzeska, with a Vortex Manifesto* (Milano: V. Scheiwiller, 1957).

30. Jacob Koppel Javits (1904–86), American politician, senator from New York (1957–80). Eugene Isaac Meyer (1875–1959), investment banker, government official, and newspaper publisher. Walter Winchell (1897–1972), American journalist in newspaper, radio, and television.

On 3 April 1958, Jeanne Foster decided that she had to do something about Pound's incarceration at St. Elizabeths. She was certain that he was not dangerous, and the country needed to free one of its own greatest poets. The imprisonment of art—or of a symbol of that art—was sacrilege to her. She wrote to J. Walter Yeagley, acting assistant attorney general at the U.S. Department of Justice, detailing her case, "as if J. Q. were looking over my shoulder," she said. She received a reply from Yeagley on 16 April, thanking her for communicating her views. He did not indicate that any action would be taken.[31]

In the meantime, on 14 April, a motion was filed in U. S. District Court to dismiss the thirteen-year-old indictment that had kept Pound from his freedom. This motion was supported by statements from prominent writers and poets, including Robert Frost. Representative Usher L. Bendich of North Dakota introduced a bill calling for a review of the case. Attorney General William P. Rogers was overheard saying, "Is there any point in keeping [Pound] there if he never can be tried?" (qtd. in Norman 1960, 454–55).

With his wife Dorothy and son Omar in the courtroom, Ezra Pound was granted his release on 18 April. For a time, he returned to his family home in Pennsylvania:

> At Wyncote, last, a summer night in 1958, St. Elizabeths freshly behind him, in bed in his old house for the last time (and aged 72), he had somehow wakened—always a brief sleeper; genius enjoys long days—and tiptoed downstairs in his pajamas, out into the dark street, and down to the Presbyterian Church, to sit on its steps looking over the moonlit lawns of great estates: sitting where a boy had sat 60 years before, his eye on trees before dawn, his mind on a poet's destiny, which should be that of dreaming old men's silences. . . .
> The man knew he had been beaten; the poet knew
>> That I lost my center
>> Fighting the world
>> The dreams clash
>> And are shattered— (Kenner 1971, 556)

---

31. JRF, interviewed by RL, 15 July 1969. Yeagley's letter is in LC.

Before many weeks had passed, Dorothy and Ezra Pound boarded a ship for Italy.

On 29 April 1960, Pound wrote to Jeanne from Rapallo. The letter suggests that other letters had been written ("if you must reprint the Wyncote affair can't you remove sentimental gosh or let me see article before inflicting"). He had read about Dr. Peter Kavanaugh, who intended to publish some of Quinn's letters without the permission of his heirs or of the New York Public Library, and he told Jeanne, who worked tirelessly to prevent the publication, that there was "no indication the bloke used any of those to me."[32]

Although the letter does not survive, Jeanne wrote to Pound in 1966 to arrange a meeting between him and William M. Murphy during Dr. Murphy's trip to Italy. Pound responded graciously that he would be happy to meet the man who was writing the biography of "the father of all the Yeatsssssss." Here is Murphy's story:

At the time [Pound] wouldn't see anyone, and people protected him. We had an automobile and went straight to Rapallo. He wrote to us in Rome and said that he would like to meet with my wife and me, but we never got the letter. We were already in Rapallo when it arrived. We were told he lived at Ambrogio, and we asked around for his residence but were told that he was away. There was a kind of "conspiracy of silence"—of protection. We stayed two or three days. During that time we met an old woman who needed some assistance. We were only too happy to help. She invited us to a party. I remember that it was held on a big balcony. One of her friends who was there was a friend of Pound. When she asked what we were doing in Venice, we told her of our disappointment. "I know Pound very well," she said. He's in Venice having some dental work done." So off we went to Venice in search of the poet, and there we found him. I remember how we were greeted by Olga Rudge. "Oh, Mr. Pound wanted to meet you because Jeanne Foster had written to him. If you are a friend of hers, he will have great pleasure in meeting you."

When I talked to Pound, he immediately asked me about Jeannie. He wanted to know all about how she was and what she was doing.[33]

32. See Bunzel 1960.
33. Murphy, interviewed by RL and JL, 9 June 1998, Schenectady, N.Y.

William M. Murphy and Ezra Pound in Venice, 1966. Photograph by Harriet Murphy. William M. Murphy private collection.

Murphy told a *New York Times* reporter in 1984 that Jeanne Foster was "a name which opens doors" (McDowell 1984, I-12). As a memento of the Rapallo occasion, Mrs. Murphy took a picture of her husband and Pound to give to Jeanne.

By the following year (1967), Jeanne was more infirm, and though she still enjoyed short visits from old friends, and though she tried her best to keep up her correspondence, her energy was waning. She had a few Adirondack poems left to finish and saved most of her time for them.[34] A newspaper report quoted part of a letter Jeanne had written to Pound in 1963:

> By now [1963] [Mrs. Foster] was virtually alone, for . . . she wrote again to Ezra Pound, saying, "I do not have a living relative; I have outlived them all." She also told the ailing poet, who meanwhile had undergone a number of surgical operations: "Looking at the pictures that I have in my collection of the Quinn days, I can hardly imagine you changed. I remember you as a very beautiful human being, one that I admired and loved. I hope the future years will treat you kindly." (McDowell 1984, I-12)

These are the last extant words from a correspondence that began during that glorious summer in Paris in 1921.

Her dear friend Ezra? In Rapallo, an old, tired poet. Hugh Kenner ends the story: "His mind on Carpaccio, on cats and stones, on butterflies visitors brought, on faces present and gone, on his own past; shrunken, slight,

34. JRF chose the titles "Adirondack Trail" and, on another occasion, "The Lost Breed" for her Adirondack book, but it was never published. Many of the poems for this book were later collected and edited by Noel Riedinger-Johnson for *AP* (JRF to Ruth Riedinger, 20 January 1960 [MC]).

no more weight than he had had half-grown, long ago, in Wyncote, he shouldered the weariness of [eighty-three] years, his resource memory within memory within memory" (1971, 560–61).

But once, this strange genius had "got his tweezers on the subject" (555).

Ezra Pound died in 1972. He was the last survivor of a group that had changed the direction of modern literature.

# 14

# The Schenectady Years

## 1928—1970

BY 1928, IT WAS GETTING DIFFICULT for Jeanne Robert Foster to maintain her life in New York City, away from her aging father and husband. Her brother Elwyn was also living at home. Although he was able to work as a salesman in a local bookstore, he suffered from chronic heart trouble. At the age of thirty-eight, he died on 11 May 1932.

In the late 1920s and early 1930s, Jeanne could still sell her writing, but not for enough to support a household, and her career as a model was effectively over. She was occasionally called on to edit articles, to promote people such as Pound, and to give readings of her work. One reading was on 20 May 1928, at a Howard University memorial service for journalist John E. Milholland.[1]

Jeanne's friendship with Milholland began early in her journalistic career and was amplified by the admiration they had for each other's dedication to social concerns. One story Jeanne told was about a dinner she and Milholland shared on 20 October 1918. During the meal, a drunk made things extremely unpleasant. Milholland had several African American friends who frequently visited his home, and the drunk was upset that a white man would demean himself by entertaining such company. Milholland became angry and was particularly distressed that Jeanne's evening had been ruined. But she used the occasion to write a humorous lyric, and she sent it to Milholland the next day, hoping to cheer him. He was delighted: "When I recall the bitterness of Saturday night's disappointment in re that . . . drunk, I

---

1. John Milholland (1869–1925) was a journalist with the *New York Herald Tribune* for twelve years.

am deeply doubly sensible of your goodness in sending me those bits of . . .
verse this morning! . . . To be soothed and sobered up by Sappho! . . . To
be 'soothed and sobered up by Sappho' is a darn good bit of Swinburnian-
ism, Jeannie Foster, and be sure you realize the fact" (letter, 22 October
1918, LC).

Always a proponent of equal rights, Milholland had supported his wife
and daughter in their fight for suffrage. Mrs. Jean Torry Milholland had
won recognition in 1910 when she published an article in the NAACP-
sponsored magazine *The Crisis*, encouraging African American women to
join the suffrage movement.[2]

Milholland's daughter, Inez Milholland Boissevain, had become one of
this nation's most ardent and effective leaders of the suffrage movement.
Tragically, she died in 1916 after giving an impassioned speech in Los An-
geles. Near the end of her talk, she "collapsed from the rigors of the cam-
paign, dramatically calling out for votes for women as she fell" (Boissevain
1998). She died on 25 November and became a martyr for the cause. She is
buried at Meadow Mount near Elizabethtown, New York, not far from
Chestertown. Her father had carried on the fight. At a memorial service for
several suffragettes in Washington, D.C., in 1923, where Edna St. Vincent
Millay read her commemorative poem "The Pioneer," organizers had indi-
cated that African Americans were allowed to attend but not to speak.[3] In
the middle of the ceremony, Milholland had interrupted:

> I feel a duty to speak out. If I did not [I] think her spirit would rise up from the
> grave and say to me, "Dad, why were you afraid?"
>
> And so I want to remind you that in the first suffrage parade, Inez herself
> demanded that the colored women be allowed to march, and now today we
> were told that it would mar the program to have these guests of mine speak.

2. The article is reproduced on the SUNY–Binghamton web site (27 March 1998):
http://www.womhist.binghamton.edu/webdbtw/Doc9.htm. Jean Torry Milholland (1862–
1939), American political activist for equal rights among women of all colors.

3. Millay read her poem on 18 November 1923 at the unveiling of a statue of three suf-
fragettes (Lucretia Mott, Susan B. Anthony, and Elizabeth Cady Stanton). In *Collected Sonnets*
(New York and London: Harper and Bros., 1941), Millay dedicated "The Pioneers" to Inez
Boissevain. Millay married Boissevain's husband, Eugen, in 1923.

I have nothing to say except that Inez believed in equal rights for everybody. (qtd. in Boissevain 1998)

At that moment, Jeanne Foster had never been more proud of her friend, and she had promised herself that she, too, would not be afraid.

And so it was that she honored Milholland with a poem after he was gone, as she had done for so many other friends. At that ceremony in 1928, Jeanne could not have known how much her friend's ideals would bolster her resolve in the years to come.

Jeanne resigned from the *Review of Reviews* in 1927, although letters between her and Shaw indicate that she continued to do some writing for him.[4] She had offered to resign twice before, in 1914 and 1922, and though the 1922 resignation may have ended a formal contract with the *Review*, Albert Shaw continued to provide her with assignments. Not until Matlack and her father died and Albert Shaw remarried did she sever her ties completely. By the mid-1930s, the *Review* was in the process of merging with the *Literary Digest*. The magazine to which she had dedicated so many years disappeared.

From 1928 until the late 1930s, Jeanne worked on the New York State Constitutional Convention with Dr. George R. Lunn in Albany, researching and writing summaries of past conventions.[5] She had served as a part-time aide to Lunn during his years as mayor of Schenectady (1912–14, 1916–18, and 1920–23), and Lucia Oliver had been one of his staunchest supporters. In 1912, he had been elected mayor on the Socialist ticket, but later had left that party to become a Democrat and was reelected several times. In 1916, Jeanne had considered running against him on the Socialist ticket, and although there was some publicity in the local paper about a probable contest, she decided against it.[6]

4. In several letters to various friends, JRF wrote that she resigned from the *Review of Reviews* in 1922, but in a *Schenectady Gazette* article, 27 May 1970, she said that she worked until 1927, which seems more likely, considering the content of Albert Shaw's letters to her.

5. George R. Lunn (1873–1948), New York State politician.

6. The information about JRF's working life, unless otherwise noted, is taken from a series of interviews of JRF by RL in the summer of 1969, dated 10 July through 15 August.

For two years, from 1930 to 1932, she also was employed part time (every Tuesday) for the head of the state police in the Schenectady area, Dr. Bradley Kirschberg. It was Jeanne's job to proofread and edit the state police bulletin. During the same period, she worked in the Woodlawn area of Schenectady as a lady on the block, as she had done so many years before in New York City. She was still making periodic trips, though more and more infrequently, to her apartment in New York City.

In the summer months, when schedule permitted, Jeanne liked to spend time at the Foster cottage in Higgins Beach, Maine. In the *Portland Sunday Telegram* of 11 May 1930, the reporter mentioned that Jeanne Foster, a part-time resident of some note, was making the family cottage "ready" for her invalid sister, Mrs. Theodore H. Smith (Cara Oliver). He quoted Jeanne:

> I love Maine—sister and I fell in love with it years ago when we both came down here on a visit. I remember it was in the summertime and we happened on Scarboro Beach and we were perfectly thrilled with the ruggedness and the wild beauty of the beach. That's how we happened to buy this little place.
>
> . . . No other seacoast, not the wild shores of Cornwall, not the red sands of Devon, nor the cliffs of the Riviera—can equal the seacoast of Maine with its hundreds of miles of inlets, beaches, capes, and promontories. (L. P. Crowley 1930, 20)

By 1933, Jeanne had sold the cottage and felt that it was time to give up her apartment in New York City. With one sister married and in California (Fanette was now Mrs. Irving) and with her brother Elwyn, Matlack Foster, and Frank Oliver all deceased, Jeanne was now the widowed and ill Cara's sole support. This situation concerned some of Jeanne's friends, to whom she recounted her responsibilities. Henri-Pierre Roché, wishing her free of family and economic burdens, wrote to her about Cara in 1937: "I can not like her, from memory, any more than John [Quinn] did, and can not feel your huge duty towards her, who appeared to me material, selfish, limited—while you could do so much to others in the world needing your soul's and your hands' company or help" (23 December, NYPL).

Jeanne continued her editorial work, but the jobs were not lucrative enough, and when they began to disappear, she knew she had to find steady employment. Mr. James McDonald, active in Democratic politics in the area, asked her to take the exam for tenant relations counselor with the Schenectady Municipal Housing Authority (MHA) because he was impressed with her previous work of surveying housing in the British Isles for the *Review*. In order to prepare herself more fully for her job, she spent part of one summer (1938) in Glens Falls, taking a course in psychology. Relying on her experience as a social worker in New York City and in Schenectady, she passed the test and began working for the MHA in 1938. After being a model, actress, journalist, art agent, and editor, Jeanne began yet another career at the age of fifty-nine.

The Schenectady MHA was the first such authority established in New York State under Roosevelt's New Deal. In the 1930s, the federal government became more involved in many Americans' lives, and social welfare was no longer the sole responsibility of local areas, some of which could not afford to help their own residents. Jeanne's job was to work with families on the public housing rolls, specifically to "watch over" them, interview them, and guide them. She did just that for seventeen years.

One day in 1947, when housing was in short supply in Schenectady, Jeanne was suddenly reminded of John Milholland. A young man asked for her help, not for himself but for his African American brothers and sisters who desperately needed housing. James Stamper was a local resident and a member of the NAACP. It had been brought to his attention that the MHA was having more than the usual difficulty in finding places for people of color. Jeanne told him that she was determined to find answers. Mr. Stamper was surprised:

I expected her to defend the Authority and say, "We've done the best we could; there is no room," but no. Jeanne Foster helped us. She told me that there were some units available. "If you have someone, send him to me," she insisted, and we did and helped people move to better housing. Mrs. Foster was resolute and didn't allow anyone to stop her from doing something she thought was right. She was a strong lady who would not cower when faced with opposition. From that time on, all the rest of the Municipal Housing Authority buildings became integrated, black with white. Mrs. Foster was a great defender of the truth, and I've lived with the memory of that special woman my whole life.[7]

Jeanne's work with the MHA also included lobbying for more low-income housing projects, specifically for the elderly, and establishing the first "Golden Age Club" in 1947 at Schonowee Village, one of the projects. The club was a popular feature for older citizens, and, as it grew, transformed itself into the Schenectady Senior Citizens' Center, a dynamic part of the community. Jeanne's role in making Schonowee a success was remembered in 1959, when the MHA celebrated the twenty-fifth year of its founding by republishing in its commemorative magazine a poem Jeanne had written for Executive Director John MacGathan. She had read the verse, titled "The Laird O' Schonowee" at Schonowee's opening ceremony in 1938.

During these years, Jeanne was not completely divorced from an intellectual life. She maintained correspondence with several scholars during the 1930s and 1940s, most notably Frank Cheney Hersey, an old friend from her Harvard days. They were still in touch as late as 1947, writing long, friendly letters filled with verse each had composed for the other. Jeanne was understandably pleased when, quite coincidentally, a young man who had been Hersey's composition student at Harvard in 1938, Dr. William M. Murphy, became her supervisor for a time at the Municipal Housing Authority.

Jeanne retired from the MHA in 1955. Her sister Fanette, who had been living for many years in California, was widowed and ill with a bad heart and a deteriorating mental condition. Once again Jeanne Foster was called on to be a nursemaid. One of Jeanne's coworkers at the MHA said that when Fan returned to Schenectady "dressed to the hilt" and exhibiting "airs," Jeanne was "most seriously displeased."[8] The prospect of living with Fan was not appealing. Jeanne had been responsible for sister Cara for a

7. James Stamper, the NAACP representative, approximated the date. Stamper, interviewed by RL and JL, 26 September 1998, Schenectady, N.Y.

8. Josephine Vrooman, interviewed by RL and JL, 26 September 1998, Schenectady, N.Y.

number of years, until Cara's death in 1947, but Cara had been gone for a long time, and Jeanne had become accustomed to being alone, except for the friendship and assistance of her housekeeper, Sarah Washington. Jeanne told her difficulties to Ezra Pound: "If my heart were sound, I could risk more in the way of work. Then my particular household is antagonistic. My sister lived 27 years in the west (L. A.) and following the death of her husband, came to live with me. The 27 years had been years of mental divergence. I met a stranger when she came and although we must—since we are the last of the clan, make a go of it, the path of everyday living is difficult for me just now" (November 1956).[9]

Even during these difficult years, she found time to write and teach. After she met Aline Saarinen in 1956, she experienced a reawakening of spirit, as she confessed to Pound on 4 October 1956: "I dared to look back, I began writing verse again. It seemed to take my mind. . . . I also joined a poetry group, and sometime this winter I have to give a talk . . . on you" (letter, NYPL). The renaissance, as Jeanne called the last years of her life, had begun.

The time with Fan ended as suddenly as it had begun. Jeanne wrote to Murphy on 11 December 1959, not long after her sister died: "I am late in thanking you for your instant sympathy and your call at my home. It was a great shock to have my sister drop dead at the telephone desk moments after we were chatting. She had been in [such] danger since last May that sometimes it seems—as I look back—as if I had not slept peacefully for months. . . . It was as we expected—a second coronary occlusion."[10] Jeanne herself was ill at the time because of torn muscles from a "slide" (not a fall, she said) in her garden. She was nearing the end of her eightieth year.

But all was not sadness in 1959. Jeanne was voted Schenectady's Senior Citizen of the Year. The citation applauded her work as a tenant counselor, as chairperson of the Housing Committee of the Senior Citizens' Center, and as the doer of many "unheralded acts of private sympathy by which you, gracious, charming, and kindly, have lightened so many a dark room;

9. A copy of the undated letter from JRF to Pound is in LC. A copy is also in the Foster-Murphy Collection, NYPL.

10. Fanette Irving died on 13 November 1959.

and as a writer whose role in the development of leading artists was unsung but immeasurable."[11]

Jeanne also became an active member of the Schenectady branch of Zonta, a service organization of executive women that promotes education and helps those less fortunate through programs such as Meals-on-Wheels. In an interview on 7 October 1997, one of her Zonta friends, Elizabeth Sarnowski, recalled Jeanne's energy: "Her heart and soul was in everything. Even when she was ill, her spirit was there. I never knew anyone who didn't like her. I don't know how she could make an enemy. Her personality and her wit were exceptional."[12]

By the time 1959 ended, Jeanne's friendship with Aline Saarinen was growing stronger, and other scholars were beginning to visit her in Schenectady. Jeanne had recently received a letter from critic John Ciardi, asking if she might accompany him to Chestertown in the spring to visit John Butler Yeats's grave site. He sent her as well an autographed copy of his latest book.[13] Warder H. Cadbury of Boston University asked to consult with her about Native North American chief Sabael, about whom Jeanne had written a poem in *Neighbors of Yesterday*.[14] And, most exciting to her, there began to be rumors about a biography of John Quinn.

As a new year dawned, Jeanne concerned herself again with the lives of Schenectady's senior citizens. She knew that many older people loved poetry but did not often have the opportunity to share it with one another, so she arranged to teach classes at the Senior Center, a job that continued in the mid-1960s. Even as late as 1964, she continued her classes and edited a book of poems and prose collected from her students. But in December she was slowed when illness struck. The Zonta bulletin reported: "Our Jeannie is going to be a shut in for a while. She 'prowled and wrote and ran,' thinking she was 30 years old before Christmas—the result—a meeting with her doctors and two heart attacks. She reports 'milk toast' holiday celebrations,

11. A copy of the citation, which was written by Murphy, is in MC.

12. Sarnowski, interviewed by RL and JL, 27 September 1998, Burnt Hills, N.Y.

13. John Ciardi (1916–86), American poet and critic. The book he sent JRF was *I Marry You, A Sheaf of Love Poems* (New Brunswick, N. J.: Rutgers University Press, 1958). JRF mentioned Ciardi's gift and proposed visit in a letter to Murphy, 11 December 1959 (MC).

14. JRF, interviewed in the *Schenectady Gazette*, 19 March 1958, 16.

but we note that she still has her unquenchable spirit" (Zonta 1965, January, n.p.).

In 1998, one of Jeanne's former Senior Center poetry students was the subject of an article in the 29 January *Albany Times Union*. Alice Wheeler was still writing verse at the age of one hundred. When she heard about the Jeanne Foster biography project, she wrote:

> I first met Jeanne Robert Foster when I was in my 60's and she was in her low 80's. I had only recently moved from the New York metropolitan area to Schenectady where I had joined the Senior Center and was enjoying singing with the Goldenaires. One day when I was walking to the Center I composed a limerick. When I walked into the Center, I recited it to Tillie Kaplan, who was Joe Mosarra's [the director] Assistant Director. She said, "You should be in Jeanne Foster's poetry class."
>
> So I did join the class. There was a room full of people—nearly twenty, I think. But the one person whose charisma filled the entire room was Jeanne. It was evident immediately that every other person in the room adored her. She had a sort of erect and regal bearing that set her apart from common clay.
>
> She had set herself quite a task—teaching poetry writing to a group whose educational background ranged from the woman who asked, "What is an adjective?" to a man who wrote a villanelle. She was very patient with her students. She arranged for an evening program where we read our poems before an audience and had the pleasure of hearing their applause. She also published a volume of our poems in each of two years before she finally retired due to failing health.
>
> I kept in touch with Jeanne at Christmas time until her death. She sent me copies of her poems from time to time, including, "Let Me Go to the Heaven Where the Birds Are." And I, now at the age of 100, still cherish my memories of a beautiful, gracious lady.[15]

A sadder tale is told by William M. Murphy. One member of the Schenectady Poetry Society thought he had an abundance of talent but, sadly, did not. His ego blinded him to this fact, and he decided that Jeanne would be the perfect person to help him hone his genius. She tried as best she

---

15. Wheeler to JL, 10 March 1997.

could to teach him the basic technical elements—meter, rhyme, rhythm, form—but he was hopeless. His work was rejected everywhere. He became enraged at editors and made no secret of what he thought of them in several letters to the local paper.

Finally, the man grew old and infirm and, because his wife was also ill, had nowhere to go but to the county home. When he died, she was unable to attend the funeral. Only Dr. Murphy and Jeanne Foster were in attendance. There was perhaps no more unlovable man in the world, but Jeanne still found something admirable in his own personal struggle to be a human being.[16]

Although the mayor of Schenectady did not know about Jeanne's kindness to the poet manqué whose funeral she had attended or of other "unheralded acts of private sympathy," he knew about much of her work and felt that she deserved even a higher recognition than Senior Citizen of the Year. On October 1961, she received Schenectady's highest honor when Mayor Malcolm Ellis made her an honorary Patroon.

A month earlier, on 10 September 1961, she had received a letter that made her think again of another time. It was from her old friend Dorothy Pound, who reminisced: "I just find it hard to connect myself with other, far off, days—J. Q. in our studio in Paris. . . . What a chaos is this world now" (NYPL).

Jeanne by now had begun corresponding with John Quinn's niece, Mary Anderson Conroy. The acquaintance was, for a time, uncomfortable. Jeanne naturally felt proprietary about Quinn. After all, she had known him better than any person still living in 1959, including his niece, who was now a grown woman with a family of her own. For years, no one had paid much attention to Quinn, and Jeanne had worked more diligently than anyone in his family to preserve his memory and his papers. But with Saarinen's book on the market, Mary Conroy was becoming interested. Jeanne wrote to Saarinen on 22 June 1961 about a pleasant day with Mrs. Conroy and her husband, who were on their way to Maine from California for a vacation. They visited with her in Schenectady and then drove her to Chestertown to see John Butler Yeats's grave site: "The old cemetery was peaceful with its evergreens and white birches and when we left the car and

16. Murphy, interviewed by RL and JL, 11 June 1998, Schenectady, N.Y.

the monument could be seen, Mary was quite moved as she was a kind of pet granddaughter—as it were—to the old man. We carried pink and yellow roses that I had in my garden and 'Rock Flower,' as I wanted Dr. Conroy to read the tribute which he did as we stood by the grave" (NYPL).

The day seemed to go well, but eight months later Jeanne remembered other events from the same visit and complained to Saarinen:

> Dr. and Mrs. Conroy came out here—on their way to Maine . . . and were agreeable. They asked me for things I never had, one J. Q.'s diary. I told them I was not aware that he kept one.[17] . . . I asked them what became of the great mass of letters that I returned to the estate (Out of 500 to JQ from John Butler Yeats, I used only fifty. There were hundreds from Pound; I included only a few of the most informative). My question was not answered. Before they left, Dr. Conroy asked me if he might walk around the house and look at things. His quick glance darted here and there and instantly I was JQ's legal investigator again. There was SOMETHING they wanted, thought I had [it] and searched to find. After they returned, they asked for my notebooks. Except for the last tragic weeks, my notebooks contained—purposely—nothing about JQ. Then, Dr. and Mrs. Conroy wrote asking me to dictate memoirs of my association with JQ. Naturally I refused. I offered them Kodak films but I wrote that after all these years I could not be sure of accuracy and that I was certain JQ would not wish me to do anything of the kind. I did not hear from them until last week although I sent cards at Christmas. Naturally, I concluded that they were angry. Last Sunday . . . Mary called me by telephone from Hillsborough, Cal. and apologized for her silence. . . . She said nothing about her requests. . . . I understand how you feel about it now; it is all in a lost world. (1 February 1962, NYPL)

Mary Conroy was being cautious about giving approval for John Quinn's biography, and she wasn't certain that Saarinen, who planned one, would be the best person to undertake it. Jeanne was perturbed. She wrote to Mrs.

---

17. JQ kept a diary of his 1911 trip to Europe. Thomas Conroy, JQ's grandnephew, sent a copy of the diary to JL in 1995 and told her that his parents had gotten it back from B. L. Reid. JRF must have given it to Reid because JQ's diary is noted in the Londraville catalog of JRF's collection (LC). Excerpts from the diary were published in 1996. See Quinn 1996.

Conroy on 30 December 1958: "I believe that if John's biography is written, Aline Saarinen should be the one to prepare it. When you have read the data in regard to what she has done, when you have read 'The Proud Possessors,' you can have little doubt that she would create a very fine biography" (NYPL).

When Jeanne wrote to Saarinen, she was not always fair to Mary Conroy. She was perhaps trying to show her loyalty. Jeanne did so more than once during her lifetime of letter writing. Sometimes she would express the greatest of admiration to a friend but in a note to someone else complain about the very thing she had complimented. Her letters to Mrs. Conroy were pleasant, and Mrs. Conroy's to her were always amiable and never accusatory, with long, detailed reports not only about John Quinn, but also about other things that would interest Jeanne. In one of the first letters, dated 15 January 1959, she mused:

> You speak of being old but you know I can't imagine you as being anything other than beautiful—young or old. I used to love to look at you—and remember particularly one rather honey-amber colored dress you wore with which you had lovely topaz jewels. Mrs. Saarinen told me you were very handsome when she saw you and we both spoke of your magnificent eyes. I don't think many people realize the terrific amount of admiration a growing, gangly girl feels for a beautiful woman. (NYPL)

It is true that Mary Conroy thought Jeanne Foster had John Quinn's diaries and had perhaps forgotten about them; she also believed for many years that Jeanne had the original manuscript to Eliot's *The Waste Land*. Dr. Thomas Conroy, or "Frank" (as he preferred to be called), thought so, too. But one day he found out how mistaken he was.

Mary had inherited a large packing box full of miscellaneous papers from Quinn. Several times while moving to different homes during the early years of their marriage, Dr. Conroy had silently cursed as he hauled the heavy box from one place to another. His wife had insisted that they keep it, however, because of her sentimental attachment to her uncle.

One day while rummaging through the papers in the hope of finding something to justify all his heavy lifting, Frank found a handsome leather slipcase and thought it might be an attractive accent on his living room coffee table. He placed it there with a cursory glance at its contents, which seemed to him a typescript covered with illegible notes.

At about that time, Dr. Conroy was preparing to leave on sabbatical from Stanford, and he agreed to rent his house to an English professor for the year. He knew the man had young children, and so he locked in a spare room his collection of HO railroad cars and track.

When he returned to Stanford after his sabbatical, the English professor informed him that although Frank had been careful to safeguard his toys, he had left the only manuscript copy of *The Waste Land* unprotected on his coffee table.

Dr. Conroy enjoyed telling this story on himself, and he loved the reaction he got from academics, who invariably cringed when they learned how *The Waste Land* had almost become scrap paper.[18]

At the time when Jeanne was first becoming acquainted with the Conroys, two of her closest Schenectady friends, Tex and Ruth Riedinger, decided to issue a reprint of *Neighbors of Yesterday* (1963). Aline Saarinen had first suggested the project in a 10 September 1960 letter and had offered her assistance. But when Eero Saarinen died in the fall of 1961, Aline Saarinen's life was forever changed, and she could no longer help Jeanne in the same way. The Riedingers produced an exact facsimile, expertly printed. Although they did not have the opportunity to advertise the book nationally, it sold well in New York State and particularly well in the Adirondacks, where stories of the old days were becoming of great interest to historians and preservationists.

After her husband's death, Aline Saarinen canceled her own plans for a Quinn biography. But in 1962, the rumors about someone else writing it became fact, and Jeanne felt that at last her work to preserve Quinn's papers and letters would be compensated. On 24 June 1962, she wrote to William M. Murphy that Dr. Benjamin L. Reid of Mount Holyoke College was going to visit her. She always tried to connect her growing entourage of scholars and so suggested to Murphy that he invite Reid "to your study and tell him of our plans to write a biography of John Butler Yeats." She reminded him that "John Butler Yeats was so intertwined with Quinn, and

18. Dr. Thomas Conroy Sr., conversations with RL, Potsdam, N.Y., 1982.

Quinn was so closely interwound with the daily life of John Butler Yeats, one would help the other, or so it seems" (MC).

It did not take long for Murphy and Reid to become friends, and it took even less time for Reid to understand that Jeanne Foster's collection of letters, diaries, and memories were especially important. Jeanne enjoyed sharing her treasures with him and helping him with Quinn's biography. Reid often sent her copy to proofread, and she was particularly delighted when he used one of her poems, "When Niam Returns," in a footnote (*MFNY*, 635–36). She wrote on 19 February 1970: "The Reid book has made even here in this small city, a great impression because of the 'salvage of the life work' (as our dean of lawyers here states) of the 'most brilliant lawyer in the country' " (JRF to RL, in LC).

Reid sent Jeanne an autographed copy. She counted how many times he mentioned her name and said that she cried over the words he had included in his acknowledgments: "Mrs. Jeanne Robert Foster has given me her blessing and her good will, as well as her warm recollections of John Quinn, the use of her papers, and the benefit of her general good sense in the arts" (*MFNY*, xi).

The New York Public Library now became more interested in its Quinn collection and took greater care with the contents. On 19 October 1968, the library gave a private dinner of celebration to which Jeanne was invited, but she decided that it would be too taxing. To her, the dinner was not as important as the public recognition that the Quinn collection was finally receiving. She wrote on 16 September 1968 that "at last, John Quinn is to have a part of his due, a due he never had while alive, and I am happy that my part in bringing it about and my contribution of mss. and photographs have been gratefully received or acknowledged" (JRF to RL, in LC).

In 1964, French author Bernard J. Poli decided to do a book on Ford Madox Ford and the *transatlantic review*.[19] He was in the United States, spending a year at the University of California as a Sorbonne Research Fellow, when he wrote to Ford's American editor for assistance and advice. Once again, Jeanne would be "making a book." She verified or corrected information Poli had gathered, and she sent him copies of her own letters

19. Bernard Poli had previously published *Mark Twain: Écrivain de l'Quest: Régionalisme et Humour* (Paris: Presses Universitaires de France, 1965).

from Ford. She gave Poli the history of the birth of the *transatlantic review*, explained her role as American editor, and gave him appropriate photographs. She steered him in the direction of other valuable sources, including Mary Conroy and Dorothy Pound (Ezra was too ill).

Others, too, contacted her. Arthur Mizener sought her advice when he was writing his biography of Ford Madox Ford, *The Saddest Story*. She read the first three hundred pages and was impressed. "It will be a great book," she wrote on 23 February 1969. "Mizener is a scholar of the highest degree" (JRF to RL, in LC). Jeanne became friends with Larry Hart, Schenectady County historian, who dedicated his book about the Sacandaga region of New York State to her, and Sidney Geist asked her to consult with him on his new book *Brancusi: A Study of the Sculpture*.[20]

When Lytton Strachey's biographer, Michael Holroyd, asked Jeanne to meet with him about his life of Augustus John, she was particularly intrigued.[21] She had met Augustus, had lived for a short time with his sister Gwen, and had been privy to many unrecorded stories. She wrote to Holroyd immediately, and he arranged a trip to Schenectady. He arrived at her door in the spring of 1969, and Jeanne liked him immediately: "Michael Holroyd spent most of Friday here," she wrote on 6 April 1969. "He flew up from New York. . . . We worked at the long table nearly all the afternoon. I loaned him all my Augustus John papers and twenty Gwen John letters and showed him other things. . . . One has no doubt on meeting Holroyd that he is a genius" (JRF to RL, in LC). When she died, she left Holroyd part of her Gwen John collection.

In 1996, when Holroyd's *Augustus John* was reissued, he remembered her in his acknowledgments:

> After reading through the Augustus John–John Quinn correspondence . . . I
> took a train to Schenectady and spent a few hours with poet Jeanne Foster
> . . . and though she was now in her early eighties and I in my early thirties,
> we seemed to hit it off very well. Afterwards we wrote one or two letters to

---

20. Larry Hart, *The Sacandaga Story: A Valley of Yesteryear* (Schenectady: Riedinger and Riedinger, 1967). Geist's Brancusi book was published by Grossman in 1968.

21. Giles Lytton Strachey (1880–1932), English writer, a member of the Bloomsbury group.

each other, but I did not see her again. A few years later I received a letter
from an American lawyer . . . to say that Jeanne Foster was dead and that she
had added a codicil to her will leaving me her Gwen John papers and pictures. The pictures arrived in their original 1920s frames as I was finishing my
biography. I was infinitely touched by this gift from beyond the grave in my
memory of our day together, which now appeared like an augury for the
book itself. (1996, xviii)

When Holroyd heard that plans were underway for Jeanne Foster's biography, he wrote to add that he was "amazed by the instantaneous spirit of intimacy" he and Jeanne had:

> We found ourselves laughing over Augustus's flirtation with her, and we
> seemed naturally to concur about the nature of Gwen's dedication—as well as
> the surprising points of likeness between brother and sister. . . . [Mrs. Foster]
> made an extraordinary impression on me. I came away feeling marvellously
> encouraged by her generosity of spirit and her power of recalling the past.
>
> Only one aspect of her life baffled me. How had she been able to love
> such an unsympathetic character as John Quinn? I almost felt indignant. Per-
> haps I was retrospectively jealous. In my *Augustus John*, Quinn appears as a
> comic villain with a single extraordinary talent: his eye for pictures. But
> when I read Jeanne Foster's letter to Gwen John about Quinn's death, I sud-
> denly felt the transforming power of her love for him, and this enabled me to
> give him, though still in a comic vein, a genuinely poignant farewell—as I
> gave Augustus John himself at the end of the book.
>
> I still have the pictures and papers she bequeathed me a quarter-of-a-
> century ago, and I consider her gift one of the most romantic episodes in my
> life. I still remember her kindness, her sense of fun, her vitality. And I have
> the evidence that she enabled me to write a better book than would have
> been possible without her.[22]

Paul Schaefer, an ardent Adirondack preservationist and one-time vice
resident of the Association for the Protection of the Adirondacks, also
sought Jeanne's assistance. On 18 October 1969, she wrote to William M.
Murphy: "I have been working . . . on the first section of [Paul Schaefer's]

22. Holroyd letter to RL and JL, 23 April 1998.

book, the chapter 'An Adirondack Cabin' " (MC).[23] On 29 December, she wrote to Murphy again, calling Schaefer "a man of great vision and of . . . inherent 'greatness.' " Not long before her death, she spoke of Schaefer with devotion: "He has tried to keep me alive. . . . More than any one else he has tried to comfort me—in many ways and save me" (MC).

Jeanne sometimes became understandably tired because scholars demanded so much of her time. In the 1960s, she was, after all, in her eighties. She made each scholar feel important, as if that person's particular project were the most important of all, but sometimes she would express her concern about one to another. She wrote on 6 April 1969: "Dr. Reid without my consent copied the John Quinn and Augustus John diary and mailed the copy to [Michael Holroyd] in England. Dr. Reid telephoned me here last week, and told me what he had done. Of course I have the original . . . but one likes to know when and where your mss. are flying" (JRF to RL, in LC). When Paul Schaefer, Ruth Riedinger, and other friends wished to honor her with a permanent home for her papers at the Lake George Institute, she gently suggested that her collection might be better placed at SUNY-Albany, her mother's alma mater.[24] She wrote more directly to others about how she wished these friends would not make such plans and that she needed to "thwart" their efforts. On 28 December 1968, she complained, "There are things being planned, I hear, that I must find a way to disrupt. I want nothing—not the publicity I have had" (JRF to RL, in LC).

Jeanne Foster never intended her friends to read each other's letters, and she wanted each to feel he was her true confidant. Some may have felt that she was being taken advantage of, but never that they were the ones increasing her burden.

Institutions began contacting her as well, adding to the demands made on her. She owned literary and artistic treasures, and wouldn't she like to make arrangements for their permanent home? At least in one instance, she handled the situation with determined grace. When Dr. Evan Collins, president of SUNY-Albany, learned of the depth and diversity of Jeanne Foster's

---

23. Schaefer's book was *Adirondack Cabin Country* (Syracuse: Syracuse University Press, 1993) and was edited for publication by Noel Riedinger-Johnson. Schaefer died in 1996.

24. Lucia Oliver graduated from Albany Normal School in 1877. Because of financial difficulties, the Lake George Institute never became a reality.

literary collection, he was naturally interested in its eventual disposition. It seemed not unlikely that she might be persuaded to leave part or all of her collection to the university's library, as her 20 January 1969 letter to Ruth Riedinger suggested.

Dr. Collins invited Jeanne to an elegant luncheon, with the rationale that he was honoring an important local literary figure. It was true enough, and the added presence of several of the university's officials at the luncheon was an honor clearly due her. But she seemed to sense more than absolute altruism in their motives. At any rate, it was a charming meal, and she told her stories with wit and energy.

At what seemed an appropriate juncture, Dr. Collins suggested that Mrs. Foster might like to inspect the new library and evaluate its facilities for preserving documents.

"Nothing would please me more," she said, "but I'm an old woman, and I'm afraid I'm getting tired."

What could anyone offer as rejoinder? Dr. Collins gallantly declared the luncheon over, with thanks for Mrs. Foster's wonderful company. She in turn praised him and his companions for their hospitality.

After arriving safely home, she turned to her escort and said, "Dr. Collins is quite the gentleman, but perhaps a bit lacking in subtlety."[25]

Jeanne became concerned about the safety of her letters and paintings by 1969, as the neighborhood around her started to deteriorate. Her house on Albany Street was located in a district that was too worn to support an influx of poorer citizens. On several occasions, she was burglarized. In one letter to Murphy on 5 December 1967, she wrote: "Am rather disturbed this morning. Teen-agers crow-barred my storage shop in the garden open, smashed the lock and the padlock. This is the third time" (MC).

Life was slowly, resolutely pushing her away. She wanted to make certain, before she left this earth, that her friends knew how deeply she cared for them. She wrote that she would not be around much longer and that she was grateful for what they had done for her. Once, Murphy gently scolded her for such talk:

25. RL escorted JRF to the luncheon. Murphy, who inherited the core of Jeanne's collection, ultimately placed it at the New York Public Library, where it is a valuable supplement to the John Quinn Memorial Collection.

I can never tell you properly how much I appreciate all you have done for me and all the things you have given me. . . . But I can tell you that I don't like to hear talk that suggests that you are even thinking about shuffling off coils. The JBY book will not be published until 1972, and for seven or eight years thereafter I hope to produce at least a volume of letters a year, or editions of unpublished Yeats material for the Cuala Press—and *you* are to be the recipient of the first gift copy of each, a difficult thing to manage if you're not around where I can reach you. So let us have no more pessimistic talk! (7 August 1969, MC)

Murphy knew, of course, that Jeanne was old and ill, and so he decided that she should be given the highest honor his college could grant, an honorary doctorate. Reasons were obvious, as he later told Edwin McDowell of the *New York Times* on 16 September 1984: "She was known in different places all over the world. . . . Anyone in the artistic and literary circles of the time knew Jeanne Foster. They all knew her name" (I-12). In addition, she had continued her work to save her beloved Adirondacks, and she had given years of service to the citizens of Schenectady. She had helped scholars, and her gifts to friends inspired books and are still doing so today. Not long after Murphy's suggestion, Dr. Harold C. Martin, the president of Union College in Schenectady, and the college trustees agreed that the degree should be bestowed.

Dr. Martin notified Jeanne in January 1970. On the same day, she received a letter from Gustav Davidson, secretary emeritus of the Poetry Society of America, telling her that her "assistance and devotion to John Quinn . . . has secured [her] a place in the annals of American Art and Letters."[26] She was overcome and wrote to Murphy on 9 January 1970, "You can understand—remembering the log house in Minerva—and the long road—that *I am in tears*. . . . But no more now . . . with my tears phantoms arise . . . only Pound survives" (MC).

In March, Murphy brought her another surprise. Over the years of work on his biography of John Butler Yeats, he and his wife had become friends with Michael and Gráinne Yeats, the poet's son and daughter-in-law. The Yeatses had visited Jeanne several times, and now their daughter Caitríona

26. JRF quoted this in a letter to Murphy dated 9 January (MC). The letter is misdated and should be 1970 (MC). Gustav Davidson (1895–1971), American poet.

William M. Murphy, Gráinne Yeats, JRF, Harriet Murphy, and Michael B. Yeats at
JRF's home in Schenectady, 1970. Note the J. B. Yeats drawings of W. B. Yeats and
John Quinn in the background, and the large portrait of JRF by André Derain on
the wall. Courtesy of Michael B. Yeats and William M. Murphy.

was in town. Jeanne was delighted. "She is like a rose-leaf," she wrote on 4
March 1970, and on 21 April that Ms. Yeats had a touch of ages past in her:
"A most phenomenal technique with the harp—one that could not have
been wholly gained in her short years . . . —I have been possessed with the
surety in my own mind that she is Florence Farr, returned" (JRF to RL, in
LC).[27]

Jeanne showed Caitríona Yeats one of her most prized possessions, a
panne velvet jacket Lily Yeats had embroidered and given to Jeanne
decades earlier as a token of friendship for the care of her father, John Butler Yeats. Jeanne felt that it would be fitting to return the treasure to the

27. Florence Farr Emery (1860–1917), an actress who worked with W. B. Yeats on his
"speaking to the psaltery" projects.

JRF with Caitríona Yeats (granddaughter of W. B. Yeats) in Schenectady, 1970. Ms. Yeats is wearing the jacket that Lily Yeats embroidered and gave to JRF. Londraville private collection.

Yeats family. After Ms. Yeats left, Jeanne entrusted the jacket to the Murphys to give to the Yeatses "when appropriate." On 13 May, she wrote a note to be included with the bequest: "This with my gratitude for—in this life—having been permitted a degree of companionship with a noble and a gifted family. If we return, or in whatever sphere we again emerge, I will beg an identical privilege . . . in all humility."[28]

On the day of the Union College ceremony, Jeanne received a congratulatory telegram from Mary Conroy and her husband, Frank: "You have done such wonderful work. We are proud to know you" (MC). The sun that day rose high in a cloudless sky, and the afternoon temperatures reached

28. A copy of the note to the Yeats family is in MC.

JRF and other dignitaries at Union College, Schenectady, New York, in June
1970, on the occasion of her receiving an honorary degree. Photographer
unknown. *Left to right:* Franklin T. Jones, retiring executive secretary, Middle States
Association of Colleges and Secondary Schools; John H. Knowles, M.D., general
director of the Massachusetts General Hospital; Harold C. Martin, president of
Union College; Jeanne Robert Foster; Samuel Fortenbaugh, president of the
Union College Board of Trustees; John P. Lewis, dean, Woodrow Wilson School
of Public and International Affairs of Princeton University; Russell Baker, observer
for the *New York Times;* and Roy W. Peters, attorney. Londraville private collection.

into the eighties. The last photograph taken of Jeanne, in her academic re-
galia, smiling in her model's pose (one leg oblique to the camera) in the
forefront of a gaggle of professors, reveals her character. She was already
suffering from the heat and strain of the day, but none of that shows on her
composed, smiling face.

She collapsed just as the ceremony ended, and she had to be helped to
her home by the Murphys. She never fully recovered. In a letter to Caroline
Fish of the Chestertown Historical Society, she explained what happened:
"I am actually in bed with a reaction from many things—(virus intestinal)

JRF, 1969. Londraville private collection.

but I must get a message to you. . . . The 'Honor' was wonderful but the College changed the site to the College Campus. I had to walk at least a mile parading, sit in the hot sun three hours and wait for diplomas to be handed to 374 students so no wonder I have 'something' " (16 June 1970, CP).

Jeanne began to fail, breath by breath, a little more each week. On 18 June, she mustered enough strength to write to Elaine Hannay, president of the Schenectady Zonta Club, which had sent her a bouquet of pink roses as a congratulatory gift. She was touched: "They were the color John Quinn dearly loved."[29] On 21 July, she wrote to William M. Murphy about what her final arrangements were, where her papers were kept, and what was to go to whom. She was concerned for Sarah Washington's future and arranged to leave the house and a "bond" for her. She had formed an attachment to Sarah's granddaughter, who wished to attend college, and Jeanne privately gave her money toward that end. "She is a nice child . . . and I wanted her to have a chance."[30] She wanted Murphy to know that she would be happy when he finished his book on John Butler Yeats, even if she was only "air": "I am afraid I am not going to 'make it,' Bill, but everything is in order signed and sealed" (21 July 1970, MC). On 3 August, she wrote again: "Guard all the lovely Irish things you have and tell Michael [Yeats] how happy I was with his family" (MC). Among her final concerns were the

29. JRF to Elaine Hannay, 18 June 1970 (CP).
30. JRF to Dora Hayes, 11 December 1969 (Adirondack Museum Collection, Blue Mountain Lake, N.Y.).

letters of John Quinn, which she hoped would be published in 1974, fifty years after his death.

Jeanne Foster died on 22 September 1970. Dr. Murphy arrived home from a lecture trip to be greeted by the news. She had passed on only hours before, peacefully, after ninety-one years and six months on this earth. She was old and frail, but the fact of her death was difficult to assimilate. It had seemed that her charms could ward off all adversities.

Somewhere over the Atlantic at this time was Professor A. Norman Jeffares, on his way from England to consult with Jeanne about W. B. Yeats.[31] Instead, he helped Dr. Murphy close up her home.

Reverend Darwin Kirby, rector of the St. George Episcopal Church of Schenectady, presided over the funeral in Schenectady. Afterward, the body was transported to Chestertown. Murphy tells the story of Jeanne's burial service:

> When Mrs. Foster died in September 1970, I was named executor of her Estate and was in charge of the funeral arrangements. She died at ten minutes after eleven on Tuesday night. The burial was to be at the Chestertown Rural Cemetery next to the grave of John Butler Yeats.[32] I set the time at eleven o'clock Saturday morning. I asked Ben Reid, Quinn's biographer, to be a pallbearer, and even though he lived a couple of hundred miles away he agreed. On the Saturday morning we were all gathered at the graveside, the friends, the funeral directors, who had driven the hearse eighty miles from Schenectady, the pallbearers—all but Ben Reid. At eleven the mortuary scientists looked at me anxiously. "Could we wait a few minutes?" I asked. At five minutes after they began glancing at their watches. At last I said, "O.K., let's proceed. It looks as if Professor Reid isn't coming." The five remaining pallbearers moved to the hearse and began carrying the coffin to the grave. There was a squeal of brakes, and into the cemetery drove Ben Reid, just in time to take his handle on the coffin. We laid Jeanne Foster to rest at ten minutes after eleven.

31. Alexander Norman Jeffares (b. 1920), noted scholar and critic.

32. Dr. Murphy owns the grave site. On 6 June 1957, JRF wrote to Murphy: "I felt that you would look after the Yeats plot and monument and that your children would carry on in the future. I wrote Mrs. William Butler Yeats but as she never had very much liking for the father of her husband she has no interest in looking after the grave plot and monument" (MC).

A few weeks later, going through her effects, I found the handbook of the Theosophical Society. In that book I came upon something that sent a chill down my spine. According to the rules laid down there, a body must not be buried until at least eighty-four hours after death, for it takes that long for the soul to escape the body fully. Jeanne Foster had died at 11:10 Tuesday night; 11:10 Saturday morning was exactly eighty-four hours later. If Ben Reid had arrived on time her soul might still be in the coffin rather than wherever it is now. Ben later explained that a big-tractor-trailer must have blocked his view of the exit sign at Chestertown, and he had driven about twenty miles too far before turning back, arriving just properly late. I have friends who believe somebody put the truck there. (1985, 52–53)

In the summer months, Jeanne's grave site, between her husband Matlack and her old friend John Butler Yeats, is a carpet of lush grass, decorated with a few wildflowers that push their way through the soil into the sunlight. In the winter, the Adirondack winds swirl, making the snow look like the ghost of Hezzie Daley, "praising God by dancing."[33] Not many visitors to the cemetery know that John Butler Yeats is buried there, and fewer still know the story of Jeanne Robert Foster. It is a quiet place, where "the mists move slowly in the ancient trees above the circled cross, and the birds sing."[34]

33. "The Dancing Man," *AP,* 59.
34. JRF, memorial poem to JBY, quoted in Fish 1970, 42.

Appendix

Works Cited

Index

APPENDIX

# The Poetry
## "Something Fierce in Me"

THE POETRY OF JEANNE ROBERT FOSTER poses a particular problem for the biographer. It is impossible to ignore the impact of her verse on her life and yet difficult to weave into her story the critical and biographical center that work represented. Although she was largely successful in constructing a narrative that softened the harsher truths of her journey, her Adirondack verse reveals aspects of her personality and beliefs that were of a darker tinge. Conversely, her other poetry, especially the poems collected in *Wild Apples* (1916) and *Rock Flower* (1923), represents a more conventional side of her psyche, one congruent with the image of the desirable, submissive woman she found most appropriate for survival in a man's world.

Foster's Adirondack poetry, although separated in time by more than half a century, should be considered as a whole. *Neighbors of Yesterday* (1916) is a more unified work than *Adirondack Portraits* (1986), possibly because the latter is a posthumous collection. Nevertheless, the strength of Jeanne Foster's poetic voice did not markedly alter in fifty years.[1] She used Browning as her model for the poetry in both *Neighbors* and *Adirondack Portraits*, and attempted to limit accents from her lines wherever possible in order to approximate the laconic rhythms of Adirondack speech. She chose poetry over prose for the same reason Alexander Pope did— that it was economical. Yes, Frost and his interest in the lives of New England farm-

---

All information not identified specifically by source throughout the appendix is from notes RL took in conversations with JRF (LC).

1. The reviews of *Neighbors of Yesterday* in papers around the country were generally very favorable: *The Times-Picayune* of New Orleans thought that *Neighbors* would "stand as history," and the *Ohio State Journal* characterized the book as "A real favor to American literature." The Riedingers reprinted the comments on the 1963 *NOY* dust jacket.

ers had been "an encouragement," but she was mostly driven to tell the tales of real individuals she had known as a child, people whose strengths and idiosyncrasies had imprinted on a young girl growing up in the wilderness. Many of Foster's characters inhabit a world indifferent to their ambitions. Their situations match those of characters in Stephen Crane or Jack London, but their language reveals little of their difficult condition. They describe their lives and those of their neighbors with humor, realism, forbearance, and understanding.

If one adds the element of technology to what is essentially an Iron Age Adirondack community, the result is the poetry of Jeanne Foster. In attempting to recount the lives of her neighbors, she tells us in addition of the forces that shape a community on the edge of an industrial and technological revolution unparalleled in history. Her unique position as a woman who began her life in such a community—and, like Alice in the looking glass, burst into another incomprehensibly varied existence—placed her exactly on the cusp between naturalism and modernism. There is in her poetry an aspect of the fatalism of the former coupled with the enormous, explosive promise of the latter. Foster's neighbors did not, in the main, escape the mechanical determinism of naturalism, but she did, and so do a few of the people—mostly men—about whom she writes. Alec Hill ("Alec Hill: The Good-for-Nothing," *NOY*, 32–36), for example, will be able to break free by the chance of being chosen as a rich man's pallbearer. In contrast, Sonny, in "Union Blue" (*NOY*, 66–70), has his fate decided by a boyish whim. He responds to a dare to stand up and be a target for "those Tennessee men" and loses his life.

Foster's emphasis is more often on the people in the mountains rather than on their surroundings. She of course had deep affection for the places she knew as a child, but she was more apt to particularize the inhabitants. It was her neighbors' reaction to the environment that most engaged her. When she wrote of the mountains, she was likely to generalize, as in "The Old Lumberjack in Exile" (*NOY*, 89–92), "The Wilderness Is Strong" (*AP*, 141), or "Crane Mountain" (*AP*, 145). We are reminded in the latter poem of the paintings of Hudson River artist Frederic E. Church, for a human figure, if included, is dwarfed in comparison to the landscape.[2] In poems such as "The Deacon's Wife" (*NOY*, 43–44) or "The Sane Woman" (*NOY*, 71–73), a significant figure appears in the foreground, as in Andrew Wyeth's *Christina's World*.[3]

To friends, Foster recounted some tales of childhood hardships that seemed to

2. Frederic Edwin Church (1826–1900), American landscape artist.
3. Andrew Wyeth (1917– ), American artist.

be fitting material for poetry. During one terrible snowstorm, for example, a line had to be tied from the house to the barn in order that those tending the animals might not wander off and be lost. She spoke of pulling on the rope with mittens that froze immediately and of seeing nothing of either the barn or the house when she was halfway.[4] There is little mention of this awesome power of the wild in her poetry, but rather the emphasis is on the people who were shaped by daily confrontation. It is as if all one's will had to be directed toward battle with nature during a crisis, and only later could that experience, through the alembic of poetry, be understood and integrated into life.

Perhaps the most telling example of this experience was her grandfather's death. What message was there in his being swept away by the torrent, leaving wife and children? Foster learned that life is precarious, that loved ones can leave with little warning, and that their leaving can affect their family for generations. "William Newell" (AP, 107), the story of her grandfather, is one of her least-successful portraits, possibly because she did not have the artistic detachment necessary for an accurate picture. In her other depictions, we can see the details that create real people in the mind's eye, but in "William Newell" there is only the blur of William's hand waving good-bye.

Foster was able to express her delight in nature in her conversations and was especially lucid about the power of the wild, but there is little of that clarity in descriptive poems such as "Shadbush" and "Poverty Grass" (AP, 74 and 104), which directly deal with wilderness. It may be that there was a fortuitous match of Jeanne Foster's talent with her subject material when she was dealing with the people (rather than with the places) of her youth. She was prone to sentimentality when she was writing more conventional work, but the assumption of a mask in her Adirondack portraits allowed her the separation and disinterestedness that characterize her best efforts.

No one else, though, could better exemplify the change from nineteenth- to twentieth-century sensibility, for Foster literally walked out of the woods and into a brave new world. But as much as her life changed, she recognized and valued her roots. The people she had known seemed to be closer to the essentials of life, although in a way difficult to document. They certainly had a more difficult life than most, yet they appeared to extract more from it. To speak of them at all was a major task, for it required an objectivity that could not be masked in sen-

4. JRF, interviewed by RL, 15 July 1968. Unless otherwise noted, all interviews with JRF were held in Schenectady, N.Y.

timentality. Foster finally decided that the best service she could do these old friends was to let them speak for themselves. Each character she wrote about gave her an opportunity to examine a life in a way that she could never fully examine her own.

The dramatic nature of her work, which most often uses a monologue by a storyteller, reproduces the sense of being told a tale on the steps of the general store or at a pause in farm work. The narrators of the poems wish to entertain their listener, but also seem to be attempting to understand something of their neighbors by telling their story. We learn of Ezra Brown's problems with faith ("Ezra Brown," *NOY*, 11–13) or of Ben Enoch's unease with women and "half-wits" ("Ben Enoch's Fools," *NOY*, 24–27) or of Jen Murdock's bad luck with chickens ("Jen Murdock's Roosters," *AP*, 15). We see first that their stories are half-realized attempts to reconcile immensities with their own experience, and then that the forces of their difficult existence are working inexorably on these people; eventually, the correspondences in our own lives begin to filter through. Finally, we comprehend that these characters are enmeshed in the same dilemmas that continue to bewilder us.

These people have little to do with a modern culture removed by almost a century in time and by a near-immeasurable technological gulf, and yet they speak to us. Jeanne Foster's poetry is like a recurring dream that insists itself on our consciousness until some awareness is reached. Her characters do not declaim; they explore, inviting us to seek for meaning with them. In the best examples, it is not message poetry, for neither the narrators nor their subjects seem certain why any particular story is being told. Even when some conclusion is reached, as in "Flint" (*NOY*, 63–65) or in "Ezra Brown," it is gentle and not dogmatic. The traits of Foster's subjects reveal themselves to us not by what she says of them, but by what they do.

Character isolated in a deed. How much more we know of these people from their actions than we ever could have discovered from reams of exposition. In Foster's best work, an action or an image makes the poem function. In her less-successful attempts, such as the introductory "Where Are the Americans?" (not paginated) in *Neighbors* or "The Old Church" and "State Land" in *Adirondack Portraits* (71–72 and 142–43), she tells us what we should feel instead of showing us how the character reacts to a situation. The action in her best poems may be as direct and defiant as fiddling on the Sabbath in "The Deacon's Wife" or as subtle as the passing of candy between the married couple in "Flint."

In the latter poem, a young teamster pauses to pass out peppermint sticks to a

group of people sitting on a porch, among them a staunch Calvinist couple whom
he had considered rigorous in pursuit of their religion and passionless in their private lives.

> I never believed they were married lovers:
> He was a hard man—and she was hard.
> . . . . . . . . . . . . . . . . . . . ..
> They never called each other by their first names
> 'Twas always "Mr. and Mrs."—stiff words
> For the breakfast table year in and year out.
> (NOY, lines 1–2, 9–11)

Yet when there isn't enough candy to go around, the wife passes the sweet behind
her back to her husband: "She couldn't bear to have the little treat / And feel that he
was not sharing it too" (lines 20–21). The image of the red-and-white candy being
passed surreptitiously encapsulates the sweetness and the privacy of their relationship like a spot of color in a black-and-white photograph.

In choosing folk narrative as her form, Jeanne Foster creates a tension between
the expected outcome and actual tale she is telling. We expect some gentle narrative as in Sarah Orne Jewett or a tall tale as in Joel Chandler Harris or Mark Twain.[5]
We get instead a twist that makes us reexamine the work. "Ben Enoch's Fools" may
be the best example. The persona, a male (although we cannot be sure until the last
line of the poem), is being told the story by another male, the successful farmer Ben
Enoch. Ben is complaining that the folks at the poorhouse had wronged him by
giving him a half-wit instead of a "genuine fool" to work on his farm:

> I kept him a spell, but never felt easy.
> There are two kinds of men to have near you:
> Smart men or fools,—real fools without cunning
> Honest and simple, who'll work for you, grateful
> For their clothes and a penny or nickel
> Fair-time to spend on peppermint candy.
> (NOY, lines 40–45)

5. Sarah Orne Jewett (1849–1909); Joel Chandler Harris (1848–1908), American
authors.

The reader is listening to a tale that might have been told by a slave owner, not as justification for his action, but as a simple recipe for success for a diligent entrepreneur. The last line of the poem has another and even more sinister development: "Women's the same; stay clear of the pert ones" (line 83). The reader has been led in one direction so that he pities the simple fool that Ben Enoch exploits, and then suddenly the narrative shifts from "genuine fools" to women. In a larger context, this simple narrative is a paradigm of the problem of slavery in the United States. Just as Ben Enoch did, slave owners were able to justify possessing others as sensible, economically sound, and even benevolent, for who would care for these "genuine fools" if they were left to their own devices? The equating of fools and women in the last line is a perfect extension of Ben Enoch's argument for control over those "naturally" unable to care for themselves.

Like T. S. Eliot, Jeanne Foster often employs an "objective correlative," an object or a situation that is the formula for a particular emotion. In her poems about women, for example, she fixes our attention on objects that we judge to be ordinary feminine adornments, but in the context of the Adirondacks become icons to remind women of their gender. For example, there is the threadbare, faded green-satin bow that the woman at the poor farm treasures in "The Green Bow" (NOY, 48–49):

> "She worships that bow,"
> Said the Wife of the Man Who Kept the County House;
> "I wouldn't wonder, if she ever lost it
> Or the thing wore out, but it might kill her."
>
> (lines 27–29)

Both this bow and the blue hair ribbon worn by Mis' Cole ("Mis' Cole," AP, 28–29) economically show the reader the importance such a gimcrack had for both women. In the first poem, the old woman uses the bow to define her as "woman":

> No one ever comes up here to see her,
> But someway,—I don't know how she got it—
> She found a green bow, a small satin thing
> Such as you'd wear at your neck,—it's her knick-knack;
> And when anyone drives up here she runs out
> And pins that bow on her drilling dress.
>
> (NOY, lines 12–17)

The image in "Mis' Cole" is a hair tie, but the first tie, "a leather thong cut from a tanned hide," is a symbol of Mis' Cole's bondage. Her new tie is "a blue hair ribbon," signaling recognition of her gender and of freedom from her old life.

> "It's the first one I've ever had,"
> She said. "I'm beholden to you."
> I packed a paper sack of victuals for her.
> "Don't forget, you'll get hungry," I said.
> "I'd hardly feel it, now I'm free, but I thank you."
> (AP, lines 34–38)

In a land where a woman is only "hands and feet," the green bow and the blue hair ribbon represent attempts to hold on to some vestige of femininity.

Foster's portraits are thematically rich. Both "Mis' Cole" and "The Green Bow" are concerned with at least one of the subjects that characterize her poetry: women dealing with adversity. Cathy E. Fagan says that "like Katherine Mansfield, Foster's depictions of the debilitating restrictions of male domination highlight the subtle, powerful, and often raging energy of women" (1998, 6). These women find themselves in a world not of their own making and deal with it in diverse ways. Mis' Cole walks away from her family and the slavery it represents; the woman at the poor farm goes mad; Silence Davis ("Silence Davis," NOY, 58–62) "died gladly."

Some Adirondack women controlled their own destiny, but their choices were still formed to a great extent by the need to survive. In the second poem in Neighbors, for instance, we meet the childless bachelor woman, Mis' Meegan ("Mis' Meegan," NOY, 1–5), who is "married / Just in name to her hired man, to keep him / From hiring out to the neighbors" (lines 5–7). Mis' Meegan has a house that "had sunk / Slowly into the ground, as the years passed" (lines 18–19). In 1927, when Foster reworked "Mis' Meegan" into her play Marthe, there is an added poignancy to the lines she had written a decade earlier:

> When you find out there's lovin'
> In the world, and going on all the time,
> Passing you by, something you've never had,
> You've got to die; I'm going to do that.
> (NOY, lines 88–91)

When Jeanne Foster wrote this poem, she was a relatively young woman in her mid-thirties, bound to one man, Matt Foster, and in love with another, Albert

Shaw. When she later recast the poem into drama, John Quinn had recently died, and she had an even stronger sense of love "passing by." The love of her life was dead, she was nearing fifty, and the future looked bleak. The critic for the *Saturday Review of Literature* (26 May 1928) grasped the sentiment, calling *Marthe* "an arresting study of an old Irishwoman living in the Adirondack region, whose hard exterior only conceals a deathless youthful passion" (913). The play won first prize in 1926 from the Pasadena branch of the Drama League of America, and Frank Shay included it in his 1928 edition of *Fifty More Contemporary One Act Plays*, under another of Foster's noms de plume, Noel Armstrong.[6]

One of Foster's recurring themes is "baby fever," which she handles effectively in "Nance Hills" (*NOY*, 111–16).[7] Fifty years later in "Day Lilies" (*AP*, 102–3) she wrote what is arguably her best treatment of a woman longing for a child. In the character Nance Hills, we see the natural and predictable grief of a young woman who has lost her baby and replaced it with a doll. She may or may not know that the doll isn't real, but her sorrow is palpable. The old woman in "Day Lilies" shows the reader that baby fever is not the exclusive province of the young and that even when children and grandchildren have left, the desire to hold and nurture a child never leaves some women. In this poem, Foster extends the conceit of her earlier work, for the old woman is able to adopt a child, only to have it die after a year, and her sole wish now is to care for that child in heaven:

> I'm waiting to be called, and I know God will let me
> Stay somewhere inside the pearly gates long enough
> To bring up that baby. I'm in a hurry
> For fear she'll get so big she won't need me.
>
> (*AP*, lines 85–8)

The old wife shows us that the pain of attachment does not lessen as we age. She appears before us as a living being afflicted with the "baby fever" as convincingly as a woman fifty years younger.

6. Frank Shay (1889–1954), American editor and author. JRF's only other play, *Black Frost*, was written about the same time as *Marthe*, but never published. JRF felt that it needed extensive rewriting and lost interest. The manuscript is in the Foster Murphy Collection, NYPL.

7. In "Nance Hills," the narrator explains, "you have crazy dreams / Of babies; and sometimes in broad daylight / You see one come and play round on the floor. . . . That's 'baby-fever'; it drives women mad" (*NOY*, lines 40–42, 47).

Women and flowers are also linked in Foster's poetry. There is first the more obvious and traditional connection as in "Her Flowers" (*NOY*, 14–18):

> Her garden bloomed from May till snowfall
> There by the fence are her lemon lilies
> And the double hollyhocks, and the asters.
> There's the herb bed set in the fence corner,
> With the green and white creeper around it.
>                                (lines 26–30)

But there is also the sense that women in the Adirondacks use flowers as a kind of charm against the encroaching wilderness. Their gardens "from May till snowfall" are oases of color and hope set against the rigors of the land, nurtured like children against the terrible winter, gathered from graves (usually of other women) as talismans. These flowers in particular seem to have a special power, for they are remembrances of dead women whose lives are extended through the slips that their friends garner. Finally, in "Simples" (*NOY*, 83–85), there is the evidence that the garden can provide far more than beauty: "But if you know the Simpler's kindly skill, / Weeds are the 'leaves of healing' given to man / In a lost Eden" (lines 8–10). Like Spenser and Milton, Foster uses the garden as a symbol of coherence. In her depiction of Adirondack life, there is a feeling of the earth just after the expulsion from paradise, when the natural world that had been embracing and symbiotic becomes indifferent and austere. It still retains its beauty, and there remains in the memory of some few the loving embrace of the prelapsarian Eden. Those who can use the "leaves of healing" can speak in poetry to those of us who have lost all contact with our previous lives.

The men of the Adirondacks had no Wordsworth to record their pastoral existence, but Foster spoke for them all in "Human Nature" (*NOY*, 6–10). The poem tells the story of a young salesman who comes to peddle his company's new reaper to local farmers. It doesn't take long for him to discover that the farmers will not buy his machine: "And I felt guilty to offer it to them. / Why should I disturb their accustomed ways?" (lines 26–27). But he has a job to do. He ties his horse to the old hitching post outside the general store and steps inside to speak with the shopkeeper, who inquires why the stranger wants to see Sam Perkins. The object, of course, is to sell: "I've come to make you dissatisfied— / That's my business" (lines 72–73). Although the salesman has little to offer that will be practical in the stony Adirondack fields, Sam Perkins, who "never has bought a machine / he could use" (lines 66–67), might be foolish enough to buy some more. We learn that Sam is not the only man dazzled by the new, for the storekeeper himself has bought from "a slick agent" (line 86) an automobile that he cannot make run. The deal is that the storekeeper will "speak right for ye to Sam Perkins" (line 89) in exchange for some free technological advice—and he is not averse to doing in Sam in the bargain.

The poem captures the personality of the Adirondack man—simple yet wily and, although resistant to change, willing to make a deal with the representative of the new. Foster has achieved freedom from the confines of ordinary narrative by creating a voice and then conjuring with it through images and symbols, giving her the ability to enter into another's consciousness. The poem is, as Alfred Kazin calls much of her Adirondack verse, "striking in its matter-of-fact plainness" and "an astonishing duplicate of Frost's slow-moving, artfully conversational pastorals." She makes us "homesick for loneliness," with pictures of life far from our crowded urban existence (AP, xii).

Adirondack men often faced enormous sacrifice, and some broke under the strain. In "The Coward" (NOY, 56–57), Dave Murdock flees from his own house because it is overrun with stray cats that he could ill afford to feed but could not kill: "The milk from two cows wouldn't feed them / And make any butter for Dave to eat" (lines 19–20). He earns the opprobrium of the narrator, a neighbor who had to "take a day off from harvesting / And shoot those beasts; they were starving" (lines 30–31).

> And [Dave] heard of it and sneaked back in the night,
> And went to farming again. After a while
> I kind of forgot he was a "softy,"
> (We don't like that kind here in this country);
> But blast me, if I didn't pass his house
> Last week, and see a cat on the doorstep!
>
> (lines 32–37)

Like Ezra Brown, Dave appears before us defined by his action. Just as we can picture the industrious Ezra sweating in his fields and hoping for a sign from God, we can see Dave daydreaming on his porch, a cat in his lap and several others mewing around him, hoping that someone will resolve his dilemma.

Foster observed that as often as some Adirondack men were clever or bore immense hardship, others were indigent and ineffectual. She loved her father deeply, but she confessed that his failures left his family, and in particular his oldest child, in peril. She tries to ameliorate his portrait in "Transition" (*NOY*, 28–31), in which the main character (whom she identified as her father)[8] makes a valiant attempt to find profitable work in town for the sake of his children. At the end of the poem, there is hope that he will succeed, but Frank Oliver's results rarely matched his good intentions. His lack of success is more attributable to the times than to his efforts.[9]

In "Alec Hill," we see the epitome of the mountain man with little or no concern for his family, his children scrambling for bones from the cooking pot, their clothes tatters. Hill seems little concerned for them or their plight. Even his neighbors' attempts at help go for naught:

> Sometimes the neighbors would give him fresh seed
> And make a "bee" for planting and hoeing,
> But after they did all that work for him,
> He would let the potatoes freeze in the ground. . . .
> His wife didn't complain;
> She was used to her life and 'most likely
> Knew he would never change, so she bore it. . . .
> She seemed to love that good-for-nothing man.
> (*NOY*, lines 41–44, 47–48)

In fact, it takes a deus ex machina to change Alex. He is chosen as pallbearer for Sam Carpenter. Although the people are shocked, they acquiesce to Sam's last wishes, but insist that Alec be presentable for the funeral. It takes a community effort to dress him, and the result is that "He was a handsome figure of a man / Even in misfits and borrowed toggings" (lines 73–74). When Alec sees himself thus decked out, he is no longer comfortable in his rags. He begins to reform, and at the end of the poem he has a steady job and a broadcloth suit, and sits every Sunday with his wife and children at church. The last stanza of the poem may tell us more of Jeanne Foster than of Alec:

8. The cast of characters' real-life counterparts were identified in a list JRF gave to friends. One is in LC.

9. JRF's affection for her father is shared by Adorna Wright, JRF's last surviving relative, who described her uncle as a hard-working man who was always looking for ways to improve his family's lot in life. Wright, interviewed by RL and JL, 9 September 1998, Warrensburgh, N.Y.

> Respectability's half in its trappings.
> Maybe if I had always worn old rags
> And never had shoes to put my feet in
> I might have been just the same as he was—
> A shiftless, out-and-out good for nothing.
> (lines 106–10)

How keenly she must have felt the irony of her success in New York and Boston when she thought of her early life and the ease with which one slips into indolence. Her own marriage and the stillborn child of that first year showed her how circumstance can intervene to smother ambition. Matlack Foster was supposed to be different, a man of substance who could protect her against the vagaries of fate, but he, too, like other men she knew, proved fragile.

There never seems to be bitterness in Foster's portraits of men, though, only a kind of concern, as in "The Mother" (*NOY*, 45–46), in which a wife (the mother) is patiently explaining to the persona of the poem (appropriately a woman this time) why she is sending her husband to visit Nance Wilson, whom the narrator describes as "a vain woman—not bad that I know of, but silly" (lines 7–8). The mother replies:

> George ain't had much of a chance.
> I thought it might perk him up to go there.
> You know men have a hankering somehow
> For women like Nance; she can talk just grand,
> George says, about what she's seen in New York.
> He gets ideas of stepping up higher
> In the world from her. What could I teach him?
> (lines 14–20)

When the narrator suggests that the mother ought to be wary of exposing her husband to such a potential rival, she answers: "You are not married; your husband is a child / After you've been married years as I have" (lines 37–39).

There is an unusual mixture here, for Foster, who wrote "The Mother" in her mid-thirties, seems to partake of the nature of all of the women in the poem. She is the outside observer, the mother, and Nance Wilson. As good poets do, Foster enters into the nature of her subjects, creating a tension among the storyteller, the ignorant but compassionate mother, and the sophisticate.

Almost all of the men in Jeanne Foster's poetry are flawed in some way, and many do not have the grit to overcome the rigors of Adirondack life. Curiously, the most successful male is Jim Pasco ("The Hunchback," *NOY,* 19–23). It is as if his deformity has given him insight denied to men without any disability. Like Jeanne Foster, Jim Pasco decided early to make the best of the hand that fate had dealt him:

> I played my part well enough, never faltered or wavered,
> Seeing myself as I should be, forgot
> At the last I was crooked—forgot it—
> For I felt I was straight, and held my place
> Among men, fooled them—even a woman
> Saw me thirty years day in and day out,
> And never knew that I was ugly as Satan.
>
> (lines 104–10)

By sheer force of will, the hunchback has transformed himself into another being, one whom the community honors and one whom a woman, seeing beyond his deformity, loves for the person he is. The young Julia Oliver felt her own shortcomings, some of them the ordinary concerns of any growing child, some more serious. She overheard herself described as someone who should hope only to be taken on as a hired girl—and she knew what kind of a future that meant in the mountains.

Many successful people suffer from an impostor complex, and Foster found it difficult to comprehend how a mountain girl such as herself had blossomed into a model, actress, and journalist. While she was modeling, she also had an awareness that her beauty would be a passport for a limited time. Jim Pasco had taught her that almost any handicap can be overcome and that she had been unusually lucky in her life—but also that one must be always prepared to take advantage of opportunity.

Almost all Foster's Adirondack men were married, and their attitude toward their wives was, as Mis' Cole says in *Adirondack Portraits,* too often that

> I'm only hands and feet to George,
> Someone to put food on the table,
> Someone to have more children for him,
> And mend and hand-sew their dresses on them
> Until they wear out in rags.
>
> (lines 21–25)

This last line works wonderfully, for not only the clothes but the women themselves finally "wear out" like the faded rags they are patching.

In "The Sane Woman," we have further evidence of how wives are valued:

> Men don't count women in their worldly lives,—
> They count their children and their farms and stock:
> They're like a river flowing—all these men—
> And if you haven't children you're no more
> Than driftwood floating on the river's breast,
> Flung in an eddy when the tide is full.
>
> (*NOY,* lines 36–41)

In the same poem, however, we see the resilience of these women in the face of such valuation: "But I am strong; there's something fierce in me / That fights back, hungers, searches all the time" (lines 42–43). Often there is terror and desperation just beneath the surface of the narrative, and these feelings contrast sharply with the easy-flowing line of unaccented verse. The reader is being lulled to sleep by rhythm, only to be jarred by a line such as "Scraping out some jig-tune on the Sabbath" at the end of "The Deacon's Wife" (*NOY*).

It is difficult to believe that Jeanne Foster intended some of her poems to be as trenchant as they are. She insisted until the last that they were simply accurate pictures of people she had known, and they may well be. But her selection shows us her feeling. More often than not, she eschews sentimental narrative for the hard edge of truth and in so doing exposes the condition of women in the Adirondacks at that time.

Foster admired the rare "love" marriage, as in "Flint," where the wife's quiet gift of candy to her husband "held all / The love we had thought they were missing" (lines 46–47). But many of Jeanne's characters—from the narrator of "Marriage" (*NOY,* 77–79) to poor Silence Davis, who died too young—are women trapped by their environment and by their men. They underscore the inevitable dichotomy: marriage is often loveless but just as often necessary:

> It was a trap, I said, and we were caught
> Netted like two unwary, fledgling birds,
>
> . . . . . . . . . . . . . . . . . . .
> My mother wept upon my wedding day,
> But she kept silence, kept the traitor pact.
>
> ("Marriage," lines 1–2; 9–10)

In "Silence Davis," the narrator tells the story of a woman "all softness and sunshine," who "died gladly" when her baby came:

> In the first flush of her young womanhood
> She married a clod—a handsome fellow
> (If you can see beauty in flesh and eyes),
> Raised on Mormon Hill, where they count women
> Less than fat cattle. They used to trade them
> Till the Government stepped in and stopped it.
> One man traded his wife for a calf and a bridle,
> Another for a colt and a halter,
> And everybody changed round once in a while.
>                                  (NOY, lines 64–72)

Some of Foster's most frightening poems are about the price that children paid for being born in such a beautiful but harsh environment. It was common for a mother to bear many children because "hands" were needed to survive on the rough homesteads. In the old days, children were, according to their ages, designated "house," "yard," or "field" children, and their lives were so shaped. But as necessary as children were, the more there were, the more mouths there were to feed. Neighbors sometime were forced to care for the neglected:

> I sliced bread and tossed it to the children.
> They snatched it from me and ran to hide,
> Just as young partridges run to cover
> When the hen-partridge krakes her note of warning.
>                          ("Alec Hill," NOY, lines 22–25)

Most of the characters in *Neighbors* and in *Adirondack Portraits* ultimately make a fragile peace with their mountain existence. Though "beset by poverty, isolation, madness, religious fervor, misspent love, and death," they survive because they must (Winter 1989, 17). Foster's characters are not limited to the Adirondacks; they are also universal types. They are women struggling for their own place in the world; men fighting for their lives against a strange and frightening environment. They are fools and ne'er-do-wells, lovers and dreamers, people battling to survive whatever life hands them. Foster's poetry is about people in transition in a land in transition, part of a larger human experience.

One of Foster's techniques for creating images for *Neighbors of Yesterday* and

*Adirondack Portraits*, in which she said she followed Yeats's example, was evocation. She would focus on an object completely, intensely, and then, in time, the "anima mundi" would awaken other images that fresh images beget. In a 7 February 1968 letter, she described her method: "There is a cure for the 'lyric answers' that 'tumble into words' if you can win the cure by Yeats's own method, i.e. EVOCATION. He meditated long on great figures. I find evocation as powerful as Yeats found it; a leaf, a tone, a memory will evoke a train of images beyond the power of the mind to create" (JRF to RL, in LC).

Foster was able to make poetry from her Adirondack experience because she saw the extraordinary in the ordinary. She froze moments and forever preserved the colloquial language of the mountain people. She fulfilled what her old friend John Butler Yeats said was the "end of poetry": "to make rich and significant with harmony the passing moment."[10] Perhaps because Foster moved easily between two worlds—the rough land of the Adirondack lumberjack and farmer and the sophisticated world of the international cosmopolite—she was able, in most cases, to escape the sentimentality that characterizes many regional writers and to create a tension by using her literary sophistication to write about simplicity. Her friends—especially W. B. Yeats and Ezra Pound—had experimented in poetry or drama, but Jeanne Foster, although she attempted many different forms, was most successful in one of the oldest, the folk narrative. What makes this form new is her ability to take the reader gently down one path while she unfolds an alternate reality that ultimately astounds her audience. It is her wonderful sense of understatement that reinforces our understanding. She tells us without shock or rancor that on Mormon Hill they devalue women and trade them for livestock and farm equipment ("Silence Davis"). What is worse, nothing seems likely to change, and only such examples as the Sabbath fiddling of the deacon's wife and Mis' Cole's walking away from her family alert us to the intolerable tension boiling just beneath the surface of this quiet community. Such examples are hardly less shocking than Ibsen's Nora slamming the door of the doll's house.[11]

The folk narrative with its naturalistic, modernistic implications was clearly Foster's forte. It is curious, then, that the same year that she published *Neighbors*, she also published *Wild Apples* (1916), a collection employing more conventional ideas and forms. It is not surprising that a poet would attempt to expand her scope, but what is unusual is the contrast between the two books. *Neighbors* is startling in the raw power and insights behind the folksy tales, whereas *Wild Apples* is merely a

10. JRF quoted JBY in a letter to RL, 23 December 1968 (LC).
11. Henrik Ibsen (1828–1906), *A Doll's House* (1879; trans. into English 1880).

pleasant enough collection of love poems, philosophizing, and esoterica that might have been written by any number of poets at that or any other time.

The disparity between this work and her Adirondack poems may be in part explained by the multitude of masks suggested by Foster's many pen names. When she was writing of the Adirondacks, her masculine personae allowed her to explore her "male genius." She then had sanction to investigate ideas more powerful than romantic love. When she declared that "all genius is male," she may have been sincere, or she may have been using the cunning necessary for a female artist to succeed in a man's world. She could under such a rubric thus explore the mistreatment of women ("Silence Davis"), the trap of marriage ("The Mother" and "Marriage"), or the insensitivity of the community to the outsider ("The Deacon's Wife" and "The Road," NOY, 74–76). Although she maintained that she was telling the tales of her neighbors without adornment,[12] there is in the best of these poems a kind of escape velocity that one finds, for example, in Robert Frost. Just as in his "Two Tramps in Mud Time" or "The Mending Wall," there is in Foster's " 'Mis' Meegan" and "Flint" (to name only two examples) the simple recounting of an event that elicits, as Wordsworth put it, "thoughts that do often lie too deep for tears."

When Foster was writing as a female poet, feminine sensibility, as she understood it, prevailed. One of her masks was that of a desirable object for powerful men. It was a pose she had created almost ex nihilo from the homely child she thought herself to be. It was as if she had made herself a beauty by sheer force of will, and that disguise was in danger of being disclosed by any discerning individual. Therefore, she had to take advantage of her appearance while it was still within her control. In her thirties, she wrote of love in a way that caused John Butler Yeats figuratively to grind his teeth and to remonstrate with her inclination to make that emotion a "maid of all work," and his gentle criticism is apt (see chapter 4). He was objecting to the imprecise in her poetry, although it was what might be expected from "woman's poetry" of that time. Such imprecision, however, was not consistent with the journalist who wrote of the treatment of women in prison and even less with the persona who wrote "Respectability's half in its trappings."[13]

It may be that Foster's insistence on the telling of "real stories" in Neighbors gave her naturalistic license to tell the truth, whereas the sonnets and couplets of Wild Apples caused her to retreat behind the pose of poet as she understood it. In Neighbors, there is a world inhabited by people responding to the inexorable laws of a natural world she rarely dealt with in Wild Apples. In the former book, she created a

12. JRF, interviewed by RL, 14 July 1968.
13. See Foster 1911a and "Alec Hill: The Good-For-Nothing," NOY, 32–36, line 108.

universe, a mythos to which her characters respond viscerally. In attempting to tell her unvarnished tales, she made a world as structured as any Greek myth.[14] In *Wild Apples*, she could not match that intensity. "The Year of the Great War: To My Mother" (*WA*, 74–75) shows the difference. It is an occasional poem written in wartime:

> Mother—Mother—
> Little Mother mine,
> Every year upon your birthday morning I have sung in rime
> Some gay rondelay for love's adorning;
> But this gray spring time
> I have neither chant nor rondel; their light measures
> Vanished from my casket of bright treasures
> Long ago.
>
> (lines 1–8)

The poem continues for thirty-five more lines, with few effective images and little tension created from form, meter, or subject.

"W. B. Yeats—Reading" (*WA*, 7–8) uses stricter form, but suffers from hero worship and hyperbole. As a tribute, it is undoubtedly sincere, but sincerity in this case doesn't make a good poem:

> I had not dreamed you—thinking you but clay
> As other men are clay—to make me weep
> Or laugh, or feel desire for,—this and all
> My outgrown selfhood. Suddenly you rose
> In the lamps' flare, grave as the dark waters;
> Forgetful of each face, sense winged beyond
> The preen of curious eyes and whispered praise.
> First the recoil: too perfect far, you seemed;
> How dared you wear God's image like a gem,
> Or lean so white a hand—a poet's hand?
>
> (lines 8–17)

14. "Myth, then, is one extreme of literary design; naturalism is the other. . . . In more realistic modes the association [of the image] becomes less significant and more a matter of incidental, even coincidental or accidental, imagery" (Frye 1957, 136–37).

In *Wild Apples*, Foster was attempting to echo the sentiments that she understood as conventional poetry. It is also true that lyric poetry, which by its nature does not have the force of plot behind it, is simply more difficult to write well than narrative.

Foster's third book of poetry, *Rock Flower* (1923), is an improvement over *Wild Apples*, but absent of the dramatic imagery she used to unify her work in *Neighbors of Yesterday* and later in *Adirondack Portraits*. She continued to work with conventional forms, but there are occasional exquisite lines and some good "poems of sentiment," such as "Your Song" (*RF*, 9):

> There was a song that I had made for you.
> I am too filled with wonder now to find
> How the words go. I think the way of it
> Was like a flower—but no, I half forget—
> Perhaps 'twas like a palace or a tomb
> Curled close with ivy, or like some wild thing
> That runs away and feels the sucking breath
> Of the hounds close behind . . . I have forgotten it.

In the poem, the reader is invited to partake of primitive nature and to feel the immediacy of pursuit and the dreamlike careening from one impassioned emotion to another. The image of the hounds' breath felt by "some wild thing" particularizes and elevates the lyric.

Foster also attempted to transfer what she learned from the visual arts to her poetry in the series "Three Colors of the Moon," which, as Cathy E. Fagan says, "calls to the mind the massing of forms present in the Cubists and Futurists": "The flawed 'Three Colors of the Moon' is in many ways Jeanne Foster's *La Danse a la Source* and *Nude Descending*. Desiring to move reality beyond reproduction, Jeanne attempted to recreate [sic] her desperate personal loss in her art" (1999, 14).[15]

Only one poem in *Rock Flower* reflects Foster's Adirondack work, "In Dimness" (84), which WCFE used in its video production to emphasize her connection to the rhythms of nature:

> I heard the wild loon and the catbird cry
> Over Sagamore Lake, and knew that I

15. "The Three Colors of the Moon" includes "The Eye of the Beholder," "Blue," "Crimson," and "Black" (*RF*, 113–18).

Heard the ancient call of race
Bidding me to my own place.

(lines 1–4)

The poem contains four stanzas, the second and the last a refrain:

I am the root of the yellow willow,
The stem of the lily leaf;
There cannot come to my marsh-grass pillow
The cry of a human grief.

(lines 5–8)

In this successful lyric, Foster combines her search for an ordered universe in a chaotic world with the foundation on which her life was built: her Adirondack experiences. The poem isolates the poet's desire to sink at last into the essence of nature, to use a blending into its vegetative soul as an escape from all human sorrow.

In *Rock Flower*, Foster also included poems about friends such as John Butler Yeats (to whom the book is dedicated), Constantin Brancusi, and Ezra Pound.[16] She wrote of Oscar Wilde, Maud Gonne, and Michael Collins, indicative of her life-long interest in the Irish. Some poems are Japanese in style—or at least in attempt—and some theosophical, such as "The Eye of the Beholder" (113), in which the Omniscient holds all of life in his Eye, and "Nothing happens that the Eye does not awaken" (line 2). W. B. Yeats expressed his approval of the book, especially the Japanese poems, in an 8 April 1923 letter to her. His comments naturally pleased her: "I am delighted with your book of poems, especially, I think, with the 'Verses for Japanese Prints.' The little fragment, 'A Pair of Lovers,' is a passionate invention—that rare thing, a new metaphor. There are other delightful things and I am particularly grateful for your poem about my father, a vivid eloquent piece of writing" (CP). George Gray Barnard, the American sculptor, found *Rock Flower* "a beautiful gift of flowers plucked from the garden of the heart," and added, "your flowers are like the shells in the sea, through the magic of the crystal waters" (letter, c. 1923, NYPL).

Critical response to *Rock Flower* was positive. Clement Wood wrote, "Mrs. Foster has achieved a place as one of the singing voices of today," and the *New York Evening Post* critic, William Rose Benet, said that the book was "filled with delicate melodiousness." *The Outlook* called her poetry "extraordinarily dowered with a rich and

16. The frontispiece of *RF* is a pencil portrait of JRF by JBY (*PF,* 469).

sane imaginative quality. . . . The book is rich in poetic values and bears the imprinted contours of an individual mind." [17] Any writer would be pleased with such reviews, but Foster said she had reservations about her verse because Pound had suggested that it was still imitative (see chapter 12).

In her later years, Foster continued to write a variety of poetry distinct from her Adirondack work. She won one thousand dollars from the Pennsylvania Poetry Society in the late 1950s for "Fey Nora," a lyric about poetic inspiration ("Announcement," LC). Around the same time, she won first prize for "The Flag Rededicates the Ground" from the Tennessee Poetry Society and second prize in the National Poetry Contest for "If There Are Ghosts," and in 1958 she was listed in the *International Who's Who in Poetry* (AP, xxxvii).

In a 21 July 1968 letter, Foster wrote about her excitement over finding a path back to direct communication with the infinite. This "reawakening" was responsible for much of the poetry in *Awakening Grace* (1977). Even if the poetry falls short of her earlier work, she found joy in its creation:

Contacting the individuals in my mss.—contacting them in mind—has made the whole summer incredible. My poetry is stronger, my plans for "time ahead" (if I have any time) are completely changed. With all my study of faiths, with all my contacts, I some way missed the return to Zen and that return you brought to me. I came to it not as an unbeliever, not as one unfamiliar, but with the joy of one who has "come home." I think you know that without knowing the discourses, the poetry, the records of the Zen Masters, I had tried to follow the Path.

I could not leap wholeheartedly in the paths of the various masters of the present day because I missed a beauty, a "dissolving" as it were, that I had once known, a beauty, even a way of expression, in words.

Together with, as I believe, recovered memories of an ancient incarnation when I knew Zen, I walk on. (JRF to RL, in LC)

These recovered memories may have been in part aided by books that Foster read connecting Zen with the practice of haiku. Always a quick study, she was able to incorporate what she learned into her work. She read some books on poetic structure, and she was pleased to learn of the particular problems poets faced in working with haiku. She was concerned that her work need paring and thought that the forced economy of the Japanese form was a good discipline. She understood that

17. The critical comments are printed on the brochure advertising *RF* (LC).

her earlier efforts in *Rock Flower* had not depended enough on simple juxtaposition of images to evoke emotion. When asked if she had any favorite haiku poets, she thought for a moment and chose Issa over Basho, who is usually considered the better poet.[18] "Technically, he's better, but I like old Issa. Basho is wonderful with animals and objects, but Issa likes people."[19]

And so did Jeanne Foster. Hers is a defining insight, and it tells us as much about herself as it does about the two Japanese poets. Basho was famous for rendering emotion through stark pictures: "Autumn evening / A crow alights / On a withered branch." Issa, on the other hand, almost always was more directly human. When his young child died, he tried to console himself with his Buddhist beliefs: "The world of dew / Is a world of dew. / And yet, and yet."[20] One could argue that Foster's best work is that in which she refrains from comments such as Issa's, but there is also the possibility that her poetry would be poorer without her attachment to people.

One of the best examples of her ability to create emotion by the juxtaposition of images is a poem she wrote to Paul Londraville in 1966.[21] He was then nine years old, and she was responding to several verses he had written for her:

I shall always keep them and never forget you. I am sending you a little verse I have made for you. It is about a beautiful picture of a branch of an apple tree and a bird. Birds and apples and indeed everything you see—as your first snow of winter—remind you of other things . . . and of something we cannot put into words.

> On my Choso print, the bird and the apple
> Show me what is pure in the mind,
> What has been planted, what has grown,
> All that disappears, yet is eternal.
> The color of the apple
> Is a caress and the bird
> Sings a clear-sounding song

18. Kobayashi Issa (1762–1826), Japanese poet. Basho (pseudonym for Matsuo Munefusa, 1644–94), Japanese poet.

19. JRF, interviewed by RL, 19 August 1969.

20. See Henderson 1958. The Basho poem appears on p. 18 and Issa's on p. 131, but both are translated here by RL.

21. Paul Londraville, eldest son of RL.

Upon the latticed bough.
And I know
All birds are on the bright bough
And apples hang forever
Among the green leaves.[22]

There is progression from her earlier attempts at such poetry. The synesthesia of caressing color and the relentless objectivity of the images in the verse, combined with the echoes of Yeats's "Sailing to Byzantium," with its understanding of "all that disappears yet is eternal," make this effort superior to similar poems in *Rock Flower*.

There is a considerable gulf between such imagism and Foster's theosophical work, which in the main fails as poetry, however effective it may be as prayer. The expression, although devout, is ordinary. In one of her poems, "Master's Grace," published posthumously in *Awakening Grace* (3), she addresses Master Meher Baba, whom she met twice earlier in her life. The hymn meter is particularly appropriate and a tune rises, inevitably, unbidden, in one's consciousness.

The Grace of a Perfect Master—
Over and over I say
These words that transform my being
The words that show me The Way.
(lines 1–4)

*Awakening Grace* is a series of hymns, thoughts, songs, and invocations more than it is a collection of poetry, and the selections are better read as devotions separate from her more polished Adirondack work. Foster probably did not intend these writings for a general audience but instead for friends and colleagues interested in theosophy. She once said that she understood her theosophical work was "not in the same universe" as *Neighbors of Yesterday* or as the poems that would eventually become *Adirondack Portraits*.[23]

One's last impression of Foster's work is equivocal. She produced some of the best vernacular dramatic poetry of the early twentieth century, coupled with some very ordinary love lyrics that seem not from the same sensibility. She was always able to write easily, and this facility may have been a mixed blessing. There is

22. JRF to Paul Londraville, undated letter (postmarked 1966). Paul Londraville private collection.

23. JRF, interviewed by RL, 14 July 1968.

enough strength in her narratives to make us wish that she had heeded John Butler
Yeats's advice to keep her work longer "on the anvil" (see chapter 4).

Today the Grasse River Players are dramatically performing Jeanne Robert
Foster's Adirondack verse in their Adirondack sketches; actress Eileen Egan Mack
is presenting her prose and poetry; and songwriters Daniel Berggren and Bridget
Ball have each recorded versions of her poems. Had she lived long enough to see
the rebirth of interest in her work, she would have known finally that it was not
merely "the scribbling of a mountain girl."[24]

24. JRF's characterization of her writing in a 4 March 1970 letter to RL.

# Works Cited

SEE "ABBREVIATIONS" for books, people, and collections cited frequently in the text, in particular Jeanne Foster's four principal books of poetry.

Alexander, Charles, and Joanne Taylor, directors. 1994. *Seasons of a Poet: The Jeanne Robert Foster Story.* WCFE Mountain Lake Television. PBS Plattsburgh, New York.

Armstrong, R. 1900. "New Leaders in American Illustration." *The Bookman* 2 (March): 49–56.

"Author of Book Born and Raised in the Adirondacks." 1964. *Indian Lake Bulletin,* 27 March, 2.

Boissevain, Inez. 1998. http://www.san-marino.k12.ca.us/~hehvfwproject/Sig.%20People/Bossevain.html. Website

Brooks, Van Wyck. 1927. "John Butler Yeats." In *Emerson and Others,* 107–120. London: J. Cape.

Brummer, Joseph L., and E. Weyhe. 1926. *John Quinn 1870–1925: Collection of Paintings, Water Colors, Drawings, and Sculpture.* New York: Pidgeon Hill.

Bunzel, Peter. 1960. "A Wild Irishman's Literary War." *Life* 48 (8 February): 103–6.

Crosman, Coral. 1968. "Who Is John Quinn?" *Schenectady Union Star,* 7 November, 24.

Crowley, Aleister [Leo Vincy]. 1911. *The Rosicrucian Scandal.* N.p: n.p.

———. 1969. *The Confessions of Aleister Crowley: An Autobagiography.* New York: Bantam.

Crowley, Laurence Paul. 1930. "Woman Poet of World Wide Fame Finds Inspiration for Literary Successes along Coast of Maine." *Portland Sunday Telegram and Sun,* 11 May, 20.

Dardis, Tom. 1995. *Firebrand: The Life of Horace Liveright.* New York: Random House.

De Tolnay, Charles. 1948. *The Medici Chapel.* Princeton, N.J.: Princeton Univ. Press.

Dill, Marshall, Jr. 1961. *Germany: A Modern History.* Ann Arbor: Univ. of Michigan Press.

Donoghue, Denis. 1976. "John Butler Yeats." In *Abroad in America,* edited by Marc Pachter and Frances Wein, 260–69. Reading, Mass.: Addison-Wesley.

Fagan, Cathy E. 1998. "Jeanne Robert Foster: An Adirondack Voice." Unpublished paper, City University of New York, March.

———. 1999. "Jeanne Robert Foster: The Artist as Subject." Unpublished paper delivered 3 March, Marquette University conference, *Women Artists and Subjects.*

Fish, Caroline. 1970. "Rediscovered in Chestertown." *Adirondack Life* 1, no. 4 (fall): 30–32, 42–43.

Fisher, Harrison. 1907–8. *The Harrison Fisher Book.* New York: C. Scribner's Sons.

Ford, Ford Madox. 1927. *New York Is Not America.* New York: Albert and Charles Boni.

———. 1933. *It Was the Nightingale.* London: J. P. Lippincott.

———. 1965. *Letters of Ford Madox Ford.* Edited by Richard M. Ludwig. Princeton, N.J.: Princeton Univ. Press.

Foster, Jeanne Robert. 1902. "Mistress Anne of Glazeal." *Rochester Democrat and Chronicle,* 5 January, n.p. available.

———. [1906]. "Character Sketch of Charles Copeland." Unpublished typescript. Foster-Murphy Collection, New York Public Library.

———. 1910. "A Republic for Boys and Girls—After Twenty Years." *American Review of Reviews* 42 (December): 705–12.

———. 1911a. "The Care of Women in State Prisons." *American Review of Reviews* 44 (July): 76–84.

———. 1911b. "Ideas about Women." *American Review of Reviews* 43 (April): 490–91.

———. 1911c. "Julia Ward Howe as Writer." *American Review of Reviews* 43 (February): 252–53.

———. 1912a. "The Abbey Theatre." *American Review of Reviews* 45 (March): 379–80.

———. 1912b. "Andrew Lang and His Work." *American Review of Reviews* 46 (September): 375–76.

———. 1912c. "The Art of the Theatre." *American Review of Reviews* 45 (March): 379–80.

———. 1912d. "The Drama and the Music." *American Review of Reviews* 45 (March): 379–80.

———. 1912e. "Woman and the Wage Question." *American Review of Reviews* 45 (April): 439–42.

————. 1913a. "Art Revolutionists on Exhibition in America." *American Review of Reviews* 47 (April): 441–48.

————. 1913b. "Forgotten Lincoln Caricatures." *Literary Digest* 46 (8 March): 514–15.

————. 1913c. "The Reason of the Cause." *New York Call* (8 June): 10.

————. 1913d. "Romain Rolland's Life of Michael Angelo." *American Review of Reviews* 47 (February): 232–34.

————. 1914. "New Volumes of Verse: Poems of Lindsay." *American Review of Reviews* 49 (February): 245.

————. 1916a. *Neighbors of Yesterday.* Boston: Sherman, French.

————. 1916b. *Wild Apples.* Boston: Sherman, French.

————. 1917. "The Vitalization of Schools." *American Review of Reviews* 56 (July): 73–77.

————. 1918a. "The Czecho-Slovaks." *American Review of Reviews* 58 (August): 197.

————. 1918b "The Czecho-Slovaks in Russia." *American Review of Reviews* 58 (October): 421–22.

————. 1918c. "The War Organization of Christian Science." *American Review of Reviews* 58 (October): 425–26.

————. 1919a. "The Music of the Czechoslovaks." *American Review of Reviews* 59 (May): 547–48.

————, ed. 1919b. "Poets' Tributes to Theodore Roosevelt." Introduction by Jeanne Robert Foster. *American Review of Reviews* 60 (July): 79–81.

————. [ca. 1921]. "Alice Masaryk." Unpublished typescript. Londraville private collection.

————. 1922. "New Sculptures by Constantin Brancusi: A Note on the Man and the Formal Perfection of His Carvings." *Vanity Fair* 18 (May): 68, 124.

————. 1923. *Rock Flower.* New York: Boni and Liveright.

————. 1925a. "Notes about the Trip to the Barnes Collection, November 1925." Unpublished typescript. Foster Murphy Collection, New York Public Library.

————. [ca. 1925b]. "Preface to the Collected Letters of John Quinn." Unpublished typescript. Foster Murphy Collection, New York Public Library.

————. 1926a. "It's Clever, But Is It Art?" *New York Herald Tribune,* 21 February, 4.

————. 1926b. "Last Interview with James Joyce." Unpublished typescript. Foster Murphy Collection, New York Public Library.

————. 1928. *Marthe.* In *Fifty More Contemporary One Act Plays,* edited by Frank Shay, 9–18. New York: D. Appleton. Reprinted in *Adirondack Portraits.* Edited by Noel Riedinger-Johnson, 147–62. Syracuse, N.Y.: Syracuse Univ. Press, 1986.

————. 1977. *Awakening Grace.* South Carolina: Sheriar.

————. 1986. *Adirondack Portraits*. Edited by Noel Riedinger-Johnson. Syracuse, N.Y.: Syracuse Univ. Press.

————. n.d.a. "Circumstances Previous to Meeting John Butler Yeats." Unpublished typescript. Not paginated. William M. Murphy private collection.

————. n.d.b. "Notes on John Butler Yeats." Unpublished typescript. William M. Murphy private collection.

Frank, Stephen. 1984. "Jeanne Foster's Quiet Life of Literary Riches." *Albany Times Union,* 16 September, H-1.

Frye, Northrup. 1957. "Archetypal Criticism: Theory of Myths." In *Anatomy of Criticism: Four Essays,* 131–239. Princeton, N.J.: Princeton Univ. Press.

Gonne, Maud, and John Quinn. 1999. *Too Long a Sacrifice: The Letters of Maud Gonne and John Quinn.* Edited by Janis Londraville and Richard Londraville. Selinsgrove, Penn.: Susquehanna Univ. Press.

Graybar, Lloyd. 1974. *Albert Shaw of the* Review of Reviews: *An Intellectual Biography.* Lexington: Univ. Press of Kentucky.

Henderson, Harold G. 1958. *An Introduction to Haiku.* Garden City, N.Y.: Doubleday Anchor.

Herbell, Hajo. 1969. "Born Between Fear and Hope." Document 23. In *Winter in Prague,* edited by Robin Alison Remington, 165–72. Cambridge, Mass.: MIT Press.

Holroyd, Michael. 1996. *Augustus John.* 1974. Revised ed. New York: Farrar, Straus and Giroux.

Hone, Joseph. 1965. *W. B. Yeats: 1865–1939.* London: Macmillan.

Hughes, R. 1993. "Opening the Barnes Door." *Time* (10 May): 61–64.

Hulsker, Jan. 1977. *The Complete Van Gogh.* New York: Harry N. Abrams.

Hunt, Violet. 1926. *I Have This to Say: The Story of My Flurried Years.* New York: Boni and Liveright.

"John Butler Yeats, Father of Irish Poet, Lies in Chestertown Grave." 1962. *Warrensburg-Lake George News,* 16 February, 10.

Kenner, Hugh. 1971. *The Pound Era.* Berkeley: Univ. of California Press.

Kobbé, Gustav. 1901. "The Artist and His Model." *Cosmopolitan* 31, no. 2 (June): 115–28.

Langdale, Cecily. 1987. *Gwen John.* New Haven, Conn.: Yale Univ. Press.

Lewis, Wyndham, and John Quinn. 1990a. "Two Men at War with Time: The Unpublished Correspondence of Wyndham Lewis and John Quinn" (Part 1). Edited by Janis Londraville and Richard Londraville. *English* 39, no. 164 (summer): 97–145.

———. 1990b. "Two Men at War with Time: The Unpublished Correspondence of Wyndham Lewis and John Quinn" (Part 2). Edited by Janis Londraville and Richard Londraville. *English* 39, no. 165 (autumn): 229–51.

Lindsay, Vachel. 1963. *Selected Poems*. Edited by Mark Harris. New York: Macmillan.

Londraville, Janis, and Richard Londraville. 1990. "A Portrait of Ford Madox Ford: Unpublished Letters from the Ford-Foster Friendship." *English Literature in Transition* (February): 181–207.

———. 1991. "A First Class Fighting Man: Frank Hugh O'Donnell's Correspondence with John Quinn." *Eire Ireland* 26, no. 3 (autumn): 60–81.

Londraville, Richard. 1968. "The Many Careers of Jeanne Robert Foster." *Biblion* (winter): 84–92.

———. 1970. "Jeanne Robert Foster." *Eire Ireland* 5, no. 1 (spring): 38–44.

MacShane, Frank. 1965. *The Life and Work of Ford Madox Ford*. New York: Horizon.

Maddox, Brenda. 1999. *Yeats's Ghosts: The Secret Life of W. B. Yeats*. New York: Harper Collins.

Mamatey, Victor S., and Radomir Luza. 1973. *A History of the Czechoslovak Republic 1918–1948*. Princeton, N.J.: Princeton Univ. Press.

Masa, Ann. 1970. *Vachel Lindsay: Fieldworker for the American Dream*. Bloomington: Indiana Univ. Press.

Masteller, Richard N. 1997. "Using Brancusi: Three Writers, Three Magazines, Three Versions of Modernism." *American Art* 2, no. 1 (spring): 46–67.

McCarthy, Jeff. 1999. Ford Madox Ford Home Page, 24 September. Available at: http://www.wcslc.edu/pers_pages/j-mccart/ford_page/fordbio.html.

McDowell, Edwin. 1984. "A New Yorker's Link with Literary Figures." *New York Times*, 3 September, I-12.

Miller, Francis Trevelyan, and Dudley H. Miles, eds., with editorial contributions by Jeanne Robert Foster. 1957. *Poetry and Eloquence from the Blue and the Gray*. Vol. 9 of *The Photographic History of the Civil War*. 1912. New York: Review of Reviews. Reprint. New York: Thomas Yoseloff, Castle Books.

Mitchell, Ruth Crawford, and Linda Vlasak. 1980. *Alice Garrigue Masaryk: 1879–1966*. Pittsburgh: Univ. Center for International Studies and the Masaryk Publications Trust.

Mizener, Arthur. 1971. *The Saddest Story: A Biography of Ford Madox Ford*. New York: World.

Morris, May, and John Quinn. 1997. *On Poetry, Painting, and Politics: The Letters of May Morris and John Quinn*. Edited by Janis Londraville. Selinsgrove, Penn.: Susquehanna Univ. Press.

Murphy, Daniel J. 1987. "Dear John Quinn." In *Lady Gregory: Fifty Years After,* edited by Ann Saddlemyer and Colin Smythe, 123–130. Gerrards Cross, U.K.: Colin Smythe.

Murphy, William M. 1971. "Jeanne Robert Foster." *The Idol* (Union College) 47, no. 1: 3–10.

———. 1978. *Prodigal Father: The Life of John Butler Yeats, 1839–1922.* Ithaca, N.Y.: Cornell Univ. Press.

———. 1985. "John Butler Yeats." In *The Craft of Literary Biography,* edited by Jeffrey Meyers, 33–54. New York: Schocken.

———. 1995. *Family Secrets: William Butler Yeats and His Relatives.* Syracuse, N.Y.: Syracuse Univ. Press.

Norman, Charles. 1960. *Ezra Pound.* New York: Macmillan.

O'Donnell, Frank Hugh MacDonald, and John Quinn. 1991. "The Stage Irishmen and Pseudo-Celtic Drama: Selections from the Correspondence between Frank Hugh O'Donnell and John Quinn." Edited by Janis Londraville and Richard Londraville. *Yeats: An Annual of Critical and Textual Studies* 9: 66–87.

Oliviere, Lucia Newell. 1928. *Old Houses.* New York: Oscar A. Rendel.

Phillips, Robert. 1978. "The Real Thing: An Interview with Marya Zaturenska." *Modern Poetry Studies* 9: 33–46.

Poli, Bernard. 1967. *Ford Madox Ford and the transatlantic review.* Syracuse, N.Y.: Syracuse Univ. Press.

Pound, Ezra. 1922. "Credit and the Fine Arts." *The New Age* (30 March): 284–85.

———. 1986. *The Cantos of Ezra Pound.* New York: New Directions.

———. 1991. *Selected Letters of Ezra Pound to John Quinn, 1915–1924.* Edited by Timothy Materer. Durham, N.C.: Duke Univ. Press.

Quinn, John. 1916. "Sir Roger Casement: Some Notes for a Chapter of History by a Friend Whose Guest He Was When the War Broke Out." *New York Times Magazine,* 13 August, sect. 5, 1–4.

———. 1983. *The Letters of John Quinn to William Butler Yeats.* Edited by Alan Himber and George Mills Harper. Ann Arbor, Mich.: UMI Research.

———. 1988. "John Quinn's 'An Evening in New York with W. B. Yeats' " [1920]. Edited by Richard Londraville. *Yeats Annual* 6: 166–85.

———. 1996. "A Visit to May Morris in London: Excerpts from John Quinn's Diary of 1911." Edited by Janis Londraville. *Journal of the William Morris Society* 14 (autumn): 25–29.

Reid, Benjamin L. 1968. *The Man from New York: John Quinn and His Friends.* New York: Oxford Univ. Press.

Reliquet, Scarlett, and Phillippe Reliquet. 1999. *L'Enchanteur collectionneur.* Paris: Éditions Ramsey.

"Reverend Enos Putnam Sleeps in Churchyard at Johnsburg." 1962. *Warrensburg-Lake George News,* 2 August, 3.

Rinzler, Carol E. 1987. "The Greatest Moments in a Girl's Life." *American Heritage* (February-March): 34–35.

Roché, Henri Pierre. 1959. "Adieu, Brave Petite Collection!" *L'OEIL* 54 (March): 34–41.

Saarinen, Aline. 1958. *The Proud Possessors: The Lives, Times, and Tastes of Some Adventurous American Art Collectors.* New York: Random House.

Salvato, Richard. 1996. " 'Dante Must Have Looked That Way': A Visit to James Joyce in the 1921 Paris Diary of Jeanne Robert Foster." *Biblion* 4: 58–72.

Spear, Athena Tacha. 1969. *Brancusi's Birds.* New York: New York Univ. Press for the College Art Association of American.

Taborsky, Edward. 1981. *President Edvard Benes: Between East and West 1938–1948.* Stanford, Calif.: Stanford Univ., Hoover Institution Press (publication 246).

Wade, Allan. 1955. *The Letters of W. B. Yeats.* New York: Macmillan.

Wells, H. G. 1934. *Experiments in Autobiography: Discoveries and Conclusions of a Very Ordinary Brain.* New York: Macmillan.

Wilson, Woodrow. 1968–89. *The Papers of Woodrow Wilson.* 69 vols. Edited by Arthur S. Link et al. Princeton, N.J.: Princeton Univ. Press.

Winter, Kate. 1989. *The Woman in the Mountain: Reconstructions of Self and Land by Adirondack Women Writers.* Albany: State Univ. of New York Press.

Yeats, John Butler. 1917. *Passages from the Letters of John Butler Yeats.* Selected by Ezra Pound. Churchtown, Ireland: Cuala.

———. 1923. *Early Memories: Some Chapters of Autobiography.* Churchtown, Ireland: Cuala.

———. 1946. *Letters to His Son W. B. Yeats and Others, 1869–1922.* Edited by Joseph Hone. New York: E. P. Dutton.

———. 1969. *Essays Irish and American.* New York: Books for Libraries.

Yeats, William Butler. 1938. *A Vision.* New York: Macmillan.

———. 1965. *The Autobiography of William Butler Yeats.* New York: Collier.

———. 1966. *Variorum Edition of the Plays of W. B. Yeats.* Edited by Russell K. Alspach and Catharine C. Alspach. New York: Macmillan.

———. 1990. "Four Unpublished Speeches from W. B. Yeats's 1903–04 American Lecture Tour." Edited by Richard Londraville. *Yeats Annual* 8: 78–122.

Zemel, Carol. 1997. *Van Gogh's Progress.* Berkeley: Univ. of California Press.

Zilczer, Judith. 1978. *The Noble Buyer: John Quinn, Patron of the Avant-Garde.* Washington, D.C.: Smithsonian Institution Press.

———. 1979. "The Dispersal of the John Quinn Collection." *Archives of American Art Journal* 19, no. 3: 15–21.

———. 1982. "John Quinn and Modern Art Collectors in America, 1913–1924." *American Art Journal* 14, no. 1: 56–71.

———. 1985. "Alfred Stieglitz and John Quinn: Allies in the American Avant-Garde." *American Art Journal* 17, no. 3: 18–33.

Zonta. 1965. *Tel-a-Zontian Newsletter.* 1965. Schenectady, New York, January.

# Index